Contents

An Introduction to Disability Studies

Second Edition

David Johnstone

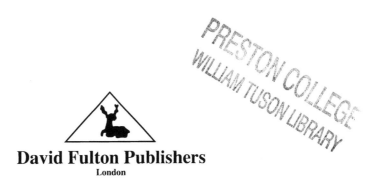

David Fulton Publishers

London

David Fulton Publishers Ltd
Ormond House, 26–27 Boswell Street, London WC1N 3JZ

www.fultonpublishers.co.uk

First edition published in Great Britain by David Fulton Publishers 1998
Second edition published in 2001

Note: The rights of David Johnstone to be identified as the author of this work has
been asserted by him in accordance with the Copyright, Designs and Patents Act 1988.

British Library Cataloguing in Publication Data
A catalogue record for this book is available from the British Library.

ISBN 1–85346–726–X

Typeset by Book Production Services, London
Printed and bound in Great Britain by The Cromwell Press Ltd, Trowbridge, Wilts.

Foreword to the second edition

The second edition of *An Introduction to Disability Studies* has offered me the chance to revise and expand portions of the text. I have also tried to reflect some of the current debates that have caused comment and discussion and expanded the bibliography. The inclusion of an appendix has provided the chance to hear the opinions of people involved in disability politics at a local level and reflects some of the concerns discussed in the chapter on disability research involving disabled and non-disabled people.

I hope that the new edition of the text will cause readers to consider whether or not there is any real and detectable change in the ways that disabled people are perceived and the ways in which they perceive themselves. The image and representation of disabled people as powerless and oppressed has been challenged, but might this simply be a form of accommodation to these legislative requirements that now apply in different parts of the world? The political strength of the Disability Movement may have helped to counter prejudiced and ill-informed attitudes towards disability and the circumstances of disabled people, but how are disabled people now regarded in post-industrial society? Disability law now acknowledges the existence of discrimination and disadvantage but, ultimately, the effectiveness of this legislation is diluted if there is insufficient economic means to sustain equality and liberation when it appears.

The messages are confused. As governments seek to reduce the costs of social security on the exchequer, personal responsibility, investment in oneself and entry to employment are perceived as potential solutions. In such a climate, individual or collective acts of altruism are still tainted with suspicion as cynical acts of charity, cheating and self-interest. For disabled people and those with health impairments this is perhaps the greatest oppression of all.

The theoretical models of disability outlined in Chapter 1 have been expanded and I have attempted to incorporate a stronger sociological analysis of the social model as an explanatory descriptor of disability. The driving force of the text continues to be grounded in and influenced by the proponents of the social model and to this end the debate between those who consider that the social model is sufficient in and of itself will be contrasted with the alternative commentators who wish to question if it is possible to link social and systemic oppression with individual pain and feelings of psychological loss arising from impairment. The intervening three years has also coincided with the rise in the number of issues relating to courses that include disability awareness in a variety of forms, in both educational and employment settings. The issues of the language of disability, disability etiquette in the workplace and the inclusion of pupils and students with disabilities and/or learning difficulties in schools, colleges and universities have also become part of a larger political agenda. Medically and ethically the debates about the rights to life and death have shifted from the mere possibilities of the human genome project to the more intense considerations, for us all, of spare part re-generative surgery, designer babies and the right to life itself. For disabled people, it might be suggested, this has uncomfortable echoes of the eugenic arguments at the beginning of the 20th century.

I would like to thank Anne Pritchard, Joan Loughran, Beverley Ward, Joan Blee and Janet Johnstone for their help in the final preparation of this text.

David Johnstone
August 2001

Introduction

Disability Studies is still of relatively recent origin, but, in the three years that have gone by since the first edition of the book, disability in an academic context has shifted from relative obscurity to a position of legitimate sociological and multidisciplinary debate.

For a number of years disability and disabled people have helped to support an industry of caring professionals, who have sustained the perception of disablement as a 'problem', an individualising and distinguishing marker of difference. The force of the Disability Movement has begun to raise a collective consciousness of the lack of rights that disabled people have. Legislative changes in the form of The Disability Discrimination Act (1995) in the United Kingdom and The Americans with Disabilities Act in the USA has been one method of responding to these inequalities. Any study of people at the margins, tends to suggest a sociological bias to the discipline and such is the case with Disability Studies. However, the study of disability crosses academic boundaries and draws on a variety of disciplines, including philosophy, sociology, psychology and history in order to analyse issues concerning the relationship between disability, social justice and political understanding.

Classical Greek theatre is effectively both the historical and the cultural starting point for linking the image of impairment with judgements about social acceptability. Hevey (1992), Barnes (1994), Thomson (1997) and Garland (1995) have developed the analysis and evaluation of the ambiguous and more frequently negative image of disablement and the threat to quality of life that disability historically carried with it for the non-disabled majority in the community. Images of disabled people have become part of both children's literature and adult horror magazines and videos. All of these representations are readily available in every home. They have tended to continue to portray a contradictory image of disabled people:

> They are either pathetic victims, arch villains or heroes. The stereotype of the disabled child is either that of the brave little lost boy/girl overcoming personal tragedy, or of the scheming malcontent determined to have revenge on society for the misfortune that has befallen him/her.

> (Johnstone 1995: 5)

Probably the most common stereotype is the image of the disabled person as pitiable and/or pathetic. This has been used to advantage by charities for the annual TV shows of *Children in Need* and *Telethon* (for an interesting discussion on this see Longmore in Mitchell and Snyder (eds) 1997). It is interesting to note how this sentimental depiction of disabled people to a non-disabled world has shifted towards the encouragement of a more critical reflection on disability issues; the self-help projects and attempts to inform the public in the appeals of *Comic Relief* are a good example.

However, Disability Studies is not so much about identifying characteristics of sensory or physical loss; nor about learning facts, although there are some to be addressed and remembered. It is not even, solely, concerned with the circumstances of disabled people. Disability Studies is more about the development of critical enquiry into those social and political forces that frame and inform our relationships with each other and the institutions of society that we have created. As with any study of human encounters there are individual and systemic ambiguities and inconsistencies that must be taken into account when deciding what disablement actually means. These can be multiplied by the additional complexities imposed by any apparent deviations from what is generally considered to be 'the norm'. However, just as there is no single accepted consensus for what is 'normal' there are few uncontested statements of agreement that can be made in relation to the construction of disability within the humanities and social sciences. This applies to disability at the level of both an individual label and, more collectively, as an area of academic enquiry.

While this text sets out to describe Disability Studies as essentially an academic discipline, it would be impossible to ignore the private experiences of loss, pain, discomfort, chronic illness and frustration that are associated with being a disabled person and the sense of psychological marginalisation. The exploration of disablement is also tempered by the intermittent experiences of ill-health that we all experience and the gradual dawning of knowledge that we are all temporarily able-bodied. These personal circumstances contrast with the more public, collective experience of overt 'disability pride' at the level of political movement towards disability rights, which is a more orthodox arena for academic debate and analysis.

Thus, disability is both subjectively experienced and objectively defined as if it were a problem that threatens both disabled and non-disabled people alike. Coleridge (1993) has indicated how the powerful negative images of disability help to perpetuate a range of emotions including fear, pity, or admiration, depending on how a person appears to be 'coping':

> Much of the apparent confusion and contradictions about disability issues can be resolved through the realisation that disability provides, for the disabled person, a certain experience or set of experiences that are not shared by other people. These experiences do set disabled people apart, but they also bind them, as it were, closer to life itself and its purpose.
>
> (Coleridge 1993: 215)

Disability Studies has emerged as a discipline for academic study in universities over the course of the last decade in parallel with the growing interest in Inclusive Learning in the UK (FEFC 1996; DfEE 2001). It has grown in schools and colleges as part of PSHE lessons, with no pedigree developed in the National Curriculum. Disability awareness has shown itself to be an area of concern, driven by curiosity but also by interest in the place and the rights of disabled people. Above all, it has emerged as disabled people themselves have begun to challenge society's definition of disablement and disabled people as involving odd, abnormal or deficient forms of behaviour (Driedger 1989; Mitchell and Snyder 1997; Thomson 1997; and Charlton 1998).

The book sets out to explore in a straightforward manner some of the key themes that link Disability Studies with wider explorations of equal opportunities and social justice. In Chapter 1 the philosophical and historical background that forms the backdrop to the differing explanatory models of disability are described. There are clearly layered hierarchies of discourse that emerge from these explanations as there are in all spheres of the social sciences. Disability Studies, in searching for a satisfactory language of explanation that can challenge preconceptions of dependency and care, shares a dilemma in common with the discourses around special needs and inclusive education. Chapter 2 attempts to develop this issue by examining some of the ideological prejudices that continue to oppress disabled people together with the part that the process of arranging educational opportunities and employment plays in structuring the boundaries of achievement that are imposed on the lives of many disabled individuals. Thus, the correlation between disability and ageing is questioned as are the attempts to construct care in the community. Chapter 3 examines the emergence of the different sections of the Disability Discrimination Act (1995) in the United Kingdom and the establishment of the Disability Rights Commission. The importance of the Human Rights Act and other European legislation is also outlined as a comparison between the legislation around disability discrimination legislation in the USA and the UK. At the heart of Chapter 4, which sets out to examine the issue of quality of life, there is an appraisal of rehabilitation programmes and an evaluation of the tension between subjective and objective indicators of both satisfaction and dissatisfaction. It is well known that disabled people experience limited choices and this isolation of their experiences serves to highlight the inequity of disablement. In emerging economies, or those societies recovering from civil conflicts, quality of life is measured on a different scale from the considerations being pursued in more settled and established communities.

It is in Chapter 5 that the ethical issues of the right to life are addressed. The historical legacy of eugenics has been associated with the marginalisation of disabled people and particularly those with learning difficulties. The re-emergence of eugenics is traced through to the current concerns with genetic engineering, pre-natal screening, the right to die with dignity and a mother's right to choose termination, versus a baby's right to live. The implications of these issues in relation to people with disabilities are discussed. Chapter 6 explores the development of the politicisation of disabled people and links to the concept of citizenship. The growth of the disability movement as a viable political force in the UK is traced through from its beginnings to its current position

Chapter 7 sets out some of the considerations for participative research in relation to the study of and with disabled people. The use of oral history as a means of recording the stories of disabled people is discussed as are the ethical concerns of disabled people as research participants rather than research subjects. In Chapter 8 the impact of some health risks from birth to adulthood are explored. The effects of dietary controls in relation to people with specific learning difficulties, e.g. hyperactivity and obesity, are also examined and discussed. Strategies for developing leisure and sport activities for disabled people and their effects on levels of fitness are also explored. Chapter 9 reflects on some of the architectural and wider environmental considerations, including access to communication aids, which offer opportunities to remove the sense of marginalisation and isolation felt by many disabled people and thus promote the development of a more inclusive society. The issues identified in Chapter 10 are reflections on the future direction that Disability Studies may need to take as it moves from being concerned with disability awareness to an identification of the issues that have informed its genesis and considerations for its continued purpose as an academic discipline.

CHAPTER 1

Why study disability?
Some explanatory beginnings

Questions

- Consider the competing explanations for the oppression and 'invisibility' of disabled people.
- What do you think might be wrong with a social model of disablement?
- What do you consider to be some of the fundamental controversies and challenges posed by the study of disability?
- Is an academic study of disability only possible in advanced capitalist economies?

Introduction

The study and explanation of disability as difference is not new; disablement as bodily difference has been a distinguishing feature marking individuals throughout the centuries. Disability Studies, on the other hand, is a relatively recent area of academic study. The applied study of disability tends to cross disciplinary boundaries and draws on a variety of disciplines including philosophy, sociology, psychology, history and the experiences of disabled people. The functional and theoretical relationships between these elements inform the boundaries of our understanding of both a personal disability identity and notions of how to identify with disability politics at a community level (Peters 2000). Ultimately, Disability Studies forms a basis for understanding both disability culture and social justice.

The conceptual underpinnings of Disability Studies has tended to borrow vocabulary and thereby definitions from other areas of the social sciences. Early discourses tended to be dominated by associating the language of disability with its history, reflected in medicine, psychology, sociology and anthropology. These disciplines conceptualised disability as a deviant individual experience within a dominant culture. But as disabled people came together in groups, new layers of meaning have been drawn to create socio/political debates of disablement. This has encouraged consideration of disability as both an individual and a public, cross-cultural experience (Peters 2000).

The distinctions between impairment, handicap and disability, developed by the World Health Organisation (WHO), have remained a universal benchmark for any documentation around 'disability'. The three terms have, deliberately or not, emphasised the layers of discrimination that link disablement with both medical interventions, individual tragedy and economic loss in post-industrial society. The WHO labels form a hierarchy of oppression and have come to be judged as inadequate, with their emphasis on functional and individual loss. This has been highlighted and emphasised in the bizarre and frequently undignified attempts by life insurance companies to justify a value-distinction on bodily loss as a result of an accident or injury; e.g. is the loss of four fingers and a thumb more or less financially traumatic than the loss of speech? The WHO categories also emphasise the sheer number of medically determined disabled people that there are in the world. The first estimates of the incidence of disability conducted in the 1970s suggested that 10 per cent of any population was likely to be disabled (WHO 1982). This estimate included disability associated with malnutrition; when this is excluded the figure is between 6 per cent and 7 per cent of the human population, equating to a global figure of 245 million disabled, impaired and handicapped people world wide (Helander 1993).

The International Classification of Impairments, Disabilities and Handicaps (ICIDH) (Wood 1980) developed by the WHO tended to inform the discourse as a starting point for causality rather than offering any analysis. Over the intervening years these definitions have been scrutinised and rejected, most noticeably by disabled people and their organisations. The assumptions that underpin the terminologies have been criticised for the way in which they perpetuate images of negativity and disability as disadvantage.

Labelling and stereotypes

There is some controversy over terminology in relation to the category or label 'disabled'; however, it would be difficult to believe that being labelled has no effect on a person's feelings about him or herself. Preconceptions about how individuals with disabilities are expected to act are held by many people and it is often believed that certain kinds of social behaviour are an inevitable consequence of the disabling condition, e.g. that children with Down syndrome 'love' music, or that a blind person is more sensitive to atmospheres.

Labelling has long been associated with disablement and the history of the Disability Movement is littered with descriptions taken from the school playground, the workplace, religious texts and superstitions. The labels themselves have emerged from the implicit disapproval and associations with 'unworthiness' that lie at the heart of society's judgement of normative differences and disability as deviance. Deviance in this context is considered as behaviour that is interpreted as being abnormal and thus unacceptable by the cultural group or society. Formal and informal law individualises deviance through labelling. Rather than transcending acts of discrimination by appearing impartial and neutral, the officers of law and the judiciary are subject to the same prejudices as those from whom it is meant to stand apart. The lack of shared meanings about the value attached to labels of disability versus ability means that the simplistic metaphor associating 'goodness' with able-bodiedness is pitted against 'evil' in the form of bodily loss or physical dysfunction.

This analogy can be extended to a consideration of the disfiguring divide that is imposed upon disabled people by prejudiced assumptions about the levels of contributions made to society by disabled people. The image of disabled people as 'crippled' or broken units of industrial production fits well with the philanthropic legacy of the alms house, the industrial revolution and the asylums. It also reinforces the historical characterisation of disability as solely a functional condition which is characterised by being cared for or as a personal deficit. The perception of disability as biologically determined reappears throughout history. It runs alongside the ancient, antagonistic associations of the evil, demonic (and frequently masculine) forces that lead to impairment, disability and handicap that are pitted against the gentler, more feminine and re-generative sources of goodness. Disability stereotypes are as contentious as those around feminism and multiculturalism. The principle features of my argument can be outlined as follows, and are worth some further consideration:

- Male stereotype as an effective unit of industrial production v female stereotype as a unit of service and reproduction.
- The emergence of 'need' builds on the more feminine stereotype of the servant/carer.
- The stereotypical image of the disabled person reinforces the image of 'crippled' or impaired production.
- Diversification of peoples performance as economic units in a post-industrial society brings the search for alternative roles.
- The structure and definition of disability shifts to include social disadvantage in different forms.
- Role diversification and new labels. Disabled people become both a source for newly feminised services and a potential labour force as service providers.

Stigma and disability

Diagnosing the physiological or psychological state of a person has long been important as a means of determining individual pathology or functional disability. It not only serves as a basis for undertaking curative or remedial treatments but is also clearly linked to medical–biological labels and explanation for individual treatments and conditions

Labels may emerge as a consequence of embarrassment, shame or stigmatisation. One of the inherent evils of labelling is that the label comes to be viewed as an attribute of the individual concerned. A learning difficulty, for example, may be associated with a disease within an individual. This contrasts with the view that learning difficulties arise as a consequence of a multilayered relationship of variables within an individual's social environment. Put simply, behaviours that constitute abnormality or emotional disturbance for one group in society may not be considered as such in another society or social situation.

Nevertheless, there are, of course, a number of arguments in support of the benefits of labels:

- It is often noted that funding and administrative decision making is based on labels and therefore labelling is necessary in order to distribute funds and allowances.
- Labelling a population helps professional carers, researchers and service providers to communicate to one another about what kinds of impairments and disabilities are being referred to (e.g. in evaluating research studies it is helpful to know the characteristics of the population with whom the investigation was carried out).
- If the present labels were to be abolished a new set of labels and/or descriptive terms would evolve to take their place. In other words people with disabilities will probably always be perceived/perceive themselves as being different. (However, people do not necessarily need a label in order to recognise that there are individual differences in behaviours.)
- Labelling helps to spotlight issues and causes for the general public. Charities, for example, have relied on the public reacting sympathetically to the characteristic stereotype of a group of people or a cause that has been labelled in accessible language.

Stigma, as an extreme form of labelling, has come to be associated with some of the more negative features of definition. Goffman, one of the main authorities to discuss the term, sees its origination in the ancient Greek culture that associated stigma with 'bodily signs designed to expose something unusual and bad about the moral status of the signifier. The signs were cut or burned into the body and advertised the bearer was a slave, a criminal or a traitor' (Goffman 1970: 21).

Stigma has, thus, become a term usually identified with a variety of socially inferior attributes that, in their turn are assumed to be associated with a group or an individual. The term concerns deviance from a supposed norm and tends to be ascribed as a permanent attribute. This may help to explain why train spotters tend to be considered merely eccentric, whereas disabled people are permanently stigmatised as individuals.

Critics of Goffman's view have suggested that this stance supports a normative view of the unchanging nature of society. Finkelstein (1979, 1987), for example, has accused Goffman of neutralising the insidious role that stigma plays in attempting to justify the maintenance of oppressive relationships between different social groups. Thus, stigma buttresses and maintains a status quo in a system where one stratum of society can continue to oppress another. If this perspective is applied to disabled people it begins to suggest that disabled people are responsible for their own suffering and that the rest of society is somehow relieved from any responsibility for its remediation. In such circumstances it is easy to see how the stigmatised are expected to seek out a role for themselves that is tantamount to acceptance and passivity. This means they also continue to maintain a view of themselves that is dependent and segregated.

Stigma, as an extreme form of labelling, tends to be associated with the victimisation of individuals or groups. The relationship between stigma, disablement and labelling theory are closely allied to the problem of prejudice:

> Disability is the product of definitions and practices that seek to exclude individuals who might be seen to deviate from the socially constructed norms of the 'able bodied'. In short, 'disability' is what a 'disablist' society decides so to call. ... It is not the inherent nature of disability that matters, but the labelling process, which categorises people by virtue of their position in relation to the dominant structures and values of the society.
>
> (Bury 1996: 25)

The evidence from labelling and stigma theory suggests that expectations concerning disabled people can be biased by stereotypes. For example Szivos (1992) reminds us that when we write and speak of 'people with learning disabilities' we are unconsciously condoning the devaluation of one of their defining attributes as a collective group. By relegating some disabilities to the status 'of an almost unmentionable afterthought' some of the positive assertions attributed to other minorities are ignored, e.g. the proud assertions of the gay pride movement and sisterhood are denied to people with disabilities:

> Would we now use the apologetic phrasing of 'people who are black' or 'people who are female' when we have the proud assertions 'black people', 'women' or 'sisters'? I think not. Perhaps it is too soon to envisage a similar slogan of 'slow is beautiful'.
>
> (Szivos 1992: 127)

Nevertheless, it is with labels and language that change takes place. With the growing consciousness of an emerging disability culture there is some evidence of self- and group identification with disability as a positive identification; although it is not necessarily central to all disabled persons' self-definition. There is also some suggestion that disabled people feel a common group identity:

> we have described ourselves as 'the unexpected minority' rejecting 'handicap' as a social construction, and embracing 'disabled' as an essential reality that has become essential to our personal identity.
>
> (Peters 2000: 590)

Impairment, disability and handicap

The search for an agreed model and definition of disability has been most eloquently explored and explained in the United Kingdom by Oliver (e.g. 1983, 1990, 1996a, 2000). Much of the early theorising of a nascent Disability Studies in the 1970s and 1980s attempted to explain disability through the dominant relationship between illness, impairments and disablement.

The current legal definition of disability in the United Kingdom is set out in the Disability Discrimination Act (1995). It is a masterpiece of ambiguity. The definition draws on terms which are themselves fraught with complexity in their interpretation:

> a person has a disability if he has a physical or mental impairment which has a substantial long term adverse effect on his ability to carry out normal day to day activities.
> (Disability Discrimination Act, HMSO 1995: 1)

The experience of disablement can immediately be seen to be perpetuating the association between disability and individual loss of function, rather than with any collective act of discrimination by society. As a result the understanding of impairment or loss as the legitimate basis for disability is reinforced.

This definition acknowledges and reinforces the link with chronic illness as the foundation for the disadvantages that disabled people experience. The causality of disability is explained hierarchically and in the context of personal health. This is consistent with the classifications devised by the World Health Organisation (WHO 1976 International Classification Document A29/INF.DOC/1):

> **Impairment** – In the context of health experience, an impairment is any loss or abnormality of psychological, physiological or anatomical structure or function.

(i.e. it emphasises any medical damage, or malfunction of a part of the body, such as a stutter, a loss of vision);

> **Disability** – In the context of health experience, a disability is any restriction or lack (resulting from an impairment) of ability to perform an activity in the manner or within the range considered normal for a human being.

(i.e. disability is considered to be an effect on bodily functions arising from an impairment. As an illustration one of the consequences of a stutter might be conversational difficulties, or mobility difficulties arising from spina bifida);

> **Handicap** – In the context of health experience, a handicap is a disadvantage for a given individual, resulting from an impairment or a disability, that limits or prevents the fulfilment of a role that is normal (depending on age, sex, social and cultural factors) for that individual.

(i.e. the handicap arises as an effect or consequences of disability in an individual's social setting or day-to-day environment. This might be illustrated by the lack of access to a mobility aid, or a pair of spectacles).

The construct of 'disability' in accordance with the WHO is seen to be a function of a hierarchy of practices and perceptions linked to certain bodily, mental or behavioural states. The associations with disability as illness are clear. Nevertheless, there are suggestions of the cultural, social and environmental variables that have come to be the defining characteristics of the social model of disability. These are more evident in the original WHO definition of handicap.

In the UK there is now a preference for the term disabled in place of the label handicap. This has been one of the significant changes to emerge from these early debates. In order for this to occur the language of definition has had to change. So too have perceptions of disability and disabled people. Theories of 'social oppression' and the emergence of the Disability Movement have increasingly challenged attitudes to discrimination and the exclusionary language employed to describe practices.

The need to reconstruct the language of disability

All academic disciplines create their own imagery and language. Disability Studies is no exception. However, the historical legacy of disability as personal tragedy means that there is a close association between disability and personal or biological loss. This has locked the study of disablement and its consequences into a hierarchy of terminologies and oppressive metaphors. For example, the dominant paradigms of care and need, in everyday usage, have been built around medical conditions and playground name calling. As a relatively new area of academic discourse, Disability Studies has borrowed terminology and definitions from the language of older and more dominant disciplines, such as medicine, psychology and education. But, there are dangers that the content and theory of Disability Studies may become reduced, rather like the study of 'special need' in education which is more reflective of a professional ownership of services that set out to resolve and compensate for loss rather than aiming to prevent problems from arising in the first place.

The most difficult level of discourse to counteract in Disability Studies is the ideological. The ideological language of 'ownership' is usually embodied in practices thought to be acceptable and 'normal' and the practices that emerge are, therefore, never considered to be discriminatory. Professional practices with and about disabled people are often perceived in this way since they have developed within an individualistic ideology that makes the disabled person believe that they must take full responsibility for their difficulties. Things are undertaken and done to disabled people for their own good, e.g. specialist categorical services, segregation in day centres or group homes. Perhaps the most insidious aspect of these dominating ideologies is that although the solutions are individualistic, they, in fact, serve to further devalue individual differences and re-emphasise certain 'normal' images of disabled people as a group or category (e.g. the derogatory 'deaf and dumb', 'people confined to a wheelchair').

Corbett (1996) has usefully identified how patterns of special language discourses have created and shaped the structure and formal process for meeting the needs of marginalised groups. Just as with the emergence of the language of special education, the dominant discourses of Disability Studies have tended to be set down in a layered hierarchy. The formal underpinning language noted by Corbett has shaped the legislative and curricular terminologies in the framework of an array of professional and academic fields that have been spawned from disability, e.g. special education. In similar fashion the shaping of the underpinning theories of Disability Studies as a critical discipline is reflected in the terminologies of different disciplines (see Figure 1.1).

**DISABILITY
ARTS
CIVIL RIGHTS
EDUCATIONAL NEEDS
POLITICAL
PHILOSOPHICAL
SOCIOLOGICAL
PSYCHOLOGICAL
MEDICAL**

Figure 1.1 The languages hierarchy of disability

These status-rich disciplines, replete with their own terminologies and alliances, sit somewhat uncomfortably on top of each other, forming a sub-text to Disability Studies. It is unlikely, for example, that the discourses that perpetuate the medical model of disability are going to be greatly disturbed or influenced by the emerging idioms of the disability arts. The voices of the disability arts, in their turn, are different from the discourses centred around political activism 'where new languages and metaphors are emerging in a creative burst of pride and assertion' (Corbett 1996: 33) among disabled people.

Extending Corbett's argument, Disability Studies provides an opportunity not only to break away from the confinement of a disablist vocabulary but to reflect the more inclusive voice of a new social movement. 'These movements often cross national boundaries, present broadly based critiques of existing economic, political and social institutions and arrangements and use a whole range of tactics to promote their ideas and goals' (Oliver 2000: 19). The cross-fertilisation of ideas from a range of disciplines in Disability Studies provides an arena that enriches and challenges the way in which we can use language. It also highlights the spirit of inclusiveness that lies at its heart. Thus, what Disability Studies offers is an opportunity to create a new model with different explanatory power instead of the vertical hierarchy of power. In Figure 1.2 there are possibilities for creating a more collaborative and inclusive discourse.

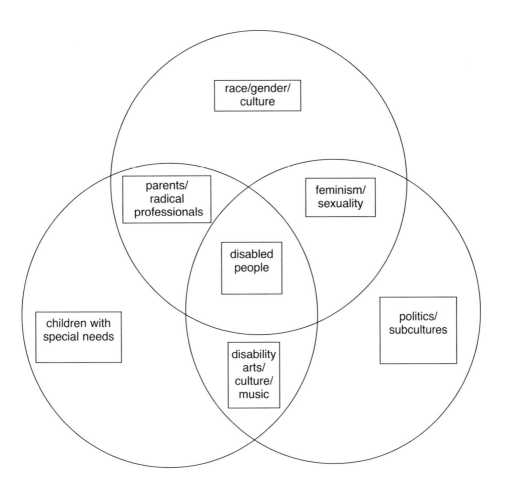

Figure 1.2 The construction of an inclusive language

In the language of this model no single voice is allowed to dominate the emerging discourse. The notions of disability as loss and restriction are removed. Instead they are replaced by the more affirmative language of inclusion, through contact with a diverse range of related and relevant participants. This creates new alliances and shared experiences. The hierarchy of oppressions and marginalisation is replaced by echoes of the 'rainbow coalition' which brought together the variety of marginalised constituencies that fought for civil rights in the USA in the 1980s and has been regenerated in relation to disability by the work of Susan Peters.

The beginning of disability pride

In 1976, the first seriously political coalition of disabled people was created in the United Kingdom. The Union of the Physically Impaired Against Segregation (UPIAS) published a monograph 'Fundamental Principles of Disability', in which disabled people gave their definitions of disability, based on their lived experience (Finkelstein 1993). These definitions only served to emphasise the limitations and confusions of the WHO classification. The UPIAS argued that medical professionals and other 'experts' were confusing both the language of definition and the contrast between, physical impairment and disability. Moreover, the UPIAS argued, people with physical impairments became disabled because they were isolated in institutions, or otherwise prevented from a full participation in social and economic life, e.g. by inadequate access, or by exclusion from the labour market. Thus, to the UPIAS a physical disability was interpreted as a form of environmental and social oppression rather than a range of limitations arising from a medical condition. Instead of the causal connection identified in the 1976 WHO classifications the UPIAS set out to deliberately differentiate and politicise the two conditions of disability and impairment:

> **Impairment** – emphasising the lack of all or part of a limb; or having a defective limb, organ or body mechanism. In other words it tends to emphasise the individual.

> **Disability** – emphasising the disadvantage or restriction of activity caused by a contemporary social organisation which takes no or little account of people who have physical impairments and thus excludes them from the mainstream of social activities.
>
> (UPIAS 1976: 14)

Some six years later Disabled People's International (DPI), developing their own causal definitions from the earlier UPIAS construction, moved the focus of causality even more to the impositions and barriers erected by society on people with impairments. By building comparisons with what might be considered 'normal life' and the restrictions placed upon people with impairments and disabilities, the DPI placed causality within the schema of community living:

> **Impairment** – the functional limitation within the individual caused by physical, mental, or sensory impairment.

> **Disability** – is the loss or limitation of opportunities to take part in the normal life of the community on an equal level with others due to physical and social barriers.
>
> (DPI 1982)

Thus, the focus of definition had shifted along a continuum, from deviation from normality arising from a functional loss to a consciousness of the political nature of disablement. As a range of socially determined and sometimes unconscious prejudices, what Oliver (1996a) has described as 'the politics of difference', the UPIAS model demonstrates the more radical end of this continuum. It suggests the beginning of a conscious disability pride, a disability culture and moreover, the restrictive boundaries imposed by notions of normality.

The original WHO conceptions of disability had tended to be established by non-disabled people speaking on behalf of and about disabled people. The DPI definition has caused a change of consciousness and a shift in the paradigm. The perception of disability was moving – away from a pathology residing within the individual person – towards disability arising from the interaction of a range of single or multiple environmental and socially imposed restrictions. Both concepts, nevertheless, assume that disabled people want to achieve some form of rehabilitation to normality and the rebuilding of old certainties. These ideas of a return to normality have increasingly come under attack as the disabled people's movement has grown in confidence:

> this is not just a matter of semantics but a concerted attempt to reject the normalising society. That some organisations of disabled people have not fully succeeded cannot be explained only as a matter of dispute between different political positions within the disability movement but also evidence of just how ingrained and deep-rooted the ideology of normality is within social consciousness more generally.
>
> (Oliver 1996b: 44)

It is also worth remembering that some people may have an impairment or disability without necessarily viewing themselves as disabled, particularly when the effects of their impairment can be reduced or controlled. For example, in circumstances where disablement is judged normatively and comparatively a person who has a slight degree of hearing loss may be said to have an impairment, but need not necessarily see themselves, or be perceived by others, as disabled because they can adopt strategies to minimise the social effects that turn this impairment into a disability. On a scale of hearing impairment they will clearly be ranked at the opposite end of the scale from a profoundly deaf person; however, if all forms of impairment were quantified in terms of the severity of the restriction on 'normal' activities, impaired hearing might be viewed as less restrictive than some forms of physical or mental impairment. Thus the person in the example would now have two separate frames of reference by which they might not classify themselves, or be classified by others as 'disabled'. In similar fashion, where two people have the same form of impairment, one may not view themselves as disabled, while the other may.

This consideration of shifts in the definition of impairment and disability moves the theory of Disability Studies to a closer examination of disability rights and liberation. These dimensions of disability are increasingly seen as the legitimate area of discourse for disability as a new social movement, although they have not emerged without the struggle of centuries of prejudice, particularly in the battle with oppressive medical and social care (see Hunt 1966). The emergence of any sort of recognition of civil rights, or participative collaboration with people with disabilities, is inextricably linked to the development of professional medicine. This includes the array of pseudo-medical professions that have also been spawned. Three conceptual models dominate the development of Disability Studies due to their clarity of interpretation. All three are associated with phases of political, historical and economic development. The models have at first glance an explanatory power that is immediately understandable and accessible in relation to planning, organisation and practices around the expansion of rights and entitlement for disabled people. However, as Finkelstein points out:

> ... models do not *explain* anything. Models should not be confused with theories or hypotheses, which do reveal the inner, or hidden laws governing the nature of things and relationships. Models, on the other hand, work best when they are used as tools to give us insights into situations which are difficult otherwise to begin explaining.
>
> (Finkelstein 1996: 1)

In other words, models are tools that should be the subject of scrutiny, tests and improvements.

Individual tragedy or medical model

Like so many other initiatives involving a group of people who have been marginalised, the beginnings of provision for people with disabilities is shrouded in some mystery. Nevertheless, from the outset it has involved the relationship of differential power between 'helpers' and 'helped', the demands of the labour market and the reification of the roles of those groups of individuals providing services.

Explanations of disability as personal tragedy for the person concerned have emerged from a long history (e.g. Edinburgh Review 1865; Hunt 1966; Finkelstein 1987; Oliver 1990; Garland 1995; Johnstone 1995; Rioux 1996; Thomson 1997). All these researchers have indicated some of the sociological and psychological adaptations that tend to be made by non-disabled and disabled people alike in their adjustments towards disabled people in society. The medical model of interpretation of disability projects a dualism which tends to categorise the able-bodied as somehow 'better' or superior to people with disabilities. It shares much in common with the earlier taxonomy established by Kurtz (1964), writing with particular reference to people with learning difficulties. The image of disabled people is identified with pity, fear and charity and it is these considerations that contribute the explanatory power of such an interpretation. The theoretical weakness and oppressive nature of the model lies in its apparent legitimation of the primitive fears associated with disability rather than in any attempts at objective rigour:

Able-bodied	v	Disabled
Normal		Abnormal
Good		Bad
Clean		Unclean
Fit		Unfit
Able		Unable
Independent		Dependent

Such descriptions have been used to justify the assumptions that it is legitimate to do things *to* people with disabilities rather than attempt to do things *with* them. Such explanations served as the rationale for large asylums and coercive control of disabled people in the guise of philanthropy that denied the right of reproduction to disabled people at the beginning of the 20th century (Gould 1996).

Yet, as has already been indicated, disabled people do not readily conform to a particular type. The creation of a taxonomy of categories does little to adequately represent the sheer diversity and range that makes up the population of people with disabilities. As Oliver (1990: 4) says, about the medical model: 'it conserves the notion of impairment as abnormality in function, disability as not being able to perform an activity considered normal for a human being and handicap as the inability to perform a normal social role'.

Rioux (1996) has argued that such explanation of disability as a taxonomy of medical/biological problems has now grown and matured to encompass characteristics of disability as a service or social problem:

> Using this formulation, the hypothesis is that the deficit lies within the individual, but the concept of treatment is broadened to include both ameliorating the condition and developing ways to enable people to develop the potential they have. From this perspective there has been no attempt to reframe the notion that the problems experienced by people with disabilities are a result of their individual impairments.
>
> (Rioux 1996: 124)

What has come to be described as the 'medical' model, emerged from the tendency of most of us to see medical practice as the epitome of a powerful professional group. Doctors carry with them an aura of God-like responsibility over life and death. This reification in turn had a profound effect on the kinds of professional services received, the education and training provision made and also the manner in which these were implemented. This powerful influence suggests that if a person has a disability the medical model of causation implies that to all intents and purposes, 'It's your own fault!' As Oliver (1990) and Johnstone (1995) have pointed out, this pervasive influence from medicine is a major factor in the individualisation of 'care' issues and it is through such means that feelings of personal isolation are compounded.

It is not difficult to see how, from their beginnings, service providers have defined the 'problem' of disablement as somehow the responsibility of disabled people themselves. For example the traditional function of the medical profession is to assess patient need, prescribe an intervention and to facilitate a cure. It is as close as any of us get to playing the Almighty. Disabled people have tended to collude with and to be dominated by, this medically defined construct as much as anyone who is 'under the doctor'. The 'medical model' is deceptively simple. Nevertheless, when it is used as an explanation for society's response to impairment and disablement it can be seen to be problematic. The interpretive strength of the medical model is grounded firmly in the principles of normalisation, and a return to 'wholeness' which is impossible to achieve (and may not be desired). The three elements of medical cure outlined in the model share many of the characteristics provided by other professional services:

- medical condition (symptoms)
- diagnosis/prescription
- cure or treatment

The model has an immediate appeal for the return of a bodily or sensory 'wholeness'. However, it is disingenuous when applied to disabled people who have, perhaps, been impaired since birth. It also emphasises the patient status and thereby carries assumptions of an anticipated passivity from disabled people. The result is an emphasis on what disabled people cannot do and what disabled people will need if their lives are to function adequately with a particular medical condition. 'An assumption is made that disabled people function at a lower rate than an able-bodied person and that, in fact, a disabled person is inadequate' (Gillespie-Sells and Campbell 1991: 15). This in turn reinforces the cycle of prejudice and discrimination that so often accompanies the treatment of a 'difficult' patient who fails to respond as anticipated, to the interventions of a caring professional:

- failure to respond (label)
- blame and guilt (low self-esteem and/or dependency on services)
- repeat presentation of symptoms to another specialist

The understanding of this interpretation of disability is premised on a shared understanding of normality. It clearly emphasises a power relationship in favour of the professionals and reinforces the personal tragedy interpretation of disablement. The message of the medical model is that people with impairments and disabilities should be grateful for their treatment and that if there is a problem it is, in effect, the fault and responsibility of the patient for failing to follow the recommended intervention.

The rehabilitation model of disability

The original meaning of the term 'rehabilitation' was associated with compensatory programmes to help people come to terms with their impairments and social disadvantages and/or newly acquired disability. Rehabilitation, therefore, emphasised the anticipated restoration of a person's dignity and/or legal status, e.g. with asylum seekers. However, in relation to the interpretation of disability as rehabilitation the term has begun to concentrate more on the interaction between people with disabilities and their environmental preparation to return to mainstream society. It is, thereby becoming more multidisciplinary and the emphasis is upon the participation of individuals in making choices.

Rehabilitation is about an expansion of the medical interpretation as it attempts to build accommodation to the non-disabled majority in society. It is about adjustment to disability as well as community integration (Renwick and Friefeld 1996). The traditional rehabilitation model is based on a liberal interpretation of care for disabled people as 'restoration'. One might hope that this interpretation of rehabilitation as a 'preparation to participate' is beginning to disappear as statutory and voluntary agencies break away from the medical model. The medical interpretation of disability is, nevertheless, integral to rehabilitation with a clear emphasis on personal care and adaptation towards disabled people and an aim of restoration to approximately normal functioning individuals. This interpretation of 'normal' is, of course, problematic. It is linked to cultural expectations and what people were like before they became disabled and thereby reinforces the association and causation of disabilities with a health condition, such as a disease, a congenital malformation, a trauma, accident or malnutrition. Once more it tends to emphasise the personal tragedy of the effect of impairment on lifestyle and the marked contrast to the functional lifestyles of non-disabled people:

> A normally functioning person does not have to grapple with the social (or administrative) model of disability which is made up of a complex interrelationship of poor access, inadequate housing, insufficient income, cash starved social services and professional control over their lives.
>
> (Silburn 1993: 224)

In such administrative and professionally dominated circumstances it is worth remembering that care and charity can still be a form of rejection. Disabled people are not objects who merely receive services, they are also participants in the processes that shape their lives. 'Revolutions begin when people who are defined as problems achieve the power to redefine the problem', as McKnight (1995) points out, and the hegemony of the professions will only be challenged when 'the client population' begins to question whether they really are the problem and starts to recognise the limitations of professional help.

The social model of disability

The medical model encourages the simplistic view that disability is a personal tragedy for the individuals concerned. It is disabled people who are seen to have, and may come to see themselves as having, 'needs'. The challenge and the strength of the social model for the interpretation of disability lies in its ability to reverse the emphasis of causation; away from the individual and personal towards shared and collective responsibility. It is an interpretation founded on the premise that it is society that perpetuates the oppression and exclusion of people with disabilities. Thus, the onus of responsibility is shifted from the individual with an impairment or disability to the restrictions imposed by the construction of the social and physical environment and the attitudes of institutions and organisations.

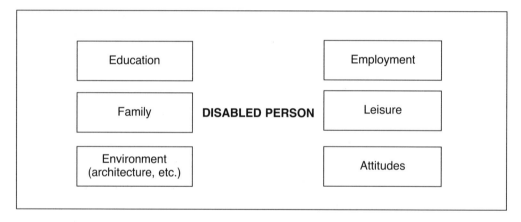

Figure 1.3 The social model

The essential difference between the medical and the social model of disability revolves around the shift in the explanatory power. The social model, unlike the medical, acknowledges the structural and personal barriers created by society. It also recognises the need for the participation of disabled people in decision making and the limitations of professional expertise. The elements of the social model can be summarised as follows.

- it recognises the interaction of structural and attitudinal variables that create disability in society;
- it recognises the voice/opinion of the disabled person;
- it acknowledges the political processes that oppress and deny civil rights to disabled people;
- it begins to put power/information within the control of disabled people and their organisations.

Criticisms of the social model of disability have begun to emerge since the beginnings of the 1990s (e.g. Finkelstein 1996; Shakespeare and Watson 1997). The social model has been accused for being atheoretical, with no firm foundation of established scientific 'truth' against which it can be measured and tested. There are also the concerns raised by disabled people who have drawn attention to the reality that some impairments involve chronic and enduring pain and discomfort that can be relieved through medical interventions (Crow 1996). These criticisms are important, but unfortunately tend to undermine what has been a useful and accessible model of interpretation and a basis for further debate.

The social model is now part of the lexicon of Disability Studies but is still only one tool for exploring the shifts in both collective and individual thinking about disability issues. It is also rather presumptuous to believe that any one model can ever fully account for the development of a theoretical paradigm, or way of understanding, for the social actions that make up human behaviour in relation to disability issues. By its nature, the social model has emerged from the lived experiences of disabled people in order to generate its illustrative power. It gained its strength from being developed by disabled people and their collective voice, standing in opposition to the medical interpretation of disablement and it focuses on showing how 'the social interpretation of disability undermines the confidence of "experts" with abilities' (Finkelstein 1996). It has been argued that its greatest strength of all lies in the uncompromising power to reject and contradict the medical interpretation of disablement. If this authority were to be lost it would be a rejection of the contribution of disabled people to a rights-based agenda. Conversely, it can be argued that the political resonance of the social construction of disability is only partial and thereby ignores the spontaneous demands of the silent majority of people with impairments and health conditions. Such an argument suggests that in order for the social construction of disability to become really useful, it should somehow begin to incorporate, rather than stand in opposition to, the medical/deficit model of disablement. By doing so, the bureaucracy and limitations indicated by the medical model come to be seen as part of the institutional limitations that are fundamental to the social model.

The limitations of the social model lie in the practical realities of impairment on people's lives. A person may be affected by more than one form of impairment but may only feel themselves to be disabled by one of these. Thus, someone with asthma, hearing loss and arthritis may find that their asthma can be controlled by medication, and that the provision of a hearing aid may give them sufficiently adequate hearing to cope with most situations, but if they cannot walk up steps and stairs they are disabled by the interaction of arthritis and the built environment. Generalising about disability is further complicated by the range and variety in the severity of the effects of forms of impairment. Throughout the research literature on disability it is apparent that for some people their level of impairment has increased and is likely to continue so to do, while for others there is no pattern of deterioration. In many cases people have 'good days and bad days' and they live their lives accordingly.

The affirmative model

By exploring the contrasting perceptions between the social and the medical interpretations of disability and building particularly on the developments emerging from the Disability Arts Movement, a new model of disability is emerging from the experiences of disabled people. This model presents a collective affirmation of the positive aspects of disability culture and has been termed as an affirmative model of disability. 'The affirmative model is emerging to strengthen the opposition of the social model to the personal tragedy model' (Swain and French 2000: 579).

The affirmative model 'is essentially a non-tragic view of disability and impairment which encompasses positive social identities, both individual and collective, for disabled people grounded in the benefits of life style and life experience of being impaired and disabled' (Swain and French 2000: 569). This is a positive way of both moving the ideas and strengthening the social model, to incorporate the sensations and emotions. It has the potential for moving on the practical and academic understanding of disablement, to a new level of inclusive and individual understanding.

The social model and the emerging affirmative model, nevertheless, appears to be grounded in liberal rather than radical conceptions of equal opportunities. It thereby suffers from some of the weaknesses associated with this paradigm (e.g. excess bureaucratisation at the point of decision making and an emphasis on fairness being perceived as individual rather than collective justice). A more radical conception of social justice within disability politics has come to be associated with a rights-based model

The rights-based model

The examination of rights and entitlements moves the discourse of Disability Studies and the social interpretation of disability into an exploration of the tensions between the private and public arenas of equal opportunities. This suggests that the politicisation of disability as personal experience needs to be articulated within a theory of equal opportunities. The narrowly private world of the individual and the personal circumstances of disabled people is not sufficient as explanation. What is required in a rights-based explanation is an articulation of the publicly accountable provision made for and received by disabled people as a movement.

The rights-based model of disability has thus emerged as a more politicised extension of the social model of disability. It has been articulated by a variety of groups at the margins of an increasingly consumer-driven society and began to emerge as a phenomenon in the late 1950s and early 1960s in Western Europe and the United States. The battles for legislation to outlaw discrimination against various groups in society – women, gays and lesbians, black people and, most recently, disabled people – have been and are being fought separately, but the underlying issues are the same. The rights-based model attempts to address some fundamental considerations that are grounded in equal opportunity theory:

- that all persons have a right to self-determination;
- individuals and groups experience unfair advantages in determining their future;
- that declines in prospects for self-determination for the less fortunate are due to social forces beyond their control;
- that as a result there is a collective obligation to improve prospects for self-determination for less well-situated groups.

It has only been in recent years that the discourse around disability has turned to a consideration of human rights. Human rights, in their turn, have been influenced by the growing strength of the disability movement and the emerging self-confidence of disabled people. A rights-based discourse spreads the dimensions of disablement to include civil, political, economic, social, cultural and environmental obligations. These rights are enshrined in a number of international charters and declarations and they should be applied to everyone. An example of rights is that developed by the Universal Declaration of Human Rights, or the United Nations Declaration on the Rights of Disabled Persons Nations (for extracts from these charters see *Disability Awareness in Action* 1993: 40–55). Most recently the European Convention of Human Rights has been implemented in the United Kingdom (in October 2000 the UK had been one of the first EU countries to sign the agreement but one of the last to implement it).

The rights-based model expands the social model of disability by moving the emphasis for change away from individuals to the requirement for changes in the collective structure of society:

- It recognises the existence of structural discrimination against disabled people in society.
- It acknowledges the collective strength of people.
- The agenda is determined by disabled people and their allies.
- It recognises legislation as a basis for establishing the visibility of the democratically enforceable rights of disabled people.
- It brings legal sanction to any act of disability discrimination.

In the United Kingdom legislation has been used to challenge and outlaw discrimination on the grounds of 'race' and/or gender. These attempts at reform, may not have been considered completely successful, but they have been used as a signal to encourage disabled people to demand similar legislation, with a major focus being on 'civil rights' rather than 'needs'. In so doing, disabled people are arguing for legislation that challenges and prevents the unfair discriminatory practices that exist both socially and institutionally, in both direct and indirect forms. While the Disability Discrimination Act (DDA) (HMSO

1995) recognises some of these concerns it still perceives discrimination against disabled people as individually rather than collectively determined. Adherence to the State or, alternatively, the Market for ensuring the maintenance of these rights is a substitute for the pluralist and inclusive democracy that an effective rights-based model of disablement implies.

Even those who have supported the enabling legislation of the Disability Discrimination Act see it as only a partially effective tool in outlawing discrimination against disabled people. In a range of arenas, within employment, transport and access to goods and services, it tends to favour a gradual path towards equality as a virtue. One major criticism is that there is a general vagueness around some of the terms and conditions laid down. Many requirements are qualified by references to what is 'reasonable', which it is argued greatly diminishes the effectiveness of the legislation. Another criticism is the protracted time scale over which the Act will be fully implemented. Some clauses (e.g. with regard to public transport) may not come into force until the second decade of the 21st century.

From needs to rights and entitlements

Major influences concerning the development of rights for disabled people are still emerging. From the United States the cause of black rights has acted as a catalyst for other groups, including the re-examination and a reclamation of disability by disabled people in the form of Disability Studies (e.g. Linton 1998; Thomson 1996; Davis 1997). A similar, but arguably, more politically focused exploration of rights and entitlements has been echoed in the United Kingdom (e.g. Oliver 1990, 1996a; Bynoe *et al.* 1991; Barnes 1994). The black experience of the civil rights movement has been fundamental in its influence on disabled people for a number of reasons:

- It re-conceptualised unequal treatments of marginalised groups into a more appropriate political context of equal opportunities and human rights. Rather than a human tragedy and, therefore, an individual 'problem', the cause was seen as a public and political concern.
- It demonstrated the possibility of achieving social change within a society. It also galvanised all people, who until then had overlooked their own role in the construction and perception of disability and special needs as a 'problem'.

The campaigns have all tended to come to successful fruition as a consequence of direct action and political activism. The Americans with Disabilities Act (1990) (Morrissey 1991) is an example of legislation that has come to be a powerful testimony to the campaigning zeal of disabled people. It is also a symbol of and justification for political activity in the development of civil rights for people with disabilities in other parts of the world. However, in the United Kingdom the evidence that disabled people are still denied their full rights to citizenship is overwhelming. It is also increasingly evident that, despite political rhetoric to the contrary, 'social disadvantage' has come to be associated with accusations of new forms of deviancy. Some forms of socially inappropriate behaviour are now akin to some of the former stigma associated with disablement. The socially disadvantaged as the new disabled – cases to be treated rather than individuals with rights – is still rather fanciful but it is interesting to see how the shift in liberal tolerance of the 'other' has moved away from fear of the body, to fear of fear itself.

It is only recently that commentators have begun to question if the very services set up to help establish a better quality of life may not instead be helping to create the problems they were designed to resolve. Bureaucratic assessment procedures and the perpetuation of segregated and residential facilities have in the past denied people the right to live where they choose. The conjunction of disability, community provision for disabled people and the philosophy of inclusive living is crucial here; particularly in terms of the realisation of individual potential and the affirmative model alluded to by Swain and French (2000) and Johnstone (1995).

Summary

In this chapter Disability Studies is discussed as a multidisciplinary subject area that sets out to explore both the private and collective experiences of disabled people. The differences between the labels of disability, impairment and handicap are outlined and critically analysed. The strongly medical definitions that are associated with the individual 'tragedy' of an impairment – e.g. chronic loss, pain, loss of status – is compared with the more politicised social construction of disability. The contrasts between these two simple models is emphasised. The emergence of a language discourse that empowers and liberates disabled people as a group, in a more inclusive and affirmative paradigm that challenges the negativity associated with marginalisation and oppression is also discussed. Shared oppression is argued as a liberating feature of the disability movement. This brings attention to a fourth explanation of disability, based on the demand for civil rights. This model has grown from the social model as numbers of disabled people have started to act collectively in order to seek access to civic rights and full citizenship. These actions, in turn, create the basis for a critical examination of community care and form the backdrop for the exploration of equal opportunities in Chapter 2.

Critical factors in community care and independent living

Questions

- Is it necessary to set the issue of disability within an equal opportunities contest?
- Do you regard it as a professional duty or an invasion of privacy to make decisions on behalf of people with disabilities?
- Should Disability Studies be concerned with raising issues that deal with conflict and prejudice?
- What do you see as the main tensions in the concept of independent living?

Introduction

The explanations of disability outlined in Chapter 1 can be viewed as the beginnings of a theoretical framework for the status of disabled people in society. This chapter sets out to critically examine the complexity of the service provision developed to meet the needs of disabled people and some of the attitudes associated with service provision. Too often the very services intended to bring disabled and non-disabled people closer have had the contrary effect of sustaining the marginalisation of disabled people – the very thing they are aiming to dispel. Finkelstein summarises this paradox as follows:

> All those working in the field of disability and earning their livelihood from this occupation are dependent on the existence of a never-ending disabled client market. They are part of the disability complex. The contention here is that the experience of the helper side of the disability relationship makes possible the generation of specific attitudes towards 'disability.' One particular characteristic of these attitudes is that, since they emerge from the 'helper' (or able bodied) side of the relationship; they focus

exclusively on the 'helped' side. Because the 'helpers' are the articulators of how disability should be described and presented to the public, these one-sided attitudes are taken as representative of the totality – of attitudes towards disability itself.

(Finkelstein 1979: 7)

Just as we cannot really be surprised if people with disabilities continue to see themselves as undervalued, we should also not be surprised when we see professional carers and educators as the 'needs providers'. For example, students and children emerging from special education courses continue to be classified as 'in need' and often, thereby, requiring the benefits of charitable and statutory services. However, having a disability or an impairment is not the same thing as having 'needs' although it might be about limited options. It is often because people have been socialised into accepting the definition of disability as a personal tragedy/need for adjustment that the concept of 'need' emerges. Nevertheless, the traditional media images associated with disabled people continue to be confused by somewhat contradictory extremes. People with impairments are either pathetic victims, arch villains or heroes. The stereotype of the disabled child is either that of the brave little lost boy/girl overcoming personal tragedy, or, in later life, the scheming malcontent determined to have revenge on society for the misfortune that has befallen him/her. Other alternative examples of disabled people who have become public figures have tended to overlook or play down the part that impairment has played in their own perceptions of their lives, e.g. President Roosevelt, David Blunkett or Frank Williams. Only recently has this begun to change with the public exposure of private circumstances, e.g. the work of Hevey (1992) and public awareness of Simon Weston, facially disfigured in the Falklands War, has emphasised the positive aspects of disabled body imagery. As it is realised that disablement is a concomitant of the human condition and that many non-disabled people have impairments such as long- or short-sightedness as we grow older, so the divide in categorisation begins to blur.

The need for disability

The 'industry of Concern' that has grown to serve the needs of disabled people has resulted in an increased sense of professional protection among the services created. The growth of professional services in Western economies in the last half of the 20th century has seen the shift from manufacturing to service industries and has created the need to redefine employment in its wake. Each year fewer people are employed to produce goods and therefore there is a need to create something else for people to do. The liberal ideal of caring and the market-led notions of efficiency have come alarmingly close together. This need for mechanised standardisation has been noted by Thomson (1997: 11) commenting on industrial modernisation: 'Efficiency, a concept rooted in the mechanical, ascended to prominence as a measurement of bodily values.'

There is a growing belief that the production of a service as a capital 'good' which can contribute to the gross national product of a country's economy equates with the industry of a factory that produces a motor car. However, when an economy is based primarily on the production of services, the essential new material is people who are in need, or who are deficient:

> Just as General Motors needs steel, a service economy needs 'deficiency', 'human problems' and 'needs' if it is to grow. ... The economic need for need creates a demand for redefining conditions of deficiency.
>
> (McKnight 1995: 29)

So, in effect, the industry of disability perpetuates the dependency it has been created to resolve. The caring services, researchers and academics that work within the disability 'industry' redefine themselves and the concept of disablement, but cannot afford to get rid of disability itself.

Disability as inequality

We are seeing in the emergence of Disability Studies a resurgence of interest in the fundamental principle of how people should be treated, particularly with reference to the circumstances of disabled people. The Disability Movement, individual disabled people and their advocates are beginning to question if the services developed to promote a satisfactory quality of life are in fact adequate. But the questions raised and the apparent paucity of adequate solutions, have illuminated wider aspects of inequality in human relations. The question of social and economic inequality goes to the heart of the meaning of social justice within capitalism and raises issues of what it means to receive a fair share of the 'national cake' of prosperity. The case of disability suggests that the way disabled people are perceived, measured and treated is far from ideal. Rioux (1996) has indicated that the dominance of the medical model has created an identifiable hierarchy within the social construction of disability and also in the determination of equality:

* a person is labelled or distinguished from others in such a way that he or she is considered as socially inferior;
* care and treatment, including professional standards and practice, law policy and political rights, are developed and legitimated on the basis of this label of social inferiority;
* a paternalistic denial of liberties and self-determination is imposed, premised on the social obligation that attaches to the status.

And through such methods, intentional or otherwise, the cycle of oppression remains unbroken.

Disability as need: the case of special education

The concept of 'need' first emerged in education in 1946, in regulations that clarified how to implement the Education Act (1944). These regulations led to the establishment of services and schools that acted on behalf of, rather than in consultation with, disabled people. This, in turn, has led until recently to a kind of passive citizenship on the part of disabled people and their families within a fundamentally needs-based provision determined by educational professionals. The legal framework of the UK has consistently portrayed the education of disabled people as a cost to the exchequer rather than as an individual's entitlement to participate in the exercise of citizenship. Indeed, such has been the determination to see special education as an extension of a form of treatment, that we have only in the last 20 years started to dismantle a special education system that deliberately excluded pupils and students with special educational needs from participation in the 'ordinary' school curriculum.

A feature of the 1944 Act was the creation of categories of handicap reflecting society's need to reflect medical pathology, rather than consider educational consequences in terms of learning. Regulations in *Pamphlet 5*, following the Act, actually stated that some pupils may require special educational 'treatment', borrowing heavily from the medical model already referred to. For young people with handicaps and disabilities, leaving school meant a probable future in sheltered or closed employment. Even in 1968 it was estimated that there were approximately 70,000 severely mentally handicapped adults in England and Wales, approximately 24,500 of whom attended adult training centres (Whelan and Speake 1977). The needs of a vocationally driven education system following the Second World War has stressed the link between education and employment. The very need to re-establish employment for returning members of the armed forces also had the effect of excluding disabled individuals from open employment, even though some of them had fulfilled important work during the war years. This trend has continued with few commentators attempting to explain or question the socio-political contexts from which they have emerged. However, unless this explanation is undertaken the levels of disadvantage experienced by many young people with special needs will remain unaltered.

The much more specific definition of learning difficulties within the concept 'special educational needs' formed part of the legal framework of the 1981 Education Act and followed from the recommendations put forward by the Warnock Committee of Enquiry (1978). This Act has in turn been replaced by the 1993 Education Act and its accompanying Code of Practice (DfEE 1994). As Booth (1992) has argued, the implications of the definitions are that children and students are to be measured using both 'within the individual' measures, e.g. standard tests of intelligence or ability (which, in themselves, suggest measuring the incompetence or failure of a person as the basis of learning difficulties) and secondly, 'environmental judgements' of the adequacy or otherwise of the resources available to facilitate and support teaching and learning. The whole concept of 'need' is problematic and confusing. For children in schools, it has led to an increase in services established for the purpose of meeting individual need and providing support. It is ironic that with the increasing consideration of legislation as the underpinning factor in establishing disability rights that some commentators have begun to question if the very services set up to help establish better learning may not, instead, be helping to create the problems they were designed to resolve (Booth 1992; Corbett and Barton 1992; Johnstone 1995; Oliver and Barnes 1998; Corker 1999).

The fundamentally child-centred ideas of the Warnock Report attempted to establish a concept of citizenship by building on the notion of need, determined by the collaboration of 'experts' and through the wider integration of children from segregated educational provision into the mainstream. In fact, it failed to alter many of the old prejudices. Had the original recommendations, for the education of all children in ordinary schools, been more adequately resourced, the current arguments for and against inclusion might not have become so strident. The present philosophical shifts in the discourses around inclusive education are themselves an acknowledgement that full integration is an ideal that may not ultimately be completely achievable or even desired for everyone with a disability. Nevertheless, inclusion does acknowledge that it is the structures of the education system that have to change, rather more than trying to attempt to fit an individual to the system. More than anything else, however, the concept of inclusion stresses the emphasis on rights. The structures for meeting special educational needs within the spirit of inclusion has, too often, failed to face up to the fundamental issue of ensuring that basic educational rights are part of every child's entitlement and every teacher's individual responsibility. As Johnstone (1995) points out, 'special educational need' has become such an abused and misunderstood term that it has diminished two perfectly honourable and worthwhile concepts: 'Care' and 'Need' which have fundamentally influenced the creation of the term in the first place. The system of meeting a child or student's 'needs' has continued to perpetuate some of the worst abuses of the old models of medical care through the imposition of bureaucratic assessment and insensitive diagnostic procedures on young people and their families. The perpetuation of segregated educational and residential facilities continues to deny the right for some people to live where they choose or understand 'the ways in which boundaries impact both physically and emotionally on people's lives [and] challenge us to expose the multiple political, social and cultural forces that have created those boundaries' (Jackson 2000).

The move towards inclusion

The relationship between community provision for disabled people and the economy is seen in the original 'philanthropic' ideals that lay behind the development of a structured system of provision in the institutions and 'colonies' that were established in both Europe and the United States in the 19th century. In some areas of the United Kingdom they continued to form the basis for residential care until the shift in policy during the 1970s towards 'Care in the Community'. Some semi-formal education and vocational training for people with disabilities and learning difficulties had been an established feature of the asylums of the 19th century. The development of activities for young men and women with disabilities and psychiatric disorders in the asylums of the 19th century have been interestingly described by a visitor to the Earlswood Asylum situated just outside London. Contemporary photographs of the building suggest that 'the asylum looks like a palatial country house. The people walking in the grounds create an atmosphere of gentility. There are no high walls. Fresh air and the opportunity for physical exercise were listed as particular benefits' (Potts 2000: 52). There was also a contemporary belief that this new kind of work with idiots could yield positive results economically:

> … It was in furthering the many schemes for the improvement of idiots, a most impor-
> tant object to enable those capable of reaping the highest advantages, to become adept
> in some useful branch of industry, and to make their work remunerative, exchanging
> their solitary and idle habits for social, industrious and productive occupation.
>
> (Edinburgh Review 1865: 56)

However, this paternalistic approach was soon to be replaced by the harsher, more custodial activities associated with asylums as arenas for the protection of society, rather than as places of refuge for disabled people. In the 'Moral Panic' that developed around eugenics, the populist demand grew for the asylums to become places of custody. This meant a shift in emphasis; from training individuals in order to protect them from the threats and exploitation from the rest of society, to the protection of society from the supposed debilitating effects of physically, intellectually (and by association morally) inadequate people. Any understanding of shared responsibility for either the causation or resolution of these circumstances was quite clearly overlooked.

The link between inclusion, integration and rights for disabled people emerged alongside concerns about the incarceration of people with disabilities; and people with learning difficulties in particular. Despite challenges to the boundaries between equal citizenship and 'civil death' (Stainton 2000) a gulf still exists between the rhetoric of rights and popular understanding. At the same time as debates are emerging about choice and opportunities for the inclusion of minority populations there are equally vigorous debates about curbing freedom, curfews and anti-social behaviour orders for young people considered to be beyond parental control (Carter 2001).

Scandinavian society has led the way in promoting non-segregation for all groups of people. Soder (1980), writing at around the same time as the policy initiative for changes in special education in the United Kingdom (e.g. Warnock 1978), has provided operational definitions of integration that divide it into four main groups:

i) Physical integration, i.e. the physical (or geographical) distance between the handicapped and non-handicapped is reduced. This is the most common form of integration of handicapped young people in Sweden, which means segregated classrooms in ordinary school and college buildings.

ii) Functional integration, i.e. the functional distance is reduced. This means that handicapped and non-handicapped students are using the same educational equipment and resources. In turn the functional integration can be divided into two branches, where co-utilization (which can be simultaneous or non-simultaneous) means that students only share material and co-operation means planned common activities.

iii) Social integration, i.e. the social distance is reduced. This means that the handicapped person forms part of a community with non-handicapped persons and comes into regular and spontaneous contact with these.

iv) Societal integration, i.e. the adult handicapped person has the same access to resources and opportunity to influence his own situation as others; he has a productive working role and forms part of a social community with others.

(Soder 1980: 10–11)

This hierarchy of form has been expanded by others who have added additional sophistication rather than radically altered Soder's original four-step model, e.g. a fourth level has been termed 'personal integration' and is given the following definition:

Personal integration is related to the developing and changing needs for personal interaction with significant persons. It includes the opportunities to have a satisfactory private life with meaningful relationships, for example for the child: parents, siblings, relatives and friends; and for the adult: relatives, friends, marriage partner and children.

(Nirje 1980: 48)

Some problems with this concept of integration have already been alluded to, but they have been subject to a good deal of critical scrutiny. Definitions of integration fit well with the widely developed and questionable construct of 'normalisation' and clearly have links with the debate about 'quality of life' (Wolfensberger 1989; Marks 1998). But, it is interesting to note that the most common forms of integration and inclusiveness in educational and community settings remain at the lower end of the hierarchy. This raises a number of questions about the appropriateness of applying levels to a concept that is in a proper sense indivisible. As Rosenqvist (1993) has pointed out, in a wholeness no exclusions are possible, since everybody is needed in forming this wholeness: 'if someone is taken away the wholeness has lost some of its contributions and is thus spoiled'.

The implementation of integration reforms in educational settings have shown that social goals of education are not always realised. Various studies have indicated that people with disabilities establish very few relationships with non-handicapped young people and that those people who have been encouraged to integrate socially often appear to become excluded even in the integrated setting (e.g. Johnstone 1995; Shakespeare 1998; Johnstone and Warwick 1999). Some of the possible reasons for this tension between the ideals of full inclusion and the reality of only partial success have been attributed to the lack of social networks that are available to disabled and non-disabled to socialise together. The closure of large institutions in favour of enclave housing is an example of the expectations that people with disabilities, and particularly those with more severe learning difficulties, will begin to establish social relations with non-handicapped people. This optimistic expectation assumes that society is ready to accept the integration of disabled and non-disabled people as unproblematic. In fact, the reality is that in the worst cases isolation has increased as large institutions have been replaced by smaller ones – more home-like, but still regulating choice and placing limits on social activity.

The transition to adulthood

The recognition that disability and education are both constructed within a political framework of rights and entitlements has been part of a process that has been given its most forceful lead in the world of further education. As has been pointed out, special education as a system is in danger of being perceived as a series of barriers rather than new opportunities. It focuses on shallow judgements of individual needs as selected needs and the business of access to buildings and the curriculum (Corbett and Barton 1992; Johnstone 1995). Rather than this, it should be considered as an issue to be studied with a proper examination of both the institutional and structural inequalities inherent in society. If, by so doing, we place the exploration of disability and special education within the context of equal opportunities, it then becomes part of a more fundamental contribution to civic awareness.

In 1995 I suggested that the development of inclusive provision for people with disabilities in the United Kingdom had become a player in a larger political poker game. I am now inclined towards another party game of pass the parcel. Thus, the concerns of disabled people have taken the form of an economic and class debate around poverty, 'family values' and 'back to basics'. Any attempts to influence change in provision for people with disabilities now has to recognise the additional responsibility for disabled people to engage in their own forms of political challenge, not simply seeking to affect legislation. The challenge is inherent in the language of debate as well as the agenda for action to build progressive transitions between the phases of school and adulthood. In order to influence the structures of power and control in the development of transition services the debates and judgements will have to be in terms of 'rights' rather than 'needs'. This may well involve the uncomfortable acknowledgement that most of the injustices towards disabled people have emerged from, and are still located in, an education system that talks of change but does little to resolve its own practices. This sense of inequity and injustice needs to touch the lives of the vast majority and not solely people with disabilities in order to bring real change.

The criticisms applied to education are equally applicable to other forms of service provision for disabled people. Provision is dominated by the notion that disabled people have traditionally been in need of care and that work was an option for some but not a requirement. But there is now a new agenda as part of the search for social inclusion; the policy shift to the 'third way' with its encouragement of disabled people to take up work (Hyde 2000; Roulstone 2000). For people with hidden disabilities of working age this has particular resonance as attempts to reduce welfare focuses on the requirement to seek employment, or to risk being seen as part of a dependent underclass. As Hyde points out, the disheartening aspect of this transition is that employment policy is still being informed by a medical model of disablement that emphasises the adaptation of people with impairments to the needs of employers rather than focusing on the removal of discriminatory social barriers.

Disabled people would more often prefer to talk about 'personal assistance', rejecting the association between care and dependency. One key demand is that instead of being provided with services, which are not necessarily tailored to individual requirements, those who wish it should receive cash payments to purchase assistance privately. Government policy has begun to encourage opportunities for local authorities to participate in such schemes (Rummery and Glendinning 1999). In those parts of the country where it has been possible to successfully publicise the scheme, e.g. Hampshire, this has been found to be successful by many people, and its availability nationally will do much to liberate disabled people from the constraints of bureaucracy. Unfortunately, in wide parts of the country there is still little experience and some suspicion of the change (Maglalic *et al.* 2000).

It should be emphasised, however, that I do not wish to imply that one potential form of oppression (service provision) should be replaced by another potentially oppressive practice (disabled people being forced to purchase care, manage their care budget, etc.), but that both options should be available. The struggles by disabled people to reclaim control of their own lives have shifted the debate away from the concept of 'need' to issues around the right to participate, which is, arguably, one of the key issues of the new century.

The right to employment

The comfortable certainties and routines of childhood are intended to serve as a preliminary to the often more informal and haphazard aspects of life as an adult. One of the most inclusive and until the 1990s ordinary things about adult life is employment. It is therefore no surprise that many of our formative childhood and 'pretend' experiences are related to jobs. In similar fashion, education and training have been expected to accommodate the expectations of employers in preparing young people for the job market; by developing personal and social skills, craft skills and qualifications as prerequisites for securing employment.

Some of the benefits of paid employment are obvious. As has been pointed out, people have defined themselves by their work throughout this century:

> They were miners, engineers, printers, draymen, tanners. And they were predominantly male. But as the manufacturing industries collapsed, more jobs were taken by women and millions of badly educated men could no longer define themselves. 'I'm a printer' could be said with pride; 'I'm on benefit' is a mark of exclusion.
>
> (Hugill, *The Observer* 1997: 29)

The combination of social interaction and feelings of self-worth that employment and the process of task completion can provide apply equally to people with disabilities. Some of the benefits of a job can be usefully summarised as follows:

1. A job provides economic independence and a better standard of living.
2. A job can empower people, by enabling them to become self-determining rather than living their lives as others dictate.
3. A job provides status that influences positive attitudes towards disabled people and public visibility.
4. Workplaces in integrated settings provide opportunities for social interaction and friendships.
5. A job is one of the ways in which the majority of people continue to learn and develop skills, competences and intellectual abilities.
6. Work gives our lives a routine and structure. Successful employment and job satisfaction gives people a sense of fulfilment, achievement, confidence and dignity.
7. Developing employment opportunities is cost-effective. A job involves people exercising their independence and choice to become self-supporting, rather than remaining dependent upon a lifetime of support services.

So, just as it is recognised that all people including those with disabilities can benefit from employment, it is also recognised that in a more competitive environment some people will require additional support if employment is to take place. In the past five years in the

UK all political parties have taken to advising the unemployed and the disabled that they should take some responsibility for the circumstances they are in. Education and training are seen as the keys to overcoming the skills deficit in the workforce. Griffiths (1990), commenting in relation to people with severe learning difficulties, claims that too often, too little is expected of people with learning difficulties and that, given suitable training and help, they are capable of working in both sheltered and open employment. The under-expectation that he and others (Hyde 2000) have highlighted is a carry-over from the protectiveness felt towards people deemed to be vulnerable. But, whereas most people grow to assert their rights, many people with disabilities remain passive and inarticulate in the face of the often well-meaning but ultimately oppressive will of others.

There are a number of significant factors which continue to act as barriers to open employment for people with disabilities. The most fundamental is the structural unemployment and under-employment arising from the skills revolution. This means that employers are demanding a workforce that is articulate, adaptable and innovative, rather than tied to the manual labour of the production line. The supply of jobs available is clearly related to the structural characteristics of the local economy, but it is also dependent upon the nature of work itself. This particularly affects the relationship between people with disabilities and the attitudes of employers and fellow employees.

The tendency to have an undifferentiated view of disabled people as a homogeneous group operates in the workplace as well as other areas of life. This means that people, with disabilities and learning difficulties in particular, are placed in low regard (Thomson 1997).Too often they are thought only capable of undertaking repetitive and 'simple' tasks and if such work does not exist then a person with a disability will not be considered as employable. Such issues are particularly pertinent in connection with jobs where 'initiative' is seen as a prerequisite for work. In the same way that special education can mean streamed or segregated provision, special work placements can become discrete enclaves set in sheltered settings where imagination and initiative on the part of both supervisors, disabled employees and their workmates is neither required nor encouraged. Attendance in these 'closed' settings limits opportunities for social experiences and any access to wider opportunities for employment promotion or changes to working practice that are usually an anticipated part of working life.

Equality of opportunity for access to employment has become a policy objective for a range of disadvantaged and under-represented groups. Nevertheless, the changing nature of Britain and the diminishing manufacturing base of the country has affected employment opportunities for everyone. The decline of manufacturing has coincided roughly with a technological revolution that has reduced the need for an unskilled workforce or even low levels of skill in the labour market. Training and education initiatives have been given an ideological steer in an attempt to restructure the political and economic fortunes of the country. As has been noted, doubts about the potency of economic performance have confronted all governments and employers in late 20th-century technological societies. As training has delayed and in some cases replaced entry to paid employment, an increasing number of young people have become alienated from what is perceived to be a hierarchy of education and training outcomes.

Educational achievement has become even more important as a primary indicator of the transition to adult status and the ultimate entitlements to the workplace. A reconsideration of the purpose of education and training has become fundamental for most people in order to gain entry level to any sort of employment or income above mere subsistence level. These issues are exacerbated for people with disabilities who are socially disadvantaged at the point of developing a career for a number of reasons. As Johnstone (1995) has commented, educational and vocational training programmes can appear to disadvantage young adults with disabilities, as can other initiatives developed as pre-employment initiatives. It has been apparent that some people can stay for years within a cycle of different, but badly coordinated, training schemes (Finn 1987; Kennedy 1997). They never actually achieve either adequate qualification or ultimate paid employment. Of those who achieve a qualification, most show only modest results. The majority, who receive special certificates or records of achievement related to elements within their training, have a qualification that still has little currency with employers. As a result, there are a number of unskilled and unqualified people fit for low-paid employment and they are always under threat of being laid off at short notice. Young women with disability in this category are doubly disadvantaged, either staying at home on completion of their formal schooling or obtaining a job that earns them so little that independent living is impossible.

The factor of age and disability

The associations between disability and age are inescapable. As a critical variable in the study of disability, age can be thought of as the ticking time bomb that each of us carries with us. Just as loss has been portrayed as the dominant metaphor in the medical model of disablement and impairment, so it also informs and operationalises perspectives about the onset and impact of the ageing process. In Britain, as elsewhere, the increasing number of elderly people is becoming an important issue of public policy. Even if the majority of older people are in fairly good health, they are responsible for a greater than average use of the health care services. The rapid ageing of the world's population is set to pose serious challenges to the global system of health care and to force many difficult decisions about the allocation of resources. It is estimated that 29 million people suffer from senile dementia, mostly Alzheimer's disease (WHO 1997) and this condition is likely to become one of the most common causes of disability in the 21st century.

Theories on ageing have tended to be dominated by the expectation that individuals should learn to accept the stage-related features of the life cycle (e.g. birth, childhood. adolescence, early adulthood, etc.). As Oliver reminds us, it is highly unlikely that any of us will reach the conclusion of our working lives without becoming more conscious of the effects of an impairment. People who grow old gracefully are assumed to be adapting normally to the ageing process. Thus, ageing has its own inevitable expectations and behaviours, 'from this perspective, successful adaptation to ageing is represented by an individual accepting the changes that he or she has experienced and ultimately accepting the inevitability of death' (Oliver 1996a: 134).

The point in the life cycle at which disablement occurs may well be crucial. In Britain people who become disabled in old age may find their situation particularly difficult owing to a declining standard of living and the fact that they frequently have multiple impairments. They may also live alone surviving on a British State pension that is both inadequate and low by average European standards. For example, the elderly person who starts to go deaf may also be blind or have an arthritic condition. They may also be living on the financial support provided by a shrinking number of workers. In future, part-time rather than full retirement may be an increasingly common option. This has obvious implications in relation to the costs and social consequences of disablement.

However, as French (1992) reminds us, too much pessimism is attached to ageing. Many older people cope with impairment and disability as effectively as younger people. An impairment incurred later in life, after one has established a social and economic position has a different meaning and significance from the sense of loss experienced as a young adult. There is research that suggests that disability contracted in old age is considered part of the natural staged process of the life cycle (Zarb 1993a, 1993b). The OPCS survey (Martin *et al.* 1988) also confirms the association between disability and old age. The census had defined disability in relation to the inability to perform particular activities. Of the 6 million people living in Great Britain with at least one form of disablement almost 70 per cent of disabled adults were aged 60 and over (Martin *et al.* 1988: 27). The very old emerged as those most likely to be affected, with 63 per cent of women and 53 per cent of men over the age of 75 being described as disabled. When severity is taken into account, the very old again predominated, with 64 per cent of adults in the two highest categories being 70 or over and 41 per cent aged 80 or over. Census data, nevertheless, suggest that the combination of an ageing population and new medical interventions which will prolong life will ensure that the number of people with an impairment or chronic illness will increase significantly in the next two decades.

While the pain of an acquired impairment is no less real, it can be argued that a disability incurred at birth may be a 'first order' marker dominating one's identity, while an acquired disability that arises from impairment in old age is a subordinate one. In other words the process of ageing and the onset of disablement is characterised by an element of 'disengagement' associated with behavioural changes and a decrease in the extent of people's social interactions and physical activity.

This concept of the inevitability of decline and decrepitude, which is associated with individual pathology, can be criticised on a number of grounds:

- It perceives ageing as a negative experience, inevitably linked to death;
- It presupposes that chronic pain and disease predominates as both the cause of disability and the natural corollary with old age. Many disorders can be linked to later life, especially arthritis, hearing loss, declining eye-sight. However, they should not be confused with the trauma and congenital conditions associated with disablement in the earlier years of life. Neither should they be considered to be inevitable. There are a number of reasons put forward to challenge the inevitability of disability associated with age.
- No account is taken of the social factors which are external to individuals, e.g. the reduction of social activity as people grow older is more likely to be linked to inadequate financial resources, than the ageing process *per se*. Zarb (1993a: 55) has noted in his research how ageing with a disability is associated with increases in satisfaction for some individuals and decreases for others. For people who already experience disability, the onset of the ageing process has been described as a 'second disability'.

The idea that disablement is a medical problem which affects only a small proportion of the population of the aged can no longer be sustained. Internationally there are around 50 million disabled people in Europe (Daunt 1991) and approximately 500 million world wide. The combination of an ageing population and new medical interventions which prolong life is bound to ensure that the number of people with an 'impairment' or 'chronic illness' will increase substantially over the next few years. Attitudes held towards old people and the very definition of what it means to be old will thus, need to be reconsidered.

The emergence of 'community care'

Towards the end of the 1970s the concept of 'community care' was emerging as the preferred alternative to institutionalised service provision. For feminist writers it presented a potential problem in that the family was identified as the location within which this community-based care would be provided and that the 'burden', therefore, was likely to fall on women (see Finch and Groves 1983). One major drawback in the planning of 'community care' is that it has assumed that families will continue to provide care. Community care has been presented as the ideal form of provision on the grounds of cost-effectiveness, moral responsibility (family members have a duty to care for one another), and as a safeguard against the abuse of individuals that may occur in institutional settings. The 'community care' bandwagon continued to gain momentum throughout the 1980s. The National Health Service and Social Services became separated and there was subsequent criticism of the fragmentary nature of service provision. The Griffiths Report of 1988 identified the role of Social Services as an enabling body rather than a service provider. In keeping with current government policies, social services departments were to make use of both private and voluntary sectors in purchasing services, and this was adopted in the National Health Service and Community Care Act (1990) (Morris 1993).

It was assumed that individuals would be assessed by a case manager and that a 'package of care' in terms of the necessary services would be purchased. Ultimately it was for social services to determine whether an individual's needs could be best met in the community or by residential care. Between 1991 and 1993 the Act was implemented, with the setting up of complaints and inspection units, the development of Community Care Plans (involving health and social service planners) and the separating of purchasing and providing services, together with the transfer from Social Security to local authority of residential care finance (Morris 1993).

Morris acknowledges the potential for good of the community care reforms but remains concerned about the unequal power relationship between professionals and disabled individuals. Services depend on assessment. Professionals, to a large extent, decide what is required and who will provide it, how, when, etc. Morris, however, is firmly committed to the notion of direct payments, under which individuals would receive and manage their own budgets, being responsible for 'hiring and firing' their own assistants. Although there was strong resistance to this the government view is now more favourable.

Since the implementation of the community care reforms there has been a gradual shift in focus to include the views of service users. Community Care Plans are put out to consultation, with individuals and organisations being encouraged to make known their opinions. Some health and social care planners use the term 'consumer' or 'customer' rather than 'user', but Wilson (1996) argues that 'user' is the most accurate term, since the other two imply a level of voluntarism that is not necessarily true. In many cases people have little or no choice about services, and very few people are in the position of paying in full for such services, therefore they are not customers although possibly reluctant consumers.

The monitoring of services and policy outcomes is an area that is currently the focus of much investigation (Vernon and Qureshi 2000; Drake 1999). Clearly it is important which service users are approached and how their views are recorded. Generally and historically, users have been unequal participants in the community care process and many may find it difficult to take part in the formal settings in which views are often sought. At the same time they may be dependent on services and fearful of giving offence by complaining. In this context there is a need for development work with users both as groups and as individuals. User involvement is a crucial element in the struggles of disabled people and those who support them. (See Beresford and Harding (1993) for examples of and suggestions regarding the development of user-led services.)

Summary

A number of variables can be distinguished as markers that highlight the inequalities experienced by disabled people and their families. The Victorian charitable association between the 'deserving' and the 'undeserving' had moved in the 1980s and 1990s towards distinctions between the 'helpable' and the 'unhelpable' and the effectiveness or otherwise of welfare as a solution to structural unemployment. This, in turn has highlighted one of the factors in society that is associated with disablement and lack of moral cohesiveness; an inadequate resource base for many services. The exclusion of disabled people from involvement in society's mainstream is demonstrated in education, employment and the services established to meet the requirements of 'care in the community'. Disablement is exacerbated by the poverty which emerges from poor employment prospects, limited educational opportunity and the inadequate structure of the welfare benefits system. The power of change through legislation forms the basis for the next chapter.

CHAPTER 3

Legislation in the UK and the USA

Questions

- Is there a constituency of disabled people that can influence change? Have disabled people a shared cultural identity?
- Are disabled people politically active? Will legislation bring more problems and serve to split the 'movement' towards social justice? Does it place unrealistic expectations on disabled people to litigate?
- Does anybody in society have rights? Where are the responsibilities that go with rights?
- Whose rights are ultimately being reinforced by legislation?

Introduction

The law plays both an important symbolic and practical role in forming the ideological systems that legitimise specific sets of values and assumptions in society. It is, therefore, fundamental in forming the framework within which both groups and individuals interpret their participation in society (Gooding 1994). However, the traditional assumptions that the law does not discriminate have to be questioned. Although appearing impartial and neutral, the officers of the law and the judiciary are subject to the same prejudices as those from whom it is meant to stand apart. 'Precisely because of law's power to define, it is acknowledged to be an important site of struggle and resource for groups seeking social change' (Gooding 1994: 30).

The emerging legislation of the United Kingdom, in relation to social justice for people with disabilities, reflects a number of shifts in public policy and a steady evolution in the recognition that rights are more central than needs in both employment and daily life. The accelerating speed of change is a reflection of the new group consciousness and political activism of disabled people. It also reflects their own preparedness to use the law, in order to shift public opinion away from perceptions of disabled people as 'defective' and incapable of full participation in the activities of daily living. Legislative change in relation to the rights of disabled people has occurred most significantly in the United Kingdom and the United States, but a rights-based agenda also drives reform in Australia and Canada. It is recognised that the Americans with Disabilities Act (ADA) has played a formative role in increasing the employment opportunities of disabled people in the USA and reduced their dependence on government entitlements (Blanch 1994). It has been anticipated that similar changes in the attitudes of both employers and wider society will emerge from the Disability Discrimination Act (1995) in the United Kingdom (Gooding 2000). Nevertheless while prejudice and indifference towards disabled people as individuals may be changing, there is still attitudinal, structural intolerance and low expectation held towards disablement. As a group with a disparate cultural identity, disabled people can still be frustrated and disadvantaged by the sheer bureaucracy of the legal process. When this is combined with the old-fashioned interpretations of the social welfare system in the United Kingdom and the exhaustion or 'greying' of the leadership within the Disability Movement, it is all the more problematic.

Discrimination and disabled people

The discrimination encountered by disabled people is not simply a question of individual prejudice, although that clearly occurs. Rather, it is institutionalised in the structures of society. Institutional discrimination is evident when the policies and activities of all types of organisations result in sustaining the inequalities between disabled people and non-disabled people. As has been indicated in Chapter 1, disabled people have been deliberately excluded from many aspects of community life and Western culture is replete with disablist imagery and language which keep the traditional fears and prejudices surrounding impairment alive. The centrality of these judgements of 'difference' applies to the marginalisation of all discriminated-against groups. But they are particularly clearly marked in relation to the accounts of disabled people in the United Kingdom.

Barnes (1994) in trenchant style, defines the discrimination against disabled people as 'the prejudiced attitudes of individuals – a combination of patronisation, pity and discomfort on the part of able-bodied people towards people with disabilities. Fear, hatred and hostility can also be present.' The Disability Discrimination Act (DDA) (1995), in contrast to Barnes, defines discrimination in two ways. First, as 'less favourable treatment' where an employer or service provider treats a disabled person less favourably for a reason relating to that person's disability, and cannot show that the treatment is justified. Secondly, it is also required of an employer or service provider to make reasonable adjustments in connection with the environment under the terms of the Act. As Gooding (2000) indicates, this is a significantly more diluted interpretation of discrimination than the race and sex discrimination laws. For example the duty to make adjustments in relation to service provisions only came into operation in October 1999 and will only require physical adjustments to the premises of service providers to be in place from October 2004.

Background to legislative provision in the United Kingdom

Within the paternalistic welfare services and capitalist economy of the United Kingdom the individualism of the law is one of its distinctive features. It has already been suggested that capitalist law tends to regard the rights and duties of all individuals as 'equal before the law' in a legal system that claims to remain impartial. Gooding (1994, 2000) criticises these inclinations towards a formal equality model of the law, arguing that such a philosophy is fundamentally flawed. The structure of the legal system tends to be confrontational and to reduce people to the status of isolated individuals; it fails to redress the inherently discriminatory behaviour which the law has shaped and continues to sustain. The legislation that has been passed throughout the century has tended, in fact, to reinforce the marginality and rejection of disabled people rather than signal their liberation (Bynoe *et al.* 1991; Johnstone 1995, 1996b; Equal Opportunities Review 1997; Freedman 1999). It would be easy to catalogue the failures of 'permissive' legislation. Numerous acts have purported to include consultation with disabled people and to defend the right of disabled people to participate. Nevertheless, the framing of the legislation has contained so many get-out clauses, or is so loosely drafted, that it has been ignored, over-ridden or simply gone unchallenged. If anti-discrimination legislation is ever to be effectively influential in reversing these disadvantages it must first of all acknowledge that equality is not a sufficient goal and that the real target for disabled people is effective representation and a visible presence: 'This will require positive social policy measures, alongside anti-discrimination laws which explicitly seek to establish substantive equality, in the sense of a fairer, more balanced society' (Gooding 2000: 538).

Nearly all acts of parliament concerning disabled people have tended to reinforce the domination of the medical model and the perception of disability as illness. The notorious Mental Health Act of 1913 had identified those who were deemed 'moral imbeciles' in order to justify the removal to asylums of pregnant but unmarried young women. Some 60 years later, The Chronically Sick and Disabled Person's Act (1973) set out to identify the incidence of disability and the needs of disabled people in each local authority of England and Wales. In both cases the expectation was that disabled people were incapable of providing their own protection, care and recreation. The paternalistic State was charged with the duty to care and take responsibility for meeting need. This has led to an ever-growing army of paid professionals and voluntary carers.

It has only been since the 1980s that the stifling grip of paternalistic law has been loosened. This was born out of an attempt by the government to address not only the discontent felt by disabled people after ten years of unsuccessful bids at legislation but also from a fear of parliamentary defeat on a private member's bill – The Civil Rights (Disabled Persons) Bill – from the opposition. This Bill was supported by the Disability Movement, but opposed by the Conservative ruling government at the time. This opposition arose from the belief that it would place too high a burden on businesses and would, thus, inhibit their abilities to compete in the economic marketplace. What has emerged is an Act designed as a form of political damage limitation to be acceptable and yet economically cost-effective to implement.

The legal basis of provision in the United Kingdom

Somewhat ambiguously the Disability Discrimination Act (DDA) (1995) has defined disability in the following terms:

> a person has a disability if he has a physical or mental impairment which has a substantial long term adverse effect on his ability to carry out normal day to day activities.
>
> (Disability Discrimination Act 1995: 1)

The Act received Royal Assent on 8 November 1995 and now forms the main focus for ending discrimination against disabled people in the United Kingdom. After a number of years of argument about its purpose and above all its costs, the DDA had established the following statutory duties:

- a right to non-discrimination against disabled people in the field of employment. This includes a duty on employers to provide a 'reasonable adjustment' to working conditions or the working environment to overcome the practical effects of disability;
- a right to access to goods and services, including the removal of barriers and provision of aids, where reasonable;
- a right to redress against discrimination in occupational pension schemes and insurance services;
- a right to access to transport infrastructure, such as railways and bus stations, together with provisions which allow the government to set minimum access criteria for new public transport vehicles (including buses, trains and taxis) to enable disabled people to use public transport more easily;
- a requirement that schools, colleges and universities provide information to disabled people about access to their facilities;
- the establishment of a National Disability Council to advise the government on issues and measures relating to the elimination of discrimination.

Criticisms of the law

The major criticism of the DDA is that an important piece of civil rights legislation has been placed on the statute book without the provision of an effective and strategic means of enforcement. Without a substantial enforcement body, such as a Commission, capable of funding and supporting disabled people complaining of discrimination, the Act was considered toothless. A Commission had been deemed necessary to monitor race relations and sexual discrimination legislation, but the government had argued that the appeals of discriminatory practice against disabled people could be observed and monitored satisfactorily by a quango with the status of an advisory body, the National Disability Council (NDC).

The law has, in effect, established or re-inforced two inter-related elements to what is termed and defined as disability:

- the physical, mental or sensory impairment of an individual;
- the social environment, artificial barriers and attitudes which prevent the individual from playing a full part in the life of the community.

Following from this, it can be seen how three types of discrimination against disabled people have been identified:

- direct discrimination, which means treating people less favourably than others because of their disability;
- indirect discrimination, which means imposing a requirement or condition on a job, facility or service which makes it harder for disabled people to gain access to it;
- unequal burdens, which means failing to take reasonable steps to remove barriers in the local environment that prevent disabled people participating equally.

The first two forms of discrimination are the same as those currently identified in the DDA. They are also similar to the discriminations identified in the areas of race and gender legislation. In the case of direct and indirect discrimination an employer or service provider is committing an offence if they treat someone unfairly because they have an impairment. In the case of unequal burdens discrimination the employer or service provider is committing an offence if they fail to adapt the environment to take account of an impaired person's incapacity when it would be reasonable for them so to do.

The concept of 'unequal burden' has nevertheless widened the definition of discrimination in relation to disabled people and is a distinguishing marker between disability discrimination and discrimination on racial and/or sexual grounds. The discrimination of 'unequal burden' 'exists when an artificial barrier, which could be removed by reasonable adaptation, prevents a disabled person from an opportunity enjoyed by a non-disabled person' (British Council of Organisations of Disabled People 1994).

Critics of the law have argued that the newly established Disability Rights Commission (DRC) will fail its credibility test if it does not involve sufficient numbers of disabled people in both enforcing the DDA and monitoring disability equality in practice. If it slides into the inadequacies associated with the Disability Rights Council, which was considered an unrepresentative body and not adequate for the task of enforcing the legislation, it will have failed its purpose. However, an effective DRC will act as a champion for disabled people and support them through the legislative process. This support is important for a number of reasons. As Gooding (2000) has observed, the lack of corroborating evidence together with the cost of taking action has deterred many people from seeking redress. Those dependent on state benefits, i.e. the majority of disabled people, are unlikely to have access to sufficient funds to pursue a claim, particularly since legal aid is unlikely to be available for such action. This concern was a major feature of debates before the Act became law. For the Liberal Democrats, Liz Lynne argued that it was a start but did not go far enough (*Guardian* 29 March 1995). Alan Howarth (then a Conservative) warned that the lack of an enforcement body would leave 'a hole in the heart of this legislation', while Labour MP Tom Clarke argued that the legislation had 'no teeth'. William Hague, at that time the Government Minister for the Disabled argued that setting up an enforcement body was bureaucratic and unnecessary, since the terms of the Act would provide for the assistance required by disabled people (*Guardian* 28 March 1995). In effect, the United Kingdom would be the only country to have legislation to prevent discrimination against disabled people but no enforcement body (*Guardian* 22 March 1995). Although the DDA is less far reaching than the Americans With Disabilities Act (ADA), it had been argued at the time of its passage through parliament that disabled people in Britain could find themselves with more rights than citizens of many European countries, so long as there are sufficiently powerful enforcement mechanisms. However, those seeking redress now have the support of the Disability Rights Commission and are not obliged to fight alone through the courts or industrial tribunals or be expected to meet the cost of such action from their own pockets.

Tom Shakespeare is unequivocal in his condemnation of the DDA. He argues that there is little merit in those who have been campaigning for the civil rights of disabled people settling for 'second-best' legislation. In his view, the prevalence of exemption clauses within the DDA effectively announce that discrimination in some instances will not only be tolerated, but condoned. With its 'well-meaning messages promising inclusion and justice for disabled people' (*Guardian* 30 March 1995), the DDA guarantees nothing. Shakespeare is concerned that not only is the DDA inferior to the ADA, but it also falls short of Canadian and Australian measure. The Australian Disability Discrimination Act became law in 1992, defines disability more broadly and 'proving the existence of an impairment that fits into one of seven categories is sufficient for coverage' (Colker 1998). In Canada disability anti-discrimination is incorporated into the country's general human rights legislation. This was passed in 1993 as the Canadian Human Rights Act. In the

United Kingdom, by contrast, the attention to the costs of implementation and the narrower interpretation of what is reasonable under the DDA indicates a more deferential interpretation of the law. The needs of employers appear to take precedence over the rights of disabled people and tend to make William Hague's statement (then Minister for the Disabled) rather hollow, that Britain will lead the way in Europe with this legislation. On the contrary, 'Britain leads the field only in reluctance to support disabled citizens ... and the pathetic substitute for civil rights legislation' (Shakespeare 1995). According to Shakespeare the United Kingdom also lags behind Scandinavia, France and Germany where the constitution has been amended to prohibit discrimination against people with disabilities.

Neither the DDA, nor any other anti-discrimination law, can be relied upon solely to dismantle structural disadvantage, the provision of exemption clauses and qualifications within the wording of the Act weaken this dimension substantially. Employers have a duty to modify their premises and working conditions, but regard will be paid to whether or not such modifications are 'practicable'. Thus, the financial cost to the employer of making changes can be taken into account, as can the employer's financial situation and 'the availability to the employer of financial or other assistance with respect to taking the step' (Disability Discrimination Act 1995: 5). In other words, there are a range of circumstances under which employers have no obligation to change working practices and conditions that discriminate against disabled people.

Employers of fewer than 15 people are exempt from the legislation. With regard to transport, provision is made for licensing authorities to apply to the Secretary of State for exemption from some or all of the regulations relating to taxis and accessibility (s: 30). Similar exemption certificates may be issued in respect of rail vehicles (s: 38). Although discrimination by providers of goods, facilities and services is outlawed, providers are only required to take 'reasonable' steps to change policies, practices or procedures that discriminate against disabled people (s: 18). Again there are a range of exemptions and circumstances in which discrimination is effectively 'justified'.

Caroline Gooding (1994) issues a warning about using the courts to pursue claims. She suggests that the judiciary does not have a particularly high regard for the importance of discrimination as an issue:

> either in terms of individual rights or of the 'public interest'. The judiciary has tended to proceed on the basis that anti-discrimination legislation interferes with the freedom of individuals to discriminate, and the public interest is therefore best served by restricting the impact of that legislation to the maximum extent, thus implicitly valuing the freedom of discriminators above the rights of individuals to be free from discriminatory treatment.
>
> (Gooding 1994: 98)

If Gooding's is an accurate perception, disabled people's chances of redress are further diminished, and it becomes difficult to view the Act other than as an empty gesture which channels the needs of disabled people further down the road towards medically determined definitions that disregard the disabling effects of society.

The Disability Discrimination Act defines disability as: 'a physical or mental impairment which has a substantial and long-term adverse effect on a person's ability to carry out normal day-to-day activities'. This definition has been challenged by disabled people and their organisations on a number of grounds:

- Does it really address protection against discrimination?
- Does it offer more opportunities for employment?
- Does it improve social and physical conditions for disabled people?

Who is protected?

The Act gives protection against discrimination to people who have or have had a disability which makes it 'substantially' difficult for them to carry out normal day-to-day activities. Only people who are (or who have been) 'disabled' under the Act's definition will be entitled to any of the new rights created by the Act:

- The disability can be physical or sensory, a learning disability or a mental health condition. It must be long term (i.e. have lasted or be expected to last 12 months) or likely to recur.
- People with a history of disability are also protected, e.g. people who have recovered from mental illness, but continue to experience prejudice.
- People with a 'severe disfigurement' are deemed to be disabled.
- People with progressive conditions such as cancer, HIV infection or muscular dystrophy are protected provided their condition has, or has had, an impact (no matter how small) on their ability to carry out normal day-to-day activities.

There are particular cases and conditions that are included as disabling under the legislation. For example, severe disfigurement is treated as a disability even though this may have no effect on a person's ability to carry out day-to-day activities. However, disfigurement excludes tattoos and non-medical body piercing. People who are diagnosed as having progressive conditions such as cancer or HIV infection are covered from the time that their symptoms affect their ability to carry out day-to-day activities. For example, people who are HIV positive will only be protected from discrimination when they develop AIDS-related symptoms. The interpretation of day-to-day activity anticipates that it must include at least one of the following categories of behaviour:

- mobility – moving from place to place;
- manual dexterity – e.g. use of the hands;
- physical coordination;
- continence;
- the ability to lift, carry or move ordinary objects;
- speech, hearing or eyesight;
- memory, or the ability to concentrate, learn or understand;
- being able to recognise physical danger.

It is, in effect, such a broad area that it is likely to be hard to define precisely. However, the concept of day-to-day activity is likely to be of particular concern to people with mental health problems or specific learning difficulties, who may be less able to claim discrimination under the Act than they are at present.

Opportunities for employment?

The Act prohibits discrimination against disabled people and seeks to prevent any significant disadvantage that a disabled person may encounter when applying for employment or when employed:

- The Act defines discrimination in the following terms, '… an Employer discriminates against a disabled person if for a reason which relates to the disabled person's disability he treats him less favourably than he treats or would treat others to whom that reason does not or would not apply, and he cannot show that the treatment is justified' (s.5 i. (a) and (b).
- Less favourable treatment can only be legally justified if it is for a reason which is 'material to the circumstances of the particular case and substantial' (s.5(4)).
- Employers have a duty to make 'reasonable' changes to the workplace or to the way in which work is done, where this is needed by a disabled employee or applicant.
- Trade unions and trade associations must not discriminate against disabled people in their provision of services and must make any reasonable adjustments which are required to make their services accessible.

It remains to be defined as to what is 'reasonable' in terms of making adjustments and when it is that discrimination can be legally 'justified'. As the Royal Association for Disability and Rehabilitation (RADAR) have pointed out it is not yet clear how easy it will be for employers to justify unequal treatment. This will only become clear when case law is established. As has already been made clear, before an employer can use a person's disability as an excuse to overlook them, they will first have to consider whether a reasonable adjustment could solve the problem (e.g. if a person's job normally requires them to drive to visit customers and they are unable to drive because of their disability, an employer would have to consider whether other means of transportation would resolve the problem). In making a decision about what is 'reasonable' change in the workplace or working conditions, employers can take into account the cost of change balanced against their resources. For example, it might be considered reasonable to expect a large employer to install a lift at the workplace, but unreasonable for a smaller company or employer to make the same adjustments.

Early research into the response of employers and service providers to the DDA has revealed a disturbing degree of complacency and ignorance about the legislation. In the first 18 months, research commissioned by the DfEE discovered a wide disparity of awareness of the legislation (Meager *et al.* 1999: 75–6). Individual examples in the research indicated that while some employers were aware of the DDA's existence they did not appear to have a detailed understanding of the regulations. Gooding (2000) reports that 80 per cent of establishments have an awareness of the DDA but that this is not matched with any detailed understanding of their obligations and provisions: 'the vast majority of establishments (about 9 in ten) felt that the DDA duties in relation to services which came into force in 1996 would have not have any effect on them' (Gooding 2000: 452).

The DDA does not, at present, apply to the police, the armed forces, prison officers and fire fighters. The Act also originally stipulated that it was to apply only to companies and organisations with more than 20 employees. This has since been amended to apply to employers with 15 employees or more. The Quota system (whereby employers of more than 25 people had a duty to have 3 per cent of their workforce as registered disabled people), which although effectively unworkable had been in existence for nearly 50 years, was abolished by the Act (s:61.7).

Improved social and physical conditions of disabled people?

While there was a strong lobby to ensure that the DDA acknowledged the social model of disability, the final legislation contains numerous clauses that appear to steer towards the interests of the provider of services, rather than recognising the discrimination experienced by disabled people. For instance, it will be unlawful to refuse to serve disabled customers in a restaurant, or provide them with a second-rate service, *unless this can be 'justified'*.

The Act indicates a number of exceptions in which a provider of services can justify treatment which would otherwise be discriminatory:

- where the treatment is necessary in order not to endanger the health or safety of any person (including the disabled person);
- where the disabled person is incapable of giving informed consent or entering into an enforceable agreement and for that reason the treatment is reasonable in that case;
- where a person has been refused treatment this must be necessary because the provider of services would otherwise be unable to provide the service to members of the public;

Policies, practices and procedures will have to be changed wherever reasonable, if they have the effect of discriminating against disabled people. Additional aids will have to be provided where this is reasonable given the size, resources and nature of the business (e.g. information on tape for blind customers, or in large print). Physical barriers will have to be removed wherever this is reasonable and readily achievable and reasonable adjustment made where this is is impossible. The same will apply where it is unreasonably difficult for a disabled person to receive a comparable service to that which is provided for other people. As an alternative to these arrangements for removing barriers, goods and services may be provided by alternative means – the goal is to ensure, as far as possible, that a service is is provided to the same standard as that received by other people (e.g. access to a cinema). Whether the reality of this aspiration means that disabled cinema-goers can sit wherever they wish appears to depend more on the ingenuity of individual cinema operators than on the legislation.

Enforcing the law

Like most British anti-discrimination law the DDA seeks to be non-confrontational and to create a climate of disincentives against discrimination in terms of either adverse publicity, financial sanctions or both. For the majority of disabled people and their organisations the DDA was, therefore, considered an ineffectual piece of legislation if it relied on exhortation to achieve compliance. Moreover, it was feared that the frequent references to 'reasonableness' would, in effect, facilitate non-compliance by both individuals and organisations, while at the same time making it difficult for those experiencing discrimination to prove their case. This lack of enforcement has now been rectified with the creation of the Disability Rights Commission in April 2000. However, until the creation of this strategic body the fears expressed appeared well founded. In the first 18 months of operation of the law there had been only nine cases of disability discrimination lodged in the services field (Meager 1999). In contrast, in the employment field, over 6,000 disability discrimination claims have been lodged with employment tribunals up to April 2000 (Gooding 2000: 542).

Although the effectiveness of the legislation has been supported by the courts and by the use of industrial tribunals in employment cases it is disturbing to see that only 22 per cent of applicants whose case went to tribunal were successful (Meager 1999: 207) and that the majority of settlements, while confidential, appear to be fixed at a low financial level. Where a case has successfully been brought it may well be doubted whether the deterrent effect of the awards is sufficiently high to prevent future discrimination. Except in exceptional cases involving high awards: 'Dissatisfied applicants felt that they should have received more for injury to feelings or been compensated more because of the stress of taking a case' (Meager 1999). However, the levels of financial compensation in relation to disability are better than settlements with other forms of discrimination. In 1998 disability discrimination saw the highest average award at £11,501, almost double the level of race awards and two-thirds higher than the awards in sex discrimination (Equal Opportunities Review 1999).

National Disability Council and the Disability Rights Commission

The 1995 Act established a National Disability Council (NDC) with the remit to advise the government on how existing and new measures to help disabled people are working and recommend further changes where necessary.

The NDC ceased to exist on 25 April 2000 when it was replaced by the Disability Rights Commission. Criticism of the limited functions of the NDC had emerged with the passing of the DDA; the NDC had no powers to investigate individual cases of discrimination. It had no powers to conduct formal enquiries in the manner of a Commission such as the Commission for Racial Equality or the Equal Opportunities Commission. Without these powers, and the status of a Commission, disability legislation would have continued to rely upon exhortation and monitoring for 'reasonableness' as a way of countering discrimination against disabled people. With the change from a Conservative to a New Labour government there was a manifesto pledge to alter the status of the Council to that of a Commission and consultations over the purpose and shape of the DRC were undertaken throughout 1998. The key aims and purposes of the Commission are outlined as follows:

- to work to the elimination of discrimination;
- to advise the government on law;
- to advise business;
- to investigate discrimination and ensure legal compliance;
- to prepare codes of practice;
- to facilitate independent conciliation between service providers and disabled people (re: access to goods and services) (DfEE 1998).

As Drake (2000) reminds us, a tone of persuasion rather than coercion is maintained with the guidance to the newly appointed Chair of the Commission 'to have appropriate regard to the interests of employers and service providers as well as to the interests of disabled people and their representatives' (Blunkett 2000). Like the Council that preceded it, the majority of Disability Rights Commissioners are disabled people (ten out of 14) and they are drawn from diverse backgrounds in business, trades unions and the voluntary sector.

If a person with a disability feels that they have been discriminated against they can instigate legal proceedings and if successful they may be able to recover damages for any financial loss suffered as well as damages for injuries to feelings. An instruction will also be issued that employers or service-providers should make a reasonable adjustment to provide access. Nevertheless, despite the expectation that individuals will have the opportunity to seek redress with the aid of the newly formed Commission, the interpretation of the law relates to discrimination as defined in the DDA. The weaknesses and gaps in this legislation, which in places permits 'justifiable discrimination' is bound to become frustrating. In employment cases a complaint can be presented at an industrial tribunal; in the case of a complaint on the grounds of goods and services the local county court can be used. As by definition unemployment and underemployment are consistently higher among disabled people than their non-disabled contemporaries it will be interesting to see how many disabled people achieve 'their day in court'.

Employers are expected to think imaginatively and to acknowledge their responsibility towards disabled employees. Meanwhile ministers in the New Labour government are squeezing as far as they can on public spending. The Disability Rights Commission is portrayed as a vehicle to secure comprehensive and enforceable civil rights for disabled people.

It is evident that employment law is one way in which improvement can be realised in relation to the circumstances of a range of disabled people. However, there are some warning signs on the horizon, emerging from the United States and also within the implications for disabled people in the Human Rights Act (1998).

The Human Rights Act (1998)

The Human Rights Act (1998) brings British legislation in line with European law. The Act forms another part of the growing number of changes relating to disabled people's rights that have emerged in the last decade of the 20th century. The Human Rights Act brings aspects of the European Convention of Human Rights into UK law. In brief it allows individuals in the UK to bring cases to UK courts rather than pursuing their rights in Strasbourg. The Act, which came into force in October 2000 makes it 'unlawful for a public authority to act in a way which is incompatible with a convention right'. Because the Human Rights Act is new legislation in the UK, previous European case law is not binding on the UK courts, although it does have to be taken into account. Article 14 sets out the right not to be discriminated against:

> the enjoyment of the rights and freedoms set forth in the Convention shall be secured without discrimination on any ground such as sex, race, colour, language, religion, political or other opinion, national or social origin, association with a national minority property, birth or other status.
>
> (s.1 Article 14 Human Rights Act (1998))

Disability is not explicitly included in Article 14, but there is little reason that the Article would not be understood by a court to outlaw discrimination on the grounds of disability as 'other status'. The role of Article 14 is not to prohibit discrimination in itself but to prohibit discrimination in the exercise of other Convention rights.

Provision in the United States

Both the United Kingdom and the United States are facing many of the same issues in relation to discrimination against people with disabilities. While there is a growing awareness of the rights of people with disabilities in the USA there is also a competing agenda for scarce resources from a population concerned with economic competition from the Pacific rim.

The United States has a population of approximately 264 million people, three-quarters of whom live in towns or cities. Unlike Western Europe, the United States is experiencing a rapid growth in population. This is a consequence of the immigration boom since the mid-1960s and especially since 1980. The new immigrants are primarily from Asia and Latin America; more than 2 million come from Mexico alone.

The United States has a federal democratic government. The Union comprises 50 states and each state has its own constitution. Local and state government deals with all matters not reserved for the federal government and the main unit of local government is the county. There are some 3,000 such counties in the 50 states. The national government has authority in matters such as general taxation, foreign affairs, federal and interstate commerce and crimes against the United States. It does not have a central role in relation to the social provision for disabled people provided by the individual states. Nevertheless, national government has passed a number of pieces of federal legislation that have had a direct impact on the interpretation of the new culture towards disabled people in each of the states of the Union.

The Americans with Disabilities Act

The Americans with Disabilities Act (ADA) became law in 1990. Unlike the DDA the ADA is a civil rights statute and a much more comprehensive piece of legislation. It has become the model for disability legislation in Canada, Australia and New Zealand and was the foundation for the Civil Rights (Disabled Persons) Bill which was defeated on successive occasions in the United Kingdom parliament in 1991, 1992 and 1993.

The ADA was founded on the recognition that disability is a natural part of the human experience. Thus 'all citizens have an interest in ensuring that the values that form the basis of The Americans with Disabilities Act pervade our national life' (Burke 1995: 6). The values embodied in the ADA – equal protection under the law, individual empowerment, freedom of association, economic opportunity – are important to and for all Americans. In passing the law, the Congress stated the following facts concerning the life experiences of people with disabilities in America:

- 43,000,000 Americans have one or more disabilities;
- national data indicate that individuals with disabilities occupy an inferior status in society and are severely disadvantaged socially, vocationally, economically and educationally;

- the continuing existence of unfair and unnecessary discrimination and prejudice denies people with disabilities the opportunity to compete on an equal basis and to pursue opportunities, costing the United States billions of dollars in unnecessary expenses resulting from dependency and non-productivity.

(Burke, E. N 1995: 5)

The ADA has been considered the 'most comprehensive federal civil rights law addressing discrimination against one fifth of the American population in all aspects of their daily lives. It is perhaps the most significant federal law since the Civil Rights Act of 1964' (Blanch 1994: 857).

Americans with physical or mental impairments that substantially limit daily activities are protected under the ADA. These activities include working, walking, talking, seeing, hearing or caring for oneself. People who have a record of such an impairment and those regarded as having an impairment are also protected. The ADA has the following five titles or sections:

- Title I   Employment;
- Title II   Public Services (including public transport);
- Title III   Public Accommodations and Services Operated by Private Entities;
- Title IV   Telecommunications
- Title V   Miscellaneous Provisions

Title I Employment

This prohibits discrimination in employment against disabled people and requires employers to make reasonable accommodations to the known physical or mental limitations of a qualified applicant or employee, unless such accommodation would impose an undue hardship on the employer. Reasonable accommodations include such actions as making worksites accessible, modifying existing equipment, providing new devices, modifying work schedules and conditions, restructuring jobs and providing readers and interpreters.

Under the ADA employers with 15 or more employees, must comply with the law. Title I also prohibits the use of employment tests and other selection criteria that screen out, or tend to screen out, individuals with disabilities, unless such tests or criteria are shown to be job-related. It also bans the use of pre-employment medical examinations or enquiries to determine if an applicant has a disability. The ADA does, however, permit the use of medical examination after a job offer has been made if the results are kept confidential. All people offered employment in the same job category are required to take these medical examinations and the results are not used to discriminate.

Title II Public Services

This section requires that all the services and facilities associated with local and state government, as well as non-federal government agencies, are accessible to people with disabilities. In addition, Title II seeks to ensure that people with disabilities have access to transportation, e.g. all new buses must now be accessible. People who cannot use the standard public transportation facilities must be provided with an alternative supplementary paratransit service, unless this presents an undue burden.

In the area of rail transportation, the ADA requires that all new rail vehicles and all new rail stations must become accessible within 20 years. Existing rail systems must have one accessible carriage per train. The network of subway, commuter or underground trains must be made generally accessible.

Title III Public Accommodations

Public accommodations are interpreted as a broad range of services that include commercial sales, rental or service to the public. It includes educational institutions, recreational facilities and social service centres. The ADA prohibits the use of discriminatory criteria for establishing the right to use a service, that may exclude or screen out people with disabilities (e.g. just as businesses hire a certain number of Spanish-speaking individuals to meet customer needs, they should be prepared to employ sign language interpreters).

It is anticipated that the Title III requirement for providing auxiliary aids will be interpreted flexibly. It is not expected to result in an undue burden being placed on business (e.g. a restaurant is not required to provide a menu in Braille, if it is possible for the waiter to read out the menu). A business is entitled to choose among a range of alternatives for providing a service as long as the result is effective communication.

Existing public buildings should be made barrier-free wherever it is 'readily achievable' (i.e. when it can be accomplished easily and without too much expense). In most cases this includes ramping. However, new buildings (e.g. public and commercial office space and shops) must be made accessible to people with disabilities. Nevertheless, lifts are generally not required to be installed in buildings less than three stories high.

Title IV Telecommunications

Title IV requires that telephone companies provide effective telecommunication relay services. These must facilitate the communication of speech- or hearing-impaired individuals who use non-voice terminal devices. Such telecommunications systems also incorporate automatic teller machines at banks (ATMs) which will need to be made to 'talk'. There is a recognition of the need to develop rules governing the confidentiality of information resulting from assisted communication via message relay systems.

Title V Miscellaneous Provisions

This relates ADA to other laws such as the Rehabilitation Act of 1973, or the Hearing Aid Compatability Act of 1988, which had required all new telephones to be made compatible with hearing aids; this section is also related to the provision of insurance.

A few longitudinal studies have addressed the effects of the ADA on the lives of the people it was intended to benefit. Pfieffer (1996) has indicated that there is a divergence of opinion. Individual disabled people feel more empowered and see the law as a positive influence on attitudes, expectations and rights. Individual people in Pfieffer's survey also commented on improved physical accessibility which increased participation in the community, 'We expect things to be better and it makes us angrier when it's not. There is a real sense of "we're important" coming down' (Pfieffer 1996: 274).

This indication of individual liberation contrasts with some of the experiences of employers and bureaucrats operating at company and officious state level in wider society. 'A personnel director said that they "have done almost nothing" and that if they "get sued they will probably do something"' (Pfieffer 1996: 274). A disabled activist also commented that:

> Most disabled people have no political savvy, no philosophical orientation so they eat up this shit and believe it until they find out that they're just as unemployed, getting in worse shape from the point of medical need, housing is not available to the mass of them, more and more of them are being found on the streets.
>
> (Pfieffer 1996: 276)

It is clear from people's experiences of the ADA that individuals feel empowered and that they do not want to go back to the way things were (Pfieffer 1996; Burke 1995). However, it is also possible that the Disability Movement in the United States is becoming less radical and more complacent as the zeal of its early leaders fails to be replaced by younger equally committed individuals (Johnstone 1996c).

There is a question about just how much this legislative change actually helps; particularly those who need help least, or those who need the most help. The argument is that affirmative action through legislation has gone too far (affirmative action is intended to establish preferences for minorities e.g. black Americans, whereby preferential recruitment is given in favour of black students on American college campuses). It was well grounded as a morally defensible goal for aggrieved minorities such as black Americans claiming reparations against white American domination '... but somewhere over the years, it changed from reparations policy to diversity policy , including not only blacks but women, Latinos any and all minority groups...' (Tomasky 1996). This stretching of diversity across oppressed constituencies has not been sustained through the weight of public opinion but by court orders and codes of practice. At a time when everyone is faced with job uncertainty, declining living standards and reduced wages, it arguably becomes harder to justify the support for affirmative action for all minorities and under-represented groups. It is in this universal climate and under such a shift in circumstances that legislative change and equal opportunities for disabled people is emerging in the United Kingdom. However, it is arguable whether affirmative action towards disabled people in the United Kingdom has the same historical and moral claim to make as that which seeks to atone for the particularly horrid history of white treatment of blacks.

The re-emergence of segregation

In the United States there is a strong recent history of tackling discrimination through legislation and through affirmative action. The Civil Rights marches of the 1950s and 1960s led to legislation that challenged racially segregated education and employment practices. These actions influenced the emergence of equal opportunities legislation for disabled people. However, the 1990s saw the beginnings of a rejection of affirmative action in the United States. Any affirmative action for disabled people could be subject to the same reversals. This has begun to be particularly noticeable in the area of services in community colleges and local communities in the USA where resources for learning support have begun to be closely scrutinised and cut back (Cooper 1996; O'Day 1996).

In the United Kingdom the limitations of the DDA are acknowledged by the majority of disability organisations. There is a real probability that disabled people, who cannot participate effectively in the democratic process and whose needs involve additional expenditure in the workplace, will continue to face the prospect of being singled out for 'special treatment'. National disability groups are growing increasingly insistent that comprehensive civil rights for disabled people have not been achieved. The Disability Discrimination Act does not give disabled people rights and they are still considered second-class citizens with second-class rights and opportunities. Discrimination in the electoral process begins at the polling stations. It has been estimated that only 12 per cent of polling stations are fully accessible (*Disability Now* 1996) and that although people with learning difficulties are entitled to vote, the problem is that hardly any do. Research by MENCAP shows that only 5 per cent of people with learning difficulties used their vote in the 1992 general election.

Summary

Both the Disability Discrimination Act (DDA) in the United Kingdom and The Americans with Disabilities Act (ADA) in the USA have defined and established disability issues within equal opportunities legislation. Both acts encourage disabled people to use litigation as a method for ensuring employment opportunities, access to goods and services, access to public buildings and access to public transport. However, whereas the ADA has been perceived as a way of empowering disabled people within the wider context of civil rights, the DDA has been viewed by disabled people as a somewhat piecemeal and negative response to civil rights in the UK. However, the effectiveness of the DDA, in the opinion of disabled people, has been bolstered by the establishment of a Disability Rights Commission and it is hoped European law, binding upon the UK. There is further consideration of the political reactions of disabled people to legislative provision in Chapter 6. There was anticipation that the DDA would go some way to improve the 'quality of life' of people with disabilities and this issue is investigated in the next chapter.

CHAPTER 4

What is the meaning of 'quality of life' and 'independence'?

Questions

- What do you understand by 'quality of life' and what are its components?
- What does quality of life mean within the context of a market economy?
- The issue of quality is relative. Simple choices are not problematic. What are some of the more complex measures of quality in terms of disability discrimination?
- What do you consider advocacy to be in relation to empowerment and the widening of choice for disabled people?
- Draw the distinction between independence as autonomy and independence as self-sufficiency. What are the implications for disabled people?

Introduction

This chapter sets out to explore one of the key issues that lies at the heart of Disability Studies and the concerns of disabled people about being independent and 'having their say'. The terms 'independence' and 'quality of life' are, however, not unproblematic. Independence is an aim that many would agree with, but like 'quality of life' it can be interpreted in different ways. Vernon and Qureshi (2000) point out there can be a confusion between professional definitions and interpretation of independence and disabled people's definitions. Independence as autonomy and empowerment is different from independence as professionally defined self-sufficiency. They draw attention to this distinction:

> Autonomy implies the ability of individuals to live the kind of life they want. Independence implies not having to rely on other people. These are not necessarily the same thing. ... Autonomy is a customer-based objective and independence is a purveyor-favoured objective because it implies lower costs.
>
> (Grimley Evans 1997: 25)

In relation to disabled people and their more pragmatic interpretation, independence is firmly equated with autonomy and choice:

> Independence does not refer to someone who can do everything themselves, a feat that no human being can achieve whether they have an impairment or not, but indicates someone who is able to take control of their own life and to choose how that life is to be led. It is a thought process not contingent upon physical abilities.
>
> (Barnes 1994: 129)

Independent living has also been linked to the debate on 'quality of life'. It has clear associations with the right to receive support and to participate in the interactions of ordinary life:

> The concept of independent living is a broad one, embracing as it does the full range of human and civil rights. This means the right to have personal relationships, to be a parent, the right to equal access to education, training, employment and leisure activities and the right to participate in the life of the community.
>
> (Morris 1993: 7)

'Quality of life' (QOL) has been defined as 'an overall general well-being that is comprised of objective and subjective evaluations of physical, material, social and emotional well-being together with the extent of personal development and purposeful activity, all weighted by a personal set of values' (Felce and Perry 1996: 52). And such a definition is consistent with an explanation that recognises QOL as a multidimensional construct. A three-element conceptualisation of QOL, containing five domains of well-being is reproduced in Figure 4.1. A model such as this also forces us to focus upon stereotypical representations of lifestyles, an issue that is particularly pertinent to disabled people and the manner in which images of disability are perpetuated in our culture. In any event, the concept of quality in daily living forces us to consider the inter-relationship between objective measures, such as health, income, housing quality, friendship networks, activity and social roles, which run alongside more loosely defined and subjective markers. These refer to constructs such as personal satisfaction with life circumstances and the rating of the feeling of well-being in a range of different life conditions, e.g. judgement of personal accomplishment at different stages of the life cycle.

Thus, independence, independent living and quality of life for disabled people are interlinked. But control over services and the opportunities to choose whom to employ and when, for the provision of personal assistance are central to the definition and maintenance of an acceptable quality of life. Those who have grappled with the development of a universally acceptable conceptual model of QOL (e.g. Taylor and Bogdan 1996; Parmenter 1992) have been criticised for focusing on the 'superficial elements of service environments ... rather than the degree of autonomy or quality of interpersonal relationships experienced on a day-to-day basis' (Marquis and Jackson 2000: 416). The work of Felce and Perry like others is a multidimensional model involving subjective and objective components based on community adjustment constructs:

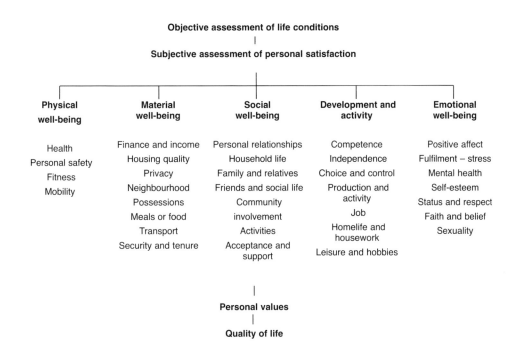

Figure 4.1 (Adapted from Felce and Perry 1996)

Many of the markers of 'quality of life' are clearly subjective and personalised perceptions of one's place in the environment and the responses that one receives from others. Brown *et al.* (1992) reporting on research conducted in Canada, have addressed the complexity of the term, indicating that quality of life is not simply about happiness and satisfaction, but also about striving and dissatisfaction (Brown *et al.* 1992). A similar attempt to measure quality of life indicators has been made in Europe (Moniga and Vianello 1995). The range of discourses suggest that there are fundamental implications for both service providers, carers and the opinions of disabled people. Research suggests that 'quality of life' is a complex concept represented not only by balances between satisfaction and dissatisfaction; primarily it is about gaining a positive self-image and a sense of empowerment and control over the mechanisms that regulate one's environment.

Quality of life: an eternal paradox?

Johnstone (1995) has indicated, with reference to the United Kingdom, and Banfelvy (1996) in a wider European context, that there is a looming crisis of confidence around the concept of quality of life in general. There are those who claim that welfare has eroded the work ethic and the moral fibre of a nation's workforce (Herrnstein and Murray 1994). As we begin the 21st century new conditions are being imposed on benefits and tough law and order measures introduced in order to control anti-social behaviour. This millennial tension is being echoed in the search for moral guidance in our leaders and our public services. The apparent failure of human relations has also disadvantaged many people who are perceived to be socially as well as sensorially, cognitively or physically disabled. Disabled people lead lives in which they will have been treated ambivalently. This often manifests itself in a kind of social inappropriateness, where disabled people perceive themselves not only as different but also as unprepared, or unwilling to adjust to all social situations. This can result in the repression of effective relationships in the home, community and the workplace.

The inability to fulfil the expectations of those around you, or the hopes of significant others, is a large burden and reactions can take the form of withdrawal and depression. At the same time there is often a disappointing lack of contact between disabled people themselves. There are few opportunities to establish and maintain intimate and mutually respectful friendships in settings that are constantly supervised. In such circumstances and with such fragile relationships, many disabled people do really need more contact with trusted companions who are capable of forming a social 'umbrella' of support to encourage them to form wider social networks and friendships. Such a network can cross the boundaries of generations, social status and gender.

Finance, or the lack of it, has already been indicated as a source of real hardship to all people without qualifications and disabled people in particular (Vernon and Qureshi 2000). The wage earned in low-paid open employment is little different from the amount paid to people on training programmes or receiving social security payments. For many people with disabilities, some of whom may be entitled to higher allowances due to disability, their welfare entitlements can far exceed their realistic earning potential. A failure of citizenship on the part of the whole society forces many disabled people to remain financially disadvantaged by a range of circumstances. Independence as financial self-sufficiency for them becomes an illusion. Either they remain living at home with their families, or they become economically dependent upon others; perhaps in the form of a spouse, partner or the State. If disabled people try to live alone or to join groups they can rapidly run into financial difficulties and confrontations with independence as autonomy and choice, in the form of bureaucratic regulations. In such circumstances, where the bureaucratic procedures of an independent adult status are only beginning to be understood, it is important to be able to turn to somebody for knowledgeable advice.

Those who are unfamiliar with handling the requirements of increasing bureaucracy may try to avoid contact with official authority, be it an institution or an agency. Quality of life may begin with the need for help in getting hold of such things as birth certificates, identity cards, passports, registration certificates, etc. There may be need for advice on how to obtain insurances and how to cancel the same if they are inadequate or too expensive. There may be need for technical support in dealing with public correspondence; for example in response to notices or demands or to know how to appeal against procedural decisions that may affect their lives. The ability to respond effectively can be a key factor in raising an individual's level of self-confidence and feelings of self-esteem.

Quality of life as an array of variables

The model of quality of life indicated in Figure 4.1 has tended towards a foundation on the lifestyles of non-disabled people and the normal social rhythms and circumstances that are so frequently considered as fundamental. As such it is an atheoretical, functional model similar to the work of O'Brien's 'Five Accomplishments' (O'Brien and Tyne 1981; O'Brien and O'Brien 1993). Research studies in the UK and Europe (e.g. Moniga and Vianello 1995; Berrington et al. 1996; Marks 1998; Marquis and Jackson 2000; Vernon and Qureshi 2000) investigating quality of life measures identified by disabled people suggest that the concept is more than a league table of those least able to benefit and should be considered as a product of a number of more complex interconnected variables. Thus, the constructs of 'independence' and 'quality of life' can be organised by both subjective and objective criteria.

- **Material well-being.** This is a potentially sensitive area. As well as income levels it might include observations and judgements about, e.g. the quality of housing, lifetime changes in relation to residence, financial circumstances, transport availability.
- **Physical well-being.** This includes any additional impairments, the need to use adaptations or prosthetic equipment. It might involve understanding of specialist services, e.g. speech therapy, chiropody, dieticians. Certainly it will incorporate an awareness of the importance of health and fitness, exercise and safety.
- **Social well-being.** This suggests community involvement as well as personal relationships. It will involve an understanding of the sources of support, aspects of everyday living and sources of help and advice in the community.
- **Development and activity.** While linked to objective measures of employment this variable is also to do with subjectively perceived levels of independence and the opportunities for choice and control in people's lives. It may refer to opportunities for education and training, including the uses made of day centres.
- **Emotional well-being** This is tied to feelings of self-worth; the levels of status and respect accorded to and subjectively assumed by people. It is also linked with the sense

of fulfilment that people attach to their lives. The legislation of the Direct Payments Act (1996) is an example of the law's potential for both expanding the sense of emotional well-being and exacerbating the stress that it induces. This long-sought legislation provides an option for personal support packages that enable disabled people to receive cash to pay for and exercise more control over the nature, purpose and quality of the assistance they receive. It is a marker of both independence as autonomy and choice and of the more questionable independence as self-sufficiency, in its potential as a cost-cutting exercise.

- **Mobility.** In order to properly develop quality of life, the mobility of disabled people has to be addressed and promoted. The awareness and removal of a number of architectural barriers (stairs and entrances to houses, toilets and public buildings) has improved across the United Kingdom and throughout Europe as a result of legislation. These considerations, together with adaptations to the means of transport (buses, trains, aeroplanes, taxis, etc. from 2004) and improvement in signage and the provision of information (e.g. sonorous traffic lights; tactile signs) are fundamental considerations for any adequate measures of effective quality of life.

- **Housing/dwelling place.** Accommodation that is unsuitable for a person's physical needs can undermine their quality of life in a variety of ways. Inaccessible accommodation can also compromise personal hygiene and dignity:

> There's no toilet downstairs here. I don't go upstairs any more than I'm forced to but I leave it until it's too late then I'm dribbling all the way upstairs, and I have to change two or three times a day. I can't put any pressure on these knees at all so going upstairs is a real struggle.
>
> (Quotation from informant, Vernon and Qureshi 2000: 264)

There are many different considerations that must be taken into account when the housing needs of disabled people are considered. On one side of the argument there are all the difficulties related to the level of autonomy of the person; on the other there are the real practical self-sufficiency considerations of people with physical and sensory impairments. We have also to distinguish between the perceived needs of those who continue to live in an institution from those in a group home, or those who share a house or apartment and those who live and support themselves independently.

- **Leisure time.** Quality of life is not only determined by the health and employment prospects of an individual, but also by opportunities that come together during leisure time and freedom of movement outside the home. Similarly social contact and companionship are important to break the monotony of being confined at home:

> Social life? I don't go out. Partly because I feel safe here whereas I don't outside. Since my wife died I've lost a lot of self confidence. But also I can't afford a social life.

I used to go dancing, I've got all the medals for ballroom dancing but I can't do nothing like that. I can hardly walk.

(Informants quoted in Cartwright *et al.* 1996: 63)

Holiday resorts, holiday houses, camping, recreational and sporting facilities must all be considered and made suitably accessible and available. There is a tendency for marked differences in this area. For example, in sport where, on the one hand, there are some activities designated only for disabled athletes and disabled sports people, while alternatively it is considered by others that sport and recreation is an ideal medium for promoting inclusion in community settings. Nevertheless, 'being able to go where you want and when you want was identified as one of the most critical factors in determining one's quality of life' (Vernon and Qureshi 2000: 264) and if such facilities can only be booked in advance this undermines the whole concept of freedom of choice and quality of life.

- **Vocational training.** Many people with disabilities are invisible to the general public following years of segregated educational provision. The majority of disabled school-leavers, it is argued, do not have the prerequisite skills for employment and this identifies them as having special training needs, regardless of whether this was evident while they were at school. These notions echo Freeman (1988) who has argued that disabled and 'delinquent' young people leaving school have been crudely redefined as not only unskilled but also as socially incompetent and in need of categorical programmes of vocational training and further training in social skills.

A great variety of vocational programmes for disabled people have been established across Europe. They are based on the principles of developing successful and satisfying placements in both the workplace and wider society. The programmes tend towards specific skills training but also teach the social behaviours and habits that are usually considered desirable in a work setting. The tension between independence as autonomy and independence as a form of social compliance, is also maintained in education and training in basic skills. With the emphasis on politically determined concepts such as self-advocacy, independence, self-determination and citizenship it is evident that education and training is in danger of emerging as an extension of professionally determined assessments of needs. The rhetoric in favour of inclusive educational principles in schools and colleges suggests that a vocational training which supports self-determination and independence will also stress the importance of changing attitudes towards disabled people. Perhaps this requires a re-negotiation of the meaning of independence and choice. If independence is about civic equity and control over one's life, this will require consideration across a wider emotional and psychological environment. This includes a reconsideration of the purpose of relationships between young people, disabled and non-disabled alike, their parents, teachers and employers.

- **Access to work/employment.** In traditional, industrial society terms, the theory of a person's value within the workplace has been argued something like this: employment potential is determined by an employee's efficiency and productivity and those people who are not capable of benefiting from training are not likely to be either economically efficient or profitable. By definition, it is argued, disabled people are less capable and more dependent than non-disabled people; therefore they are both at a disadvantage and more expensive. These attitudinal barriers are deeply rooted and while special training initiatives have expanded for all young people, they have also helped to provide a new justification for the subtle perpetuation of prejudices that limit the social and economic position of an increasing number of disillusioned and alienated young people. At the same time, work opportunities for disabled people are in danger of being redefined in order to include a growing population of those described as the underclass – people who are socially and economically deprived rather than disadvantaged through impairments. As jobs have disappeared and special services have been redefined in order to incorporate this underclass, we are beginning to see the expansion of special provision for those deemed as failures, deviating socially, economically and vocationally. Whether this has arisen as a result of deliberate strategies by successive governments, committed to driving down costs, rather than through the privately determined actions of individuals is worth some consideration.

Until recently there have really been only three alternatives for the employment of disabled and handicapped people: normal placement in a working place with some adaptations; employment in a sheltered facility; or unemployment with the possibility of therapeutic earnings. Recent legislative changes, in relation to disability discrimination, have influenced some changes in the working opportunities of people with sensory and physical impairments. However, the legislation will only apply to companies that employ more than 15 people and is, thereby, of little consequence to the majority of the employers in the UK.

The deliberate denial of quality of life

The emergence of the disability movement in the United Kingdom is integral to the understanding of 'quality of life'. The exercise of choice and the opportunity to take control of the organisation of one's own life is one of the first markers of quality. It is significant that for many people with disabilities this is still an aspiration rather than a reality. Campbell and Oliver (1996) have assembled an eloquent testimony to the many disabled people who have been – and are still – involved in raising awareness of the exclusion of disabled people in society. Quality of life is a human rights issue.

In industrial economies with relatively sophisticated and affluent political and economic systems, an infrastructure of professional services has been built to provide extensive support designed to enhance the quality of life of disabled people. The decision to compensate individuals for loss of income arising from disability, through the payment of lump-sum benefits, is a case in point. Other examples of improved quality of life could include subsidised, adapted housing and transport services. Specialist services have begun to be developed as groups of people with specific conditions have formed themselves into powerful organisations to promote the interests of self-recognised groups with 'disease specific' impairments, e.g. asthma, allergies, arthritis, dyslexia.

The physical health of young people with disabilities is often a factor in the accumulation of multiple disadvantage or accredited disabilities. Poor hygiene, poverty or alternative lifestyles are not automatic correlates with disability but they clearly affect levels of physical and psychological self-confidence. While at school, physical development and patterns of health can be observed and monitored as part of the curriculum and school life. If necessary, medical services and treatment can be arranged. The government targets for improving health and fitness set out in *The Health of the Nation* (HMSO 1992) have included a suggestion for more 'competitive' games for people with disabilities. These may not usefully relate to the promotion of health but they do at least recognise the place of activity in physical growth as an aspect of quality of life.

The promotion of health and sport during school years is unavailable outside the formal years of education. There is no mandatory requirement nor a prescribed curriculum in sports and health in further education colleges and neither is there any medical monitoring. The opportunities for organised sport for disabled people may be reduced as individuals are left to their own devices. However, it is now widely acknowledged that lots of non-competitive activities, e.g. dance, yoga, aerobics, swimming are ultimately better for the development of health than organised team games. These might be better considered in discussions about measures of quality of life for all people, but particularly those with disabilities. Attention has been drawn to this dimension of QOL:

> It has been argued that it is not the impairment but social isolation and lack of support which makes some lives unbearable. The assumption that certain impairments automatically lead to an unacceptably low quality of life is not rooted in an accurate understanding of the experience of impairment. Rather it is a failure of imagination and the pathologisation of disabled people.
>
> (Marks 1998: 38)

It is clear from the above that many people with disabilities can become multiply disadvantaged by a lack of basic care in the area of personal hygiene, laundry and sometimes reasonable nourishment, etc. If you lack basic amenities and have only a temporary address you are immediately disadvantaged in terms of employment. 'No dwelling, no job' is a basic rule for all people of lower status in society and this includes many people with disabilities.

Successful living in a community is fraught with prejudice and economic inequalities. The 'community' can itself be highly oppressive and unjust. As this text has already indicated, at certain stages in history, communities have demonstrated extremes of intolerance towards minorities. Gould (1996) outlines and chronicles how systems of control are frequently predicated on deliberate prejudice and have been used to oppress a range of minorities. We need to recognise that the community itself can be a force for oppression, exhibiting a level of intolerance that continues in society to the present day.

As has been noted by many writers (e.g. Corbett and Barton 1992; Johnstone 1995) empowerment can only come about if the powerful are prepared to relinquish power – or alternatively, if there is sufficient momentum for the powerless to mobilise and seek self-determination. The isolated experiences of the majority of disabled people mean that it is unrealistic to expect that they will set out to claim power. As we are reminded, this in itself, becomes its own form of oppression. There is a considerable issue here, that challenges the purpose of what constitutes 'real help'. As the numbers of self-help groups and support networks increase there is a growing and visible solidarity among a range of minority groups, including disabled people. This, inevitably, challenges the role and function of the 'professional'. However, as we have seen, professionals are often involved in the setting up and maintenance of self-advocacy groups and they have to face up to the often disturbing realisation that their involvement sustains the oppression that the groups are intended to overcome. The repercussions of real choice and effective empowerment, mean that there will be some inevitable conflicts. This involves professionals and parents having to readjust to a range of new and often uncomfortable realities.

> The argument that empowerment lies at the heart of 'quality of life' is a mark of a mature society. In supporting empowerment, professionals have to shift their practices and also their mind set – moving beyond tokenism and 'fix it quick' solutions. All too often the status quo is maintained under the guise of innovation; 'speaking for yourselves' is confined to curricular programmes and simulations in classrooms:
>
> To challenge it involves a fundamental and courageous shift of roles. Only through this creative process will new and innovative identities be forged. If tolerance is to be fostered, this will help define the perimeters of what constitutes 'successful' living.
>
> (Corbett and Barton 1992: 76)

Successful living and quality of life leads us back to the consideration of the deeper set of values that underpin the exploration of liberation. As Coleridge (1993) has pointed out, basic needs are lacks which need to be supplied – like food, shelter and health. However, there is a clear problem if the development of quality of life is restricted to the process of meeting needs in this way. At the heart of the problem lies the fact that such needs are passive. Quality of life needs are also active.

There are other needs which are just as basic. There is: 'the need to be creative, to make choices, to exercise judgement, to love others, to have friendships, to contribute something of oneself to the world, to have social function and purpose' (Coleridge 1993: 52).

If these needs are not met the result is the impoverishment of the human spirit. In Coleridge's view any enquiry into disability and the social and political forces that surround the concept, brings us all face-to-face with the purposes of survival, the way justice does or does not happen and the central question of human relationships. The areas of life that contribute to 'quality' are ultimately the same for us all. They apply to everybody. We cannot use the argument that they apply to some and not to others. We certainly cannot say that it only applies to that portion of the population that is classified as disabled: 'We can start by accepting that disability exists. It is part of human life, part of the way things are. Let us engage with it, enquire into it, make friends with it. Disabled people do it from the inside, people who are not yet disabled need to do it from the outside' (Coleridge 1993: 216).

The community base in the development of quality of life

Quality of life in any country has to take account of the ecological, socio-economic and cultural characteristics of the geographic area concerned. This principle lies at the heart of the move towards inclusive community provision and away from institutional rehabilitation with its centralised, capital-intensive emphasis on normalisation.

With few exceptions, established community groups and charities still see QOL and disability as basically a medical problem. 'The concept of QOL is not an objective, value-free measure of the extent to which the needs of a population are met, but rather as one laden with cultural prejudices that justify the removal of individuals deemed to be a burden' (Marks 1998: 42). Nevertheless, this utilitarian philosophy has had some pragmatic and beneficial solutions. For example, some housing associations in the UK have started to construct accessible houses and apartments, using the Scandinavian 'Fokus' system as a model. Charitable organisations like the Community Service Volunteers (CSV) have established community-based support systems. However, there is an important difference between their approach and that of the movement of disabled people campaigning for disability rights and attempting to move away from narrow rationalist criteria for the values accorded to people and their lifestyles: 'Local Authorities, Health Authorities and charities tend not to see independent living as a basic human right as we do. For them independent living is still a welfare issue' (Bracking 1993).

Community-based rehabilitation (CBR)

It was in a serious attempt to de-institutionalise, de-mystify and de-professionalise rehabilitation that the concept of community-based rehabilitation (CBR) was born. At its heart it shares much in common with other philosophies that are humanistic and aimed at promoting personal dignity. The term has, nevertheless, been widely misapplied and is still a generally misunderstood process. Community-based rehabilitation sets out to promote awareness and responsibility for rehabilitation within local communities; it deliberately targets self-reliance. Disabled people, their families and all members of the community are expected to take an active part in the process of building their own common solutions.

The premise of CBR is deceptively simple: a local supervisor is recruited from the community and receives training; the supervisor then trains the immediate and extended family of the disabled person in basic rehabilitation skills supported by 'the community'.

Quality of life within a CBR programme is thus based on two rather old-fashioned assumptions:

- that the greatest resource for helping a disabled person is his or her own family;
- that the community around the family can be mobilised for the development of support.

The role of the family is fundamental for building relationships and social development in most societies. However, its relationship to the QOL of disabled people in the community is more problematic. The family has always been one of the main sources of learning support and help to a disabled child. But, the quality of this provision varies and is not always guaranteed, e.g. there may be emotional or practical factors that prevent a family from helping in all circumstances. At a practical level, there may be simply not enough time or money to provide an adequate amount of rehabilitation for an individual. This need not imply a lack of care, but is simply an illustration of the fact that absolute poverty concentrates the mind to focus on the absolute essentials of life. As Coleridge (1993: 86) reminds us: 'As soon as services become available, parents will use them for their children, but they may not have the energy or time to do systematic rehabilitation themselves.'

At the emotional, more affective level, the function of the parent is different from the role carried out by the paid professional therapist or counsellor. The relationship between parent and child carries a set of emotions that do not exist between the child and a therapist operating outside the family. The birth of a disabled child may have produced an undercurrent of guilt in the parents, and led to the often described cycle of overprotection and under-expectation associated with parenting a disabled child. Overprotection, rather than neglect, is more frequently a cause of underachievement in people with disabilities.

The other important feature of CBR is the involvement of community action. However, it is extremely difficult to impose a community approach by government decree, i.e. in a hierarchy of authority, from the top. The concept of 'community' is an organic one that grows and changes. But an effective community is not a collection of bland assumptions that builds on the belief that everyone is prepared to work together harmoniously. Families, neighbours, health services, social workers, local authorities, employers, carpenters, etc. all play their part in meeting the needs of disabled people. But the subtle dynamics of communities will always need to be considered and development workers should tap into existing community patterns and interests rather than attempt to set up projects that may result in the destruction of existing community strengths.

The development of community-based rehabilitation (CBR)

Social justice is at the heart of disability theory and changing morality in the Western world. Debates on QOL have interlinked with changes in medical knowledge and intervention treatments to create new philosophical debates on old ethical dilemmas. Community-based rehabilitation, on the other hand, was originally developed to meet the needs of communities in isolation from generic medical and educational services (Thorburn and Marfo 1990; Miles 2000). It has been particularly applicable to remediation and rehabilitation programmes to address childhood disability in developing countries and to people in rural economies (e.g. those engaged in agriculture, farming, fishing, etc.). The World Health Organisation and UNESCO/UNICEF have established numerous functional, 'basic needs' and community-based rehabilitation programmes. These have addressed instruction and training in the non-formal and more functional areas of selection and maintenance of safe water supplies; methods of waste disposal; growing, storing and consumption of more and better quality foods and nutritional education.

Community-based rehabilitation is centred around generic 'home-grown' interventions and can be traced back to the activities of WHO in 1976 (WHO 1982). By the early 1980s WHO was claiming that CBR was 'an appropriate, effective, feasible and economically viable approach to provide the most essential rehabilitation to the disabled persons not now reached by services in the developing countries. CBR should form part of the primary health care programme' (WHO 1982: 19).

Community-based rehabilitation is designed as a three-tiered model of comprehensive rehabilitation intended to build on the resources of the community. The model has been commented upon by many authors (e.g. Miles 1981, 1990; Kalyanpur 1996).

The first level of basic community provision comprises disabled people and consumers, their families and community workers, together with existing community agencies (both statutory and voluntary). A community health worker, called the local supervisor, is recruited and trained in the application of simple and basic rehabilitation techniques using the CBR Training Manual (Helander *et al.* 1983). The local supervisor identifies the individual with disabilities, assesses the severity of the condition and then trains a member of the individual's family to provide ongoing rehabilitation. More sophisticated and professional rehabilitation would require referrals to the next two levels of specialisation. The second, or intermediate support level involves existing general health services with staff that have a higher level of competence and more sophisticated resources than those found at the community level. Since services at this level are not disability specific, personnel such as physicians, nurses, teachers, midwives, social workers will be required to receive training in the areas of disability prevention and rehabilitation. The third and final specialised service level consists of speciality areas, including medical, vocational rehabilitation, special education and social services. The quality and quantity of these rehabilitation services varies throughout almost all developing countries.

Community-based rehabilitation projects have been commended for their pioneering efforts to involve community and family members. The techniques have also been praised for their emphasis on functional rather than clinical treatments. However, critics have argued for revision of an underlying philosophy that assumes a pre-determined inclination towards people with disabilities where, in fact, none exists (e.g. Miles 1996, 2000).

Werner (1987) states that the model assumes a considerably sophisticated level of coordination of health, vocational, educational and social services in countries and regions where disability issues are a low priority. This point is illustrated by early evaluations of CBR in India (Ephraem 1984; Hariharan 1982), where attempts to incorporate CBR within the rubric of primary health care services soon began to meet with opposition from village health workers. Despite monetary incentives, the community health workers resented the additional responsibilities and complained of work overload. According to Hariharan (1982), traditional prejudice against disabled people accounted for the reluctance among the local supervisors to provide rehabilitation services.

Further criticisms directed at CBR have centred on the three-tiered process of implementation. Far from empowering people it is claimed that the system prevents people from gaining access to information and resources (Miles 1985, 1990; O'Toole 1987). In his review of CBR across developing countries Miles (1985) has stated that as parents become increasingly dependent upon the local supervisor for technical advice, they cease to use their own creative resources to develop alternatives. In addition the responsibility for caring for the disabled person falls exclusively upon the immediate and extended family. Circumstances such as this beg the question of the meaning of community responsibility. In reality the process develops into little more than the mobilisation of people's resources subsidising government-controlled programmes. Miles (1981) had been among the first to note that CBR tends to impose a top-down approach that is entirely inappropriate for some parts of the world:

> The concept of individual 'self-fulfilment', stressing one's 'maximum potential' being 'normalised' and 'integrated into society' are part of a Western package of ideals and philosophy. … The value inequality of human beings, by reason of birth, caste, skin pigmentation, economic and social status, is a fundamental tenet throughout Asia, whereas the educated Westerner tends to cherish an ideal of value-equality, while being highly competitive, individualistic and intolerant of under-achievement.
>
> (Miles 1981: 7)

Threats to quality of life from deliberate action

No systematic studies have yet been carried out to assess the extent to which warfare and violence contributes to disability. Where impairments arise as a consequence of violence, this in turn can lead to social abandonment and disablement (e.g. the physical impairments arising from the estimated thousands of amputations on soldiers and civilians surviving the conflicts in former Yugoslavia, Vietnam and Northern Ireland). Similar deliberate atrocities have resulted as a consequence of abandoned, booby-trap landmines and have been reported by Save the Children in Afghanistan, Mozambique and other parts of the world. A study by UNICEF from Somalia, covering four district hospitals each serving about 100,000 people, indicates that abuse is not constrained within national boundaries:

> it was surprising to find that in the hospital records dating two years back, the only patients admitted for treatment in the hospital consisted of hundreds of cases listed as 'wounds'. The hospital staff described these 'wounds' as resulting from domestic violence and other forms of community fighting.
>
> (Helander 1993: 28)

As a further example, in Cambodia it has been estimated that some 7 to 10 million landmines were abandoned from civil conflicts and that they continue to injure and maim some 60 to 70 people a month (Barron, *The Mine Clearers,* Radio 4, 6 November 1996). Despite the publicity derived from the work of Diana, Princess of Wales, and the signing of the Ottawa Convention in 1999, it is still estimated that worldwide 25,000 people a year are being maimed or killed by abandoned landmines (*Guardian* 8 March 2001). The associated trauma and unfortunate mental health complications resulting from such violence is the much more common experience of victims, rather than physical disablement. Severe psychiatric diseases or disturbances are seen among many who have either participated in or lived through war. However, psychiatric scars can arise from trauma that is far closer to home.

Family conflicts, and the abuse of disabled people have only recently begun to be uncovered. The grotesque stories of rape and the suspicion of sexual attack on disabled women have been neglected and overlooked. Though under-diagnosed and hidden, the abuse of people with disabilities is frequent and there is a high incidence affecting people with learning difficulties. Disabled people tend to be more reliant upon other people for a range of physical and personal activities. They may also be weaker and less able to defend themselves. They may need to be helped to take baths, use a toilet or get dressed. They are vulnerable and at the same time used to having their privacy and their personal physical space invaded. 'Given the lack of autonomy and the perpetually threatened integrity of the body, disabled people are often used to switching off and disassociating themselves from what is happening to the rest of the body' (Shakespeare *et al.* 1996 : 143). The case can be made more bluntly, 'if a child has never been allowed to say "No" to being touched by doctors, nurses or even parents, how can we expect the child, or later the woman, to resist a sexual attack?' (Degener 1992: 154).

Disability and quality of life in developing countries

Historically, provision for people with disabilities has been ignored in developing countries where the economic and material basis for living tends to be impoverished There has been an absence of suitable textbooks describing the circumstances and needs of people with disabilities in the developing world. Those that have been available are usually adopted from a Western European cultural perspective. Any detailed discussion that does emerge is frequently based on generalisations that are assumed to be held in common, but, in reality, are of relatively minor importance. Baine (1988) and Kalyanpur (1996) both suggest that this has served to diminish discussion around those issues of major concern and real community needs. For example, the tests and methods of special education recommended for use in Western countries are quite inappropriate for use in developing countries. Any tests normed on Western children will usually be culturally biased; materials, specialist personnel and physical facilities recommended and anticipated in the classrooms of Europe are simply not available in developing countries. Pre-supposed considerations about the quality of life of disabled people developed in England, Europe and America have little relationship with the day-to-day circumstances of the countries to which they have been imported.

Our consideration of quality of life has so far indicated how both a business ethos and the ideology of the marketplace have influenced and defined the understanding of disability in both capitalist and centralised economies. The new rationale for the provision of services in developing countries is to give a more fundamental meaning to the concept of quality of life as liberation. This includes equal access to educational opportunities for all learners, regardless of their physical, emotional and intellectual impairments. However, these objectives cannot be achieved without an adequate understanding of the wider political marginalisation of disabled people. Nkabinde (1993), writing with reference to the emerging political order in the new South Africa, has suggested that there is a rising number of young people with disabilities at risk due to political violence, neglect, torture and abuse. This factor can be linked to the effects of AIDS and the demands that this health condition alone is placing on stretched resources. It is evident that, in such circumstances an understanding of the social model of disability can play a significant role in changing social conditions and the quality of life.

In developing countries, as with everywhere else, cultures and belief systems tend to spring from the basic premise that the community is a hierarchically ordered unit that is superior to the individual. In India, for example, independence and 'quality of life' are defined very differently from Western conceptions:

In the West the child is encouraged to 'grow up', to 'be a big boy' to do things for himself, and he is praised for taking such initiatives. The situation is quite the contrary in India ... I have seen boys of five and six years of age sitting quietly while mother or servant or relative feeds them ... The situation is similar with the processes of bathing and dressing. This is a factor to be considered in the care of the handicapped child, in light of our desire to make him as independent and 'normal' as possible.

(Nimbkar 1971: 8)

This emergence of disability awareness in the developing world runs in uncomfortable parallel with the examination of disability as a legitimate area of study in general. Any discussion that emerges cannot, however, avoid exposure to many of the underlying prejudices of racial segregation and the uncaring treatment of many black and Asian people with disabilities.

From rehabilitation to self-advocacy '... nothing about me, without me ...'

There are a variety of considerations of the term advocacy. Among the most common are:

- **legal advocacy**, which usually refers to lawyers helping people exercise or defend their legal rights, but can also include people like Welfare Rights Services assisting people with benefits entitlements and representing people at benefits appeals;
- **group advocacy**, which refers to people uniting to campaign on issues affecting a particular group or cause. It is particularly associated with the function and role of pressure groups;
- **citizen advocacy**, which involves partnership between a vulnerable person and a member of the public on a long-term basis in order to establish and protect the person's long-term interests;
- **self-advocacy**, which often means individuals exercising their skills, to express their views on their own behalf. Sometimes self-advocacy involves people coming together through self-directed peer groups. This encourages and enables members to gather the confidence to speak up for themselves. Good examples of this development would be the development of self-advocacy groups by people with learning difficulties creating the People First Movement, or in the mental health field, Survivors Speak Out.

If we recognise how the inequality of people with disabilities has been constructed, and continues to provide a basis for a social policy of exclusion, where does this leave the concept of quality of life in relation to self-advocacy? The inequalities inherent in the social structure of our institutions have been touched upon in this chapter, but the emphasis has been on the State. The development of services and the subject matter of instruction has tended to ignore the daily life experience of people with disabilities. What is required is a shift towards a new framework for measuring the quality of life and a re–definition of the so-called problems of disability. Rather than seeing the problem as something rooted in people with disabilities, it needs to be recognised as a feature of the inequality that is inherent in the social and economic structure of society. Rioux (1996) encapsulates this point:

> If we wish to work towards societies that are distinguished by a culture of justice and the public ownership of private disadvantage, we have to find a framework that takes into account and makes policy that includes all people, including those who do not fit conventional norms. This deconstruction of inequality will have to be addressed by concerted coherent action.
>
> (Rioux 1996: 131)

Self-advocacy is a fashionable term for an old concept which is integral to any understanding of 'quality of life'. It as about seeking and gaining additional information about rights, responsibilities and entitlements for oneself or a group. Trade unions provide a good example of group advocacy; offering people who feel marginalised the infrastructure and opportunity to come together to gain strength through a collective voice. Self-advocacy, therefore, continues the act of making choices and decisions and bringing about desired change for oneself. Crawley (1988, 1989) has suggested that any activity that involves self-determination, or people asserting themselves rather than having their interests advanced by others can be called self-advocacy. This means that it can include very simple things, such as indicating whether you like the food you are given or not, to more complex actions such as choosing whether or not to go on strike for higher wages.

Both advocacy and self-advocacy are thus on the same continuum but at opposite ends of the scale of autonomy and assertiveness. The need for advocacy stems from the difficulties that we all face in modern societies from time to time. Self-advocacy emerges from strategies for self-determination. It is a truism that all individuals feel marginalised at certain times and somebody speaking on our behalf can help to facilitate change. The relative distribution of power in society means that some individuals are not always in a position to represent their own interests. This can arise as a result of intolerance, prejudice and fear. It can be due to the restrictions imposed by an individual impairment or due to the disabling or restricting environment in which someone lives. People without the means of access to power, or organisations through which their views can be heard or listened to, are doubly disadvantaged. For example, those who are deemed too old, too disabled, too poor, or somehow too far beyond the pale of society's cultural norms, are diminished in terms of their citizenship. Advocacy is a tool for challenging this disempowerment and attempting to re-establish people's sense of self-respect, dignity and self-confidence. It can be conducted on a personal and/or a group basis. But above all else it is about getting your voice heard.

The principles of all advocacy work are founded on respect, dignity and empowerment. This is particularly the case in relation to people with disabilities. As far as possible, advocates work to support individuals to help themselves and to ensure that the advocate does nothing to further disempower the individual by taking control or imposing their own agenda.

Within a social policy context, the need for effective advocacy for disabled people was officially first recognised in 1986. The Disabled Persons (Services Consultation and Representation) Act acknowledged that disabled people need to have access to independent advocates. Although the relevant sections of the Act have never been implemented, the legislation has reinforced the importance of the role played by independent advocacy groups in lobbying and campaigning for single and collective causes. The importance of this function has been emphasised and strengthened by the establishment of the Disability Rights Commission in the monitoring of the DDA (*Equal Opportunities Review* 93, 2000). The requirement that local authorities must be seen to be consulting with end-users of services has also been reinforced by recommendations in *The Health of the Nation* (HMSO 1992) initiative which has stressed the importance of gathering the views of service-users and opportunities for access to independent advocacy.

Challenges and issues for advocacy services to address

One of the main functions of an advocacy service has become the requirement to help people interpret the changes that have taken place in the provision of services. There is a need to translate official 'jargon', as Health and Social Services have moved towards commissioning services in the marketplace that has formed in the split between purchasers and providers. Language is often a major barrier to people accessing the services they need. Vernon and Qureshi (2000) have noted that the outcomes of community care and definitions of service quality are viewed differently by different stakeholders. Providers of social care services now apply the language of the financial markets to describe both the purpose of services and their infrastructure, personnel and the implications for users who are now customers. This uncomfortable association of personal care with the language of accountancy means that people become statistics and cuts in services become cost-saving 'measures' and 'down-sizing'. It is alien to most people.

There are also indications that there is an extensive need to develop both access to and interpretation of information about the range of services available to disabled people in community settings (Berrington *et al.* 1996; Chapman *et al.* 1997; Drake 1999; Priestley 1999; Vernon and Qureshi 2000). The Community Care Act (1990) was supposed to ensure that responsibility for coordinating support and access to services for individuals with disabilities was to be placed in the remit of one agency. Social services departments were given this statutory responsibility. Understandably, departments have neither the time, nor the levels of knowledge, to completely meet this challenge. There is finally the fear and suspicion that accompanies the concerns of individuals when personal circumstances become part of professional discourses.

Social workers have traditionally seen themselves as advocates for a range of service users, including people with disabilities; it is often why people have joined the caring professions. This can lead to a somewhat proprietorial sense of territory for both the social worker and the individual concerned and this, in turn, can lead to resentment of 'outside' people meddling in what they feel they both know best. The changes in the conditions of service for those involved in the 'caring services' have nevertheless made it more important, rather than less, that independent advocacy is available to vulnerable people. However, it is important to remember that most professionals and administrators have never been truly independent and so can never be true advocates. As the agenda for social work and care moves increasingly towards the rationing of services, the atmosphere and environment of professional concern has changed. Social workers are increasingly perceived as the withdrawers, rather than the providers of services and the internal market places an emphasis upon the detailed assessment of disabled people as clients, rather than helping them to provide a better quality of life for themselves through resistance to the prevailing structural allocation of resources.

Summary

In this chapter it is argued that quality of life is best judged by the way in which we treat people at the margins. Quality of life measures are made up from a complex array of variables that have become increasingly challenged by the imposition of the internal market. Quality of life is nevertheless central to the provision of services for disabled people and the enhancement of subjective and objective measures of well-being remain an overarching goal of all who work in the caring services. For people in developing and impoverished economies the promotion of community-based rehabilitation (CBR) is considered to be one way of developing self-help for, and a communal commitment to, disabled people.

Finally, the tension between CBR and self-advocacy is examined together with some of the reservations about what it is really possible to do for other people, who ideally should be empowered to act for themselves.

CHAPTER 5

Euthanasia and the new eugenics

Questions

- Is it reasonable for society to support the findings of genetic scientists in relation to the lives of disabled people?
- How is it possible to develop a positive recognition of disability while accepting a mother's right to choose to abort a foetus?
- Is it legitimate to practise population control?
- Critically consider the implications of 'the right to die' in relation to the lives of people considered to be in a permanent vegetative state.

Introduction

Eugenics: ... 'the study of production of fine human offspring by control of mating' ...

(Concise Oxford Dictionary 1989: 104)

... I have known so many women whose lives were devastated by having to take care of a helpless elderly parent or spouse. And of course, I have read about, or heard about many more ... Proponents of the welfare state may object that in a properly run country, it should never be necessary for anyone to become a burden upon anyone else. That if one does become decrepit, one ought to be properly cared for by trained professionals at the public expense. But, I ask you is such a utopian solution realistic?

('Do We have a duty to die?', *Voluntary Euthanasia Society Newsletter,* January 1988)

The sex instinct in defectives is often violent and unrestricted; and in a feeble-minded male, may lead to outrages as brutal as they are repulsive. Healy (an American eugenicist) goes so far as to urge a drastic surgical operation, not merely to prevent the

creature from propagating others of his type, but also to root out these vicious inclinations from the criminal himself.

(The Young Delinquent, Burt 1925: 319)

The natural in man is due to inborn heredity, the cultural to his acquired heritage.
Congenital heritage is received during gestation, perinatal and post-natal at the moment
of birth and throughout human education.

(Wolf Children and The Wild Boy of Aveyron, Malson and Itard 1972)

We no longer parade our freaks in fairgrounds, we put them in the courtroom for
general public consumption instead. ... The right to life is not an absolute. It is inextricably and untidily linked in almost every case with social and psychological considerations.

('Two into one', *The Guardian* 8 November 2000)

The late 19th century saw the emergence of eugenics as a science, but the construct has
a longer history. As we enter the twenty-first millennium the issue of eugenics has moved
from the narrowly defined consideration of heredity and moved more towards issues
related to pregnancy, abortion, euthanasia and genetic engineering. The aim of this
chapter is to expand the debate away from the perception of genetics as a dangerous
science and to focus instead on gene technology as a dimension of effective therapeutic
strategies and personal choice.

While human behaviour may not depend on heredity alone, the system of biological
needs and functions carried by the genotype are passed on at conception and relate us in
some way to all other living creatures. How much of an individual's intellectual ability is
determined by environmental factors and how much is already decided by a person's
genetic make-up is one of the oldest debates in the area of disability studies. Heredity may
set the limit that one may reach in intellectual capacity, but the environment determines
how close one comes to achieving the potential within each of us. The relationship of
genetics to the circumstances of people with disabilities brings us to a consideration of
the capricious workings of the laws of mutation and the principles of inheritance, dominance and recessive genes.

There is a long history of attempts to build the case for a congenital link between criminal and/or moral deviancy and educational backwardness and mental retardation. This
was particularly prevalent at the beginning of the 20th century. Goddard (1912) made a
careful, but ultimately selective, study of two lines of descent, traced from Martin
Kallikak – one normal, the other feeble-minded. Kallikak is reported by some writers (Ray
1983) to have been a soldier in the American revolutionary wars but is more likely to be a
pseudonym contrived by Goddard from the two Greek words *kallos* for beauty and *kakos*
meaning bad, to cover investigations into an extended family line. Martin Kallikak
fathered both a legitimate line of children and an illegitimate son with an inn-keeper's

daughter, or tavern wench, and so started two parallel lines of descent. The members of his legitimate family were judged to be psychologically normal, while the offspring of the illegitimate line were deemed to be full of mental defectives. A similarly notorious study is the investigation of the Jukes family (Dugdale 1877). The descendants of Max Jukes, who was described as a drunken vagabond from the backwoods of New York State, were traced by Dugdale. By 1915 they totalled 2,094 people and among them were claimed to be 140 convicted criminals (7 of whom were murderers), 300 prostitutes, 310 beggars and 600 cretins.

In more recent times the historical echoes of enforced sterilisation on people considered to be socially marginalised has been resurrected. For example, the racist claims that blacks are intellectually inferior to whites, as a result of inherited characteristics, has been raised by Herrnstein and Murray (1994) in their provocative account of the dispersion of IQ. The Nordic policy of forced sterilisation on people with developmental disabilities, as practised in Scandinavia between 1934 and 1976, has been brought to public attention and criticism (*Guardian* 3 September 1997: 13; Haydon 1997). It is a reminder that delusions of racial purity lurk just beneath the surface of the collective human psyche.

The study of genetics is complicated by more than spurious and racist judgements; there is a number of more central ethical and practical dilemmas related to the families of people with disabilities. As Shakespeare (1998: 666) points out, 'genetics currently promises more than it can deliver, particularly in the area of gene therapy'. Geneticists are first of all unable to experiment directly on human subjects and so tend to work with the short-lived, but prolific and more readily available, fruit fly. The study of genetic make-up is also complicated by the sheer complexity of the genetic structure of the human species. The number of genes involved and under investigation must be numbered in tens of thousands and this is before account is taken of possible combinations that may arise. Breaking it all down into distinguishable traits that can be mapped and analysed was the purpose of the human genome project.

The human genome project

The human genome project was started in the United States in the 1980s to trace and map out the genetic structure and variability of the entire human population. It is due to be completed in 2003. In effect, this world-wide exercise in mapping the structures that make up human biology is liable to change medicine from pure disease management to prevention of individual risks. It thus has the potential to both forecast and eradicate impairment and disability through biological therapy and improved understanding of the construction of genetic material. At this point it is probably worth recalling that the nucleus of a normal human cell contains 23 pairs of chromosomes making a total of 46 chromosomes altogether, and as is well known a human being is formed from these 23 pairs of chromosomes. Chromosomes are composed of the essential genetic material – genes. Each gene within 22 of the chromosome pairs has a duplicate gene in the 'matching' chromosomes; the 23rd pair is sex-linked, and its genes may be identical (XX for females) or different (XY for males). Research to date indicates that these chromosomes provide each of us with some 80,000 genes. The average gene has 2,000 base pairs; of the expected 80,000 genes only 6,000 are known, i.e. less than 10 per cent.

The sheer enormity of the project can perhaps be better understood when it is realised that only 5 per cent of the human genome is currently under investigation. 'The other 95% of the genome is still unknown' (Hameister 1996: 32). At the dawn of the genome project, molecular geneticists often focused on simple genetic diseases. For example, in one of the first important accomplishments of positional cloning (the process that is now widely used to link genes to traits) researchers in 1983 found a location on chromosome 4 linked to Huntingdon's disease: 'This kind of one gene, one disease formula, enticed scientists with the prospect of making relatively easy progress in the understanding and treatment of inherited diseases' (Allen 1997: 34).

Such optimism has turned out to be somewhat of a false dawn. Other key linkages have been proclaimed and either dismissed or quietly forgotten, e.g. an obvious case is the controversial 'discovery' in 1993 of a homosexuality gene. It may be that some diseases are relatively easy to account for, Huntingdon's disease and sickle cell anaemia among them, but the variations in the gene mutations may be so large and involve so many other variations and combinations as to be almost unknowable. However, while the spectre of a relatively simple genetic determinism may be disappearing within the scientific community this does not mean that the possibilities for determining a genetic basis for a whole raft of disabling conditions can be dismissed from the collective psyche of the general population. This populist argument for genetic determinism has guided many people's atavistic judgements in relation to disablement, phobias, neuroticism and the wish to exercise control.

Moral and ethical considerations

It would normally be accepted that ethical principles should be closely related to legal consequences. Ethics, or 'the principles by reference to which we organise our lives and decide what we ought or ought not to do' (Kennedy 1980), are not therefore the preserve of any one group. However, as a result of their day-on-day involvement with disabled people, doctors, care workers, social workers and managers tend to be delegated to make judgements about other people's lives. This is expected of them; they are held responsible for knowing what ought to be done. It would, therefore, be comforting to believe that the judgements made are based on the technical expertise and training that they have received. It is, nevertheless, unlikely that all the decisions made about the lives of disabled people are technical, or that they are a matter for any one profession alone. The judgements to be made are about fine judgements of truth and honesty and whether or not it should be waived. Moral and ethical determination lies at the heart of the approval of society and these judgements rely more upon the prevailing cultural and spiritual values of society than any technical expertise.

Is it a doctor's responsibility alone, for example, to decide whether it is ethically correct to treat a baby born with a severe impairment when, if untreated the baby will normally die, through what has come to be called benign neglect? Such dilemmas of moral judgement also arise each time a social worker has to decide on the needs for respite care, or a doctor weighs up what to do with an elderly person paralysed by a stroke; it applies to the disabled person, with deteriorating eyesight, living alone in their own home. As Kennedy stated in his Reith Lecture: 'There is no mechanic's manual, no technicians guide, which indicates when treatment is justified.' What happens instead is that professional judgements are made on the basis of some rough and ready index that anticipates an individual's future 'quality of life'. These life and death decisions are not technically determined but more often fashioned around human fallibility (Kennedy 1980).

For people with disabilities the human application of genetics carries with it a variety of ethical and practical risks. Scientists are clearly interested in the over-riding concern to see the use of bio-technology in the diagnosis and cure of genetic disease. As such it is linked to disabled people's lives as an attempt to relieve any suffering arising from avoidable impairments. This rather weak association between genetics and eugenics was dramatically brought to public attention in the UK when in the summer and autumn of 2000 the conjoined (Siamese) twins Jodie and Mary became the focus of public debate. The *Guardian* encapsulated the ethical, legal and eugenic agenda:

> … this has been an obsessively interesting news story, followed in gripping detail as the parents strive to stop the doctors officiously keeping alive this monstrous abnormality that might or might not be two people. The doctors want to save one child at the expense of the other, the parents don't. How everyone has relished the moral, ethical and legal dilemma. How intellectually enthralling the arguments in court have been. What a field day for the lawyers, with 'Mary' represented by the official solicitor, while 'Jodie' and the parents each have barristers of their own.
>
> (*Guardian* 8 September 2000: 10)

However, according to Shakespeare (1998) eugenic attitudes for the termination of foetuses seem to be determined more by the directive advice to pregnant woman from obstetricians. 'For example, in cases of Down's syndrome, 94% of genetic nurses, 57% of geneticists, but only 32% of obstetricians reported counseling non-directively. The majority favoured termination of foetuses with open spina bifida, anencephaly, Huntingdon's disease, Down's syndrome and Duchenne muscular dystrophy …' (Shakespeare 1998: 668). There are also commercial and industrial outcomes to genetic medicine that cannot be ignored. For families at risk of genetic conditions that may contribute to impairments the implications of genetic engineering are somewhat confusing and disturbing. For example it has been suggested that life insurance companies may begin to demand that people undergo genetic testing as a condition of insurance. Thus insurers may begin to take a harder look at the premium loadings of people who have already had genetic tests (*Guardian* 20 February 1997: 14). Both the Association of British Insurers and the National Consumer Council are concerned that there should be no practice of identifying policy holders of life insurance who are at risk of genetic disorders (Gillott 1997).

The fear that this might serve to create a 'ghetto' of such policy holders of life insurance is unlikely. Life insurance tends to be taken out by people in their adulthood when a progressive disabling condition is most likely to be already evident. The premium loading will have been set accordingly. The real insurance risk lies with long-term illness and permanent health insurance as it falls increasingly upon the individual and less upon the state. This has been particularly noticeable in the United States (Allen 1997).

Clearly arguments about and related to the ethics of genetic research, fertility treatment, reproductive technology and abortion are not new. Added to this are the implications around genetic cloning, following the breakthrough treatment in the creation of Dolly the lamb born from a test tube conjunction of an embryo and the cell of an adult sheep (*Guardian* 24 February 1997: 7; *Guardian* 26 February 1997: 6). There is no practical reason why it should not now be technically possible to clone, or grow, a new human being from the fusion of a cell from a human adult with an egg. However, the creation of a new genetic underclass of human beings is unlikely as well as being morally unacceptable. The method is likely to be used more helpfully to treat a range of life-threatening conditions. For example, if someone has bone marrow problems a cell could be extracted from the body and fused with an egg which would then be fertilised. Fresh bone marrow cells could be extracted from the resulting fusion and put back in to the body where healthy bone marrow could grow. This debate about the positive aspects of stem cell research has been brought to public attention by MPs Anne Begg and Fiona Mcaggart:

> I have a single gene defect and about five or six years ago after having adjusted my whole life to having a slowly progressive degenerative disease I suddenly found there was an enzyme replacement treatment. Had I not gone on it I'm fairly sure I wouldn't be here today ...
>
> (Anne Begg *The Times* 16 December 2000: 16)

> There are two quite significant things that are wrong with me. One is that I am infertile and the other is that I have multiple sclerosis. At the moment there are two fertilised embryos of mine in a medical facility, which are available for research. It is ironic that they could be used in research that could help to deal with my infertility and not be used in research, which could be of help to deal with the thing about which I am most anxious, my multiple sclerosis.
>
> (Fiona Mcaggart *The Times* 16 December 2000: 16)

The relationship of eugenics theory to disability

Historically, eugenics has certainly existed as a deliberate response to control unwanted impairments since the Greeks and their mythology. Artistic portrayals of procreation between the gods and earthly mortals in a union of bodily perfection, practical accomplishment and intellectual agility are exhibited in art galleries and literature. The Greek civilisations, obsessed with bodily perfection, also served to justify the practice of abandonment and death, through the exposure of new-born babies considered to be imperfect. This ultimate form of subordination of disabled people continues today in a variety of more diluted forms of prejudice (see Thomson 1997; Garland 1995).

Barker (1983) has provided a well-argued analysis of the belief systems that underlie eugenics theory. In summary, he indicates the three assumptions upon which the proposition is built:

- human characteristics could be determined by inheritance according to laws that are knowable;
- it was possible to identify 'desirable' and 'undesirable' human characteristics;
- social policy should encourage the increased fertility of those with 'desirable' characteristics.

Desirability, as bodily wholeness, has historically remained in an image of masculinity and male dominance. The physically strong, lean and active male body is contrasted with the traditional and stereotypically passive female body. The female is doll-like, acted upon, dressed and undressed. Feminists suggest that this desire to manipulate the body is reflected in the institutional motives of the fashion, health and pornography industries (Marris 1996; Wilson 1985: 3; Thomson 1997).

Biological determinism continues today in the life histories of thousands of disabled people who have lived through the brutal realities of institutional conformity and prejudice. The renewed threats to the 'right to life' of disabled people has also re-emerged as the implications of the human genome project come to be more widely considered and understood. Some commentators see this project as a breakthrough in gene therapy while others in the community of disabled people fear that it 'has given massive impetus and renewed rhetorical weight to the claims of biological determinism' (Shakespeare 1995: 23).

The practical reality beyond any discourse about the right to life (and the right to die) is the very deliberate killing of people at either the beginning or the end of their lives. Disabled people and their parents are at the centre of this. Proponents of this killing claim it to be justified on the grounds that disabled people are surplus to the requirements of society. The debate has become more urgent as scientific knowledge begins to move more rapidly in advance of both our moral interpretations of the findings and the legislative processes that frame their resolution. Furthermore, the term 'new' eugenics highlights some of the ethical dilemmas that face us all in relation to the sort of global society that we are becoming.

The oppression of disabled people occurs across different cultural groups and manifests itself in different ways. Racism is the most obvious example of stereotyping and discrimination based on and shaped by prejudice. The pseudo-scientific ideology of racism that has been used as a justification for institutional oppression of Black people has its parallels in the power and prejudice of eugenics as a justification for the covert exploitation experienced by people with disabilities. The attempts to construct a science of measurement formed around the genetic basis for intelligence and human potential has shaped much of the history of disabled people in the 20th century. The relationship between statistical science and eugenics links the statistician, Sir Francis Galton, with his cousin Charles Darwin – whose notion of the evolutionary advantage of the fittest forms the basis for eugenics. The possibilities for a scientific explanation of intelligence, rather than divine intervention, caused an explosion of interest in attempts to measure differences. Francis Galton seriously believed that 'the heredity-chances of becoming famous are twenty four times greater for a child with a famous father' (quoted in Malson and Itard 1972: 16). He also believed that it was possible to determine a gene for intelligence and that 'survival of the fittest' required the elimination of 'defective stock' in society.

The rejection of disabled people in its most extreme form has been dramatically advocated in the ideology of fascism. The fascist glorification of the 'perfect' human being resulted, under Hitler, in a deliberate effort to exterminate disabled people as 'imperfections which contaminate the genetic stream' (Coleridge 1993: 45). The Nazi euthanasia programme attempted to justify the elimination of disabled people on the grounds that they made no contribution to society and were a drain on resources; they were perceived as 'useless eaters' of resources without capital to contribute to the human lot. The Nazis and eugenicists may belong to history, but the emergence of newer forms of social Darwinism continue the assumptions that only the fit and fully functional have a right to real life (see Levine 1985).

The false logic of eugenicists who attempt to link the deterioration of social order in society with the size of families and unchecked reproductive practices has been ruthlessly exposed (e.g. Gould 1996). However, renewed interest in biological determinism is evident in the reactionary responses of the new right and 'back-to-basics' biology, encouraged by the mass media and spurious academic research studies such as that by Herrnstein and Murray (1994) linking IQ with class, race and genetic causation.

Opposition to genetic diagnosis

The traditional position of those opposed to abortion is centred around a concern for the status of the foetus. Abortion is thus part of the agenda of genetic testing and reproductive technologies. From the perspective of disability rights an additional argument emerges around the status of disabled people in society. The disability rights agenda opposes genetic diagnosis on the grounds that it devalues the lives of disabled people. There are clearly value judgements implicit in the decision that it is better to be born free from a known impairment than to have one. Genetic testing, like antenatal screening, gives families the option of avoiding having a child with a known impairment or genetic condition.

The criticisms of genetic testing have also centred around the question of parental choice in relation to prenatal diagnosis. It has been argued that choice is a consequence of the process of diagnosis and the technology employed rather than a moral decision. Parents, themselves, become de facto practising eugenicists: 'when medical interventions are particularly heroic, as with infertility treatments, foetal surgery and embryo genetic screening, women can find themselves having "chosen", yet feeling that it was not "this" that they wanted' (Rose 1994: 175).

Rose has argued that these choices are eugenic in their nature because they are premised on the marginalised status of disabled people: 'the underlying message is "screen, abort or fix." For this discourse, both the rights of disabled people and the complexity of decision are undervalued. The old and powerful mechanism of devaluing the victims and blaming mothers has been activated and can run and run' (Rose 1994: 196).

Beck equates the medical avoidance of genetic disorders with the more explicit eugenic removal of people with genetic diseases, as practised by the Nazis. His argument is that genetic testing is a form of contemporary barbarism to which society has not yet awoken:

It gains access through the clinics, laboratories and factories of the new biochemical industries. Its victory parade does not begin with street brawls, the persecution of minorities or people's assemblies, the dissolution of parliaments and the abolition of constitutions. This time it steps on to the stage of world history dressed in white coats, of self-confident research, the good intentions of doctors and the desire of parents to do their 'best' for their children.

(Beck 1995: 32)

It is clear that concern for the rights of disabled people is a particularly powerful influence on the debates around abortion and genetic testing. Contemporary commentators continue to support a woman's right to choose in relation to abortion. However, as the genetics interest group (GIG) have pointed out, worries about the rights of disabled people have been woven into the argument alongside the related concerns that modern genetics is creating a society in which people are intolerant of anything less than perfection. The experience of GIG is that parents who use genetic diagnosis to avoid the birth of a child with a genetic condition, after having a first child with the condition, love the child no less as a result of the choices they have made (GIG briefing paper 20 December 1996).

Euthanasia

Eugenics and euthanasia are not new. The premeditated extermination of disabled people has a long and shameful history. Both philosophies gather their strength of argument from associations with medicine and have as their premise an assumption that human social actions, of necessity, must be regulated. The theory of eugenics can be traced back to the belief that all human social action arises from genetic endowment and to inherited characteristics. However, euthanasia is arguably the more insidious doctrine seeking to justify the assisted murder of disabled and elderly people on economic grounds and medical expediency. Both are essentially socio-biological, medical and individualistic theories that continue the process of placing the ultimate responsibility for fitness to live on the state of health of an individual, rather than the environmental and social inequalities which cause them to be in pain.

The development of medical science in the area of genetics has given us the ability to both perpetuate and eliminate life. The act of deliberately killing a person can take place before birth, in the abortion of a human embryo or in the withdrawal of life for a demented elderly person. The discourses around euthanasia perpetuate and extend the personal tragedy model of disability that has already been alluded to.

Although neither is currently legal in the United Kingdom, euthanasia and infanticide are widely advocated in discourses around the 'quality of life' debate. In Australia's Northern Territory, the right 'to die with dignity' through voluntary euthanasia was legalised in July 1996 and has helped four individuals achieve a legally agreed form of assisted suicide. This legally sanctioned right for terminally ill Australians to commit suicide with a pill or lethal injection has subsequently been overturned, less than a year later in March 1997, after being contested by the Church, Aborigines and doctors *Guardian* 20 March 1997: 15 and *Guardian* 25 March 1997: 3). Other concerns about patient consent in relation to legally sanctioned forms of doctor-assisted suicide have arisen in Oregon on the northern Pacific coast of the USA and in the Netherlands. Mercy killings within strict legal guidelines can be carried out, and euthanasia became technically legal in the Netherlands in the spring of 2001 (*Guardian* 11 April 2001).

The moral and practical complexities of mercy killing are best exemplified in relation to people considered to be in a permanent vegetative state (PVS), notably the case of Tony Bland who died in 1993, having survived the football ground tragedy at Hillsborough, Sheffield in 1989 (Scraton 2001). The circumstances of Tony Bland have paved the way for a series of 'right to die' cases. Bland had his life-support terminated following a judgement in the High Court that he had no useful cortical function. However, euthanasia is too controversial an issue to be decided on the basis of case law. Other cases, since Bland, have shown that some recovery of function is possible even in the most severe cases. Dominique Bauby, the editor of *Elle* magazine, who died following a stroke, managed to dictate/type a manuscript of 130 pages (Bauby 1997) using the only part of his body that he could use, his left eyelid. Andrew Devine, who was massively injured in the same football tragedy as Tony Bland, had, eight years after the incident, started to become aware of his surroundings and was communicating with his family through a series of presses on a touch sensitive switch (*Guardian* 26 March 1997: 1). At the same time and almost in the same week as the Devine revelation, another family was seeking a legal declaration to discontinue the life-sustaining support for their daughter who had been diagnosed as suffering PVS (*Guardian* 21 March 1997: 12). Such tragedies as these show how diagnosis is, in itself, part of a continuum of severity. Andrew Devine was never considered to be as seriously brain damaged as Tony Bland; however, misdiagnosis of any condition is serious, misdiagnosis in the case of PVS is particularly alarming and too awful to contemplate. The challenge facing clinicians is to ensure that any acceleration of death for terminally ill people in extreme pain is properly debated on both clinical and moral grounds.

In the case of people with impairments assumptions about the 'inevitable' poor quality of life have influenced the development of prenatal screening and abortion. The express aim of screening, such as amniocentesis, is to offer abortion where impairment is indicated (section 1(i)(b) of the Abortion Act 1967 permits abortion if 'there is substantial risk' of the child being born with a severe handicap). At the same time there are clear financial 'costs' associated with the 'right to life'. As long ago as 1985, during a House of Commons debate on abortion, Peter Thurnham MP stated 'that to abort a handicapped foetus could well save the country one million pounds over the course of a life time'. However, while it is true that disability can amount to high economic costs, the level of debate may be better served if more consideration were placed on improved effectiveness in the distribution of resources rather than on absolute costs. As has been pointed out, where foetal screening indicates impairment, 86 per cent of the general public in Britain 'approve' of abortion (de Crespigny with Dredge 1991). 'Screening is rarely offered so that parents can plan for their child. These approaches have created a huge research industry and foetal screening and abortion are now major users of impairment-related resources' (Crow 1996: 64).

Summary

The foetal screening for abortion and the implicit acceptance of infanticide for babies with significant impairments are based on assumptions that the lives of disabled people are not worth living. Discussion of medically assisted suicide and living wills has exposed the same assumptions about euthanasia and the resources required to keep disabled people alive. This demonstrates the tension and paradox in the 'quality of life' debates in relation to disabled people. The re-emergence of the medicalisation of disability in the form of genetic testing suggests that the multiple experiences of disability, are forms of difference-within-difference and this needs to be better understood. The social restrictions of external barriers are central to the social model definition of disability. However, as has already been noted in Chapter 1, impairment *is* relevant. For some individuals impairment as well as disability causes disadvantage. Any attempts to reject or diminish the impact of medical interventions within a multifaceted social construction of disability can only serve to illuminate some of the misunderstandings about Disability Studies. This tension is echoed in conservative academic circles that fail to see a clear rationale for Disability Studies as a discrete discipline. It is either part of psychology, or part of sociology, or at best perceived to be a cross-disciplinary exploration into the margins that exists in society.

If the multiple experiences of illness, impairment and social restriction are not acknowledged within Disability Studies, including the moral dilemmas that surround the right to life, the disabled people's movement lays itself open to misinterpretation and misappropriation. The concerns of disabled people about genetic screening and euthanasia have been used to strengthen the arguments of pro-life groups, which does not necessarily promote a wider understanding of the purposes of the Disability Movement. As Crow reminds us:

> Although mainstream interventions are presented as being for the benefit of disabled people, in fact they are made for a non-disabled society. Ingrained assumptions and official directives make it clear that there is an implicit and sometimes explicit, intention of population control. Abortion, euthanasia and cure are presented as 'quality of life' issues, but are also justified in terms of economic savings or 'improvement' to populations.
>
> (Crow 1996: 64–5)

CHAPTER 6

The emerging politics of disability

Questions

- What distinguishes a politics of disability from other forms of politics?
- Why do we need a politics of disability?
- What are the principal components of a politics of disability?
- How has the politics of disability developed in the last decade?

This chapter seeks to outline the development of the politics of disability from charity for the 'deserving', dependent and disadvantaged to empowerment for a 'minority' who are discriminated and prejudiced against in an 'able-bodied' society. In order to simplify a complex history of legislative reform, political struggle and developing radical ideas, it presents the changing politics of disability in five models, in a broadly chronological order:

- liberalism, conservatism and the 'deserving', dependent disabled;
- post-war social democracy, welfarism and state-directed citizenship;
- the Disability Movement, the struggle for rights and equal opportunities;
- the resurgence of liberalism, New Right citizenship and the duty to disabled people;
- the radical retort: Marxism and radical democracy as paths to empowerment.

These five models give an understanding of the range of options for the politics of disability. These options can be differentiated by three themes, which will be outlined prior to exploring the models:

This chapter and its revision has been developed in collaboration with Paul Reynolds.

- the shift in focus from individual pathology to social change;
- the shift from legislation and individual rights to collective citizen rights and empowerment;
- the shift from *doing for* the disabled to disabled people *participating in* political decision making.

These themes are important in identifying key shifts and developments in the development of a politics of disability that enable us to begin to answer the questions at the beginning of this chapter.

The politics of disability: critical themes

The emergence of a distinctive politics of disability came from the larger social transformations and political struggles of the 1960s. Driedger (1989) claimed that the disabled movement was 'the last in a long series of movements for rights – labor, black, colonized people, poor people, women – and now people with disabilities' (p. 1).

The development of a disability movement politics created a divergence between the policy community – charities, interest groups, clinically defined and categorised self-help or voluntary support agencies and policy bureaucrats within state agencies – and disabled activists in three respects:

- There has been a shift in the conception of disability from personal tragedy and impairment to a broader social critique of 'able-bodied' society. Focusing on the individual or their disability in the personal tragedy model confined the politics of disability to deciding on and administering policy provision and services to a passive, dependent and different part of 'normal' society. The dissatisfaction of disabled people with policies and services was explained as responses to incidences of poor policy making or 'sour grapes' from those who did not get what they wanted and would not accept that in democracies not all wants can be met.

    The shift to a critical analysis of the assumptions and prejudices of 'able-bodied' society and preconceptions of normality and abnormality – or ability and disability – changed the terms of political debate. The agenda moved from service provision to social change through the recognition of disability rights and the need for disabled people to *be integrated and active*, rather than *marginalised and ministered for*, in their society. The powerlessness of disabled people and the social and economic inequalities they suffer began to be seen as directly related not to assessments of individual capacities, but to the ideas and values of able-bodied society, which perpetuated a political system that subjected disabled people to prejudice, discrimination and unequal life experience as part of its 'normal' functions.

- There was a growing pessimism as to the scope for change through legislation and policy change, and a greater interest in initiating social change through political struggle that empowers people with disabilities. The development of legislation, policy and service provision for disabled people is determined by civil servants and experts who approach these developments as they would any other policy problem – as distinctive features of more generic policies such as transport, employment or social policy. Disabled people are always preconceived the 'minority', the 'different' or even the 'deviant', and are one of a number of categories of 'client' or 'customer' that can be inserted into the 'equation' for arguments about special preferences or necessity for public services within the dominant cultural values and ideas of contemporary, 'able-bodied' society. As Erlanger and Roth observe:

> disability policy is in fact an aggregate of a variety of policies, each with quite different origins and purposes, … it has been most often seen as a subset of some other, more general policy area such as labor, veterans or welfare policy.
>
> (1985: 320)

Oliver (1990: 3) noted that the development of disability politics has been in part about the transition from campaigning for services to campaigning for rights and liberties – from demands for individual service responses to the needs of different forms of disability to societal changes in meanings, values and attitudes for the benefit of all disabled people. This shift involved a widening of the input of disabled people from disabled services and policies to the range of legislation, policy or political decision making. The '*ends*' of disability policy and services, while important in improving the quality of life of disabled people, were seen as important as part of the *means* by which rights and empowerment can be asserted. Oliver and Zarb (1989: 237) regard the Disability Movement as developing significant influence in policy making in Britain, to the point where they 'will come to have a central role in counter-hegemonic politics and the social transformation upon which [disability politics] will eventually be based'. Disability politics, then, is about political change and not simply policy 'wish-lists' – although the struggle for these 'wish-lists' is often the entry point for disabled people to become political.

- Finally, the politics of disability shifted from administration *for* disabled people by experts, professionals, politicians and policy managers to participation *by* disabled people in their struggle for empowerment or a more dignified advocacy. Participation in the struggles for disability rights – from attending and voicing concerns at local meetings of charities, self-help groups or local authorities to blocking traffic and being chained to the railings at the Palace of Westminster – is seen as a positive experience. Participation brings personal dignity, collective support, solidarity and a refusal to be silenced, ignored or marginalised. Media campaigns, participative lobbying of politicians and visible and voluble protest mobilises public support and increases pressure for change in policy and politics.

These three factors are central to understanding the emergence of disability politics and of disability movements as political actors. While they have created some divergence with the 'policy community', they do not exclude entering into processes and relationships that formulate legislation and policy provisions for disabled people. Driedger (1989) outlines the progress of disabled rights movements in developing an international movement (Disabled People International) that has embedded itself into the policy deliberations of international bodies such as the UN and UNESCO, as well as providing an overarching structure for influencing national governments.

The distinction between disability interest groups and movement groups is nevertheless critical in understanding the politics of disability. It is centred around how disabled people 'plug into' the economic and political systems and social and cultural values and ideas that constitute society. Accepting a degree of overlap, it is evident in the propensity for interest group politics to work within a system that acts *for* disabled people (i.e. charities) and movement politics to be founded on the actions and ideas *of* disabled people. Oliver (1990) provides a useful typology that illustrates these difference in organisations: patronage (*for*)/partnership (*of*), economic (*for*)/parliamentarian (*of*), consumerist (*for*)/self-help (*of*), populist (*for*)/activist (*of*), umbrella (*for*)/coordinating (*of*) (pp.117–8). He identifies four characteristics that are distinctive of disability organisations as movements: a peripheral position in the political system; a critical view of the structure and ideological ethos of 'able-bodied' society; post-materialist values; and an international agenda (pp. 118–23). Oliver (1990) cites Liggett (1988) in assessing the relative costs and benefits of interest politics: '… in order to participate in their own management disabled people have to participate as disabled … the price of being heard is understanding that it is the disabled who are speaking' (p. 106).

Movement politics reject the entry of disabled people and their advocates into the policy forum in a position rendered powerless in 'able-bodied' society. They argue for radical and participative struggle against that powerlessness, and the development of strategic alliances that build power for the dispossessed and aimed at the vagaries of social inequalities. Alliance building is a positive politics in two respects. As Borsay (1986) observes, struggle unites a heterogeneous disabled population around a politicised agenda against the disabling character of contemporary society rather than dividing them into their different categories of impairment. Oliver (1990) adds that it offers linkage with other politicised 'minorities' such as ethnic groups, gays, lesbians and feminists, which opens up its radical potential for social change (pp. 127–33).

Participative politics also creates a bridge between the political agendas of activists in the development of legislation, policy and service provision and the personal worlds of disabled people themselves. It links with the subjective experience, values and attitudes of disabled people with political agendas for social change. Issues such as the suppression of the sexuality of many disabled people, or the subjective perception of charities as reinforcing pathologies in their provision of welfare services can be linked to policy and political decisions. This form of politics has been the focus for other critiques of oppressive or exclusive society – and 'mainstream' politics – such as feminist and anti-racist critiques, which stress that 'the personal is political'.

These three characteristics of the development of a politics of disability since the 1960s have to be placed within their historical context. They are part of a politics largely confined to academic radicalism and a minority of political activists. To understand the continuing persistence of the conventional disability politics of the policy community with its focus on services and policy provision and the presumptions of passivity and dependency that spread from public servants and politicians, charity workers or volunteers to disabled people themselves, there needs to be some understanding of how the larger political context of welfare, inclusiveness and rights in society has changed. This context is sketched below in five stages, giving rise to five models.

Liberalism, conservatism and the 'deserving', dependent disabled

Prior to the development of the modern welfare state, disability was conceived as a product of individual personal tragedy. Whether this tragedy was by birth, accident or injury, it was regarded as something individually experienced and generally, from the industrial revolution onwards, wanting of sympathy and support – manifest by family care, charity or institutional incarceration in asylums or suchlike. Disability was regarded as *impairment* – it impeded the capacity of disabled individuals to live or act as 'able-bodied' individuals, and so impeded their enjoyment of rights and liberties. Their disability rendered them 'invisible'.

This was reflected in the dominant ideologies of industrial society: liberalism and conservatism. Both of these ideologies provided interpretations of society propagated by those with power, whose interests they prioritised. Ideologies – as coherent sets of ideas and values that formed 'world views', or ways of looking at, interpreting and explaining the world – persuaded others to believe and embrace these dominant interests' 'world view' of the way society worked. Dominant ideologies defined and captured the 'common sense' or truth with their interpretation. Dominant ideologies are propagated as inclusive of all segments of society unless they explicitly exclude undesirables – as with racist ideologies that pathologised black people and characterised them as sub-human. Disabled people were made 'invisible' through these ideologies because they did not 'fit' within dominant ideologies. Their impairment deprived them of the ideal of the competitive individual at the centre of liberalism and conservatism. Those in power had an 'able-bodied' perception of the world and gave only sympathy or contempt for the impaired.

Liberalism represents society as an aggregation of individuals, with society simply a product of the sum of all market transactions between these individuals. Individuals form private voluntary associations – family, business, social – and accept the need for a political authority – government – to maintain law and order. They are perceived as self-interested, free to enjoy their liberties and choose to compete with varying success in the market – be it for property and wealth, partners or other forms of self-aggrandisement. In liberal society, individuals are idealised as educated, informed, enterprising and competitive in the market. Their rights are codified as 'natural rights' – life, liberty and property – with the assumption that their individual intent and effort, with the legal protection of a minimal state, will achieve just rewards.

Set against this liberal model, disabled people are impeded in their competition in an 'able-bodied' society. The degree of their impairment corresponded to their impediment in acquiring knowledge, qualifications and the capabilities as individuals to take opportunities and make choices with positive outcomes. Their impairment constrains their participation in market society, which *disables* them. The 'liberal individual' represents an ideal that disabled people cannot meet, so disabled people are regarded as 'lesser' individuals. Instead, the medical model of disability, supported by the morality of liberalism to offer individual charity or minimal state support, encouraged their definition as deserving and dependent.

Disabled people in a liberal society enjoy the status of individuals through the goodwill of those they depend on. The conditional nature of their 'join' with society formed a barrier between ability and disability that few could cross. Only if the disability was manageable and invisible, or they had money or the disability was caused by an act of social status – such as the maiming of an officer in wartime – could disabled people expect to be seen in the same way as individuals who were 'able-bodied'.

Likewise, conservatism argues for conservation of the fundamental cultural and political character of society through adapting and absorbing change into a hierarchically ordered, socially authoritarian society, drawing identity from class, nation and race, through the monarchy, custom and tradition. Conservatism has been historically intertwined with liberalism in modern societies, preserving individual liberties and market organisation in society within the context of the national community. Disabled people occupy a low place in 'able-bodied' hierarchy, largely powerless and the subject of paternalism through their 'deserving' status. Accidents of birth might give different disabled people a life of sumptuous if invisible luxury or a life of institutional incarceration or poverty, but the autonomy of disabled people was strictly conditional on family or class position. Neither liberalism nor conservatism, regardless of the charity, compassion and goodwill expended upon disabled people, empowers them. They are locked into a structurally weak position in society, dependent, invisible and powerless.

Post-war social democracy, welfarism and State-directed citizenship

The development of social democracy after World War II altered this invisibility. Post-war social democracy was founded on the development of the Welfare State and an inclusive notion of citizenship in society, which involved a commitment to *social* justice, rather than *individual* care. Social Democrats – or Reformists – have a concept of society that recognises diverse minorities and develops a welfare and policy community to draw them into a supportive relationship with the state. The role of the State is central to the recognition of the needs for and responsiveness to minorities. The ethos for change is 'piecemeal social engineering' – social change derived from the state responding to democratic demands from all social interests for a better society. The welfare state, funded by progressive taxation and so supposedly redistributing resources from rich to poor, exemplified the social justice implicit in social democracy.

T. H. Marshall (reproduced in Bottomore and Marshall 1992) developed the social democratic concept of citizenship in his lectures 'Citizenship and Social Class'. The State was at the centre of this model, reflecting the democratic political will and safeguarding the civil/legal, political and social rights of the individual. It initiated the realisation of rights through legislation and policy, and was the enabler of rights by providing services. It acted as a focus for public duty and obligation to 'minorities', though personal charity was encouraged. It set the terms for inclusion through policy communities and service provision.

The extension of the welfare state, the development of professionalised state services for disabled people and support for self-organisation by and support organisations for disabled people would seem to meet a disability politics agenda. This agenda, however, was largely written for, rather than by, disabled people. While their voice can be heard, it is channelled into a care and support orientation that incorporated them rather than encouraging change within society to reflect their politics or identity. Levels of service became the measure of rights and liberties, and the focus was still individual – the benchmark of social improvement was still the enablement of individual disabled people or self-defining groups, through technology or advocacy which alleviates dependency. Oliver (1990: 78–94) identifies individualism and dependency as key constraints on the empowering potential of social policy.

The social democratic model was also limited in the tangential and consequential nature of rights. As Taylor (1989) observes: '... social relations must be situated in the context of underlying power ... These power relations structure the spaces of the market and the State and thus limit the extent to which either can fulfil the ideal of citizenship' (p. 23).

Social democratic citizenship implies that disabled people would have a voice in both acquiring and defining provision, but power remained with the experts and vested interests within or networked into the State, who determined the deployment of resources.

Social democracy delivered social welfare, ensured political rights and preserved fundamental civil liberties, but did so retaining a focus on disabled people as individuals with
impairment. Its limitations were in the lack of power that disabled people gained as citizens. The omnipresence of the State arguably *disabled* rather than enabled people with
disability by treating them as objects of policy provision. One result can be policies that
suit vested interests as much as disabled people – such as the scandal over profiteering
from the *Motobility* (disabled mobility) scheme in the late 1980s and early 1990s – or
emerge from professional orthodoxies influenced by the medical model. Because this
model of citizenship is based upon a reforming and not transforming society, it is vulnerable to the determinants of fundamental characteristics of society: in a capitalist society
profit and wealth through participation in the market are primary objectives, and the
economics of disability service provision is dependent upon the continuation of prosperity and acquisition for those who are powerful and wealthy. Disability rights are conditional to capitalist economics.

Within the context of 'able-bodied' capitalist societies, disabled people have neither
market nor State power, but rather rely on the affordability of welfare and the altruism which
capitalism can fund. Further, disability policies become not just a feature of social welfare
ideology and a form of social control and regulation. They may encouraging social cohesion,
the idea of community and support for the democratic consensus, but they also lock disabled
people into a more benign but still unequal hierarchy. Oliver (1990) warned: '... to engage in
an uncritical relationship to the state, is to risk at best, incorporation or absorption, and at
worst, isolation and marginalisation, and perhaps, ultimately, oblivion' (p. 128). Oliver (1996a)
is equally clear about the development of welfare for disabled people in capitalist Britain:

> discrimination against disabled people is institutionalised throughout society and ...
> welfare provision has compounded rather than alleviated that discrimination ...
> providing welfare services on the basis of individual need has failed disabled people.
> ... providing welfare services on the basis of individual need has aided the process of
> excluding disabled people from society rather than facilitated their inclusion.
>
> (Oliver 1996a: 76–7)

The Disability Movement, the struggle for rights and equal opportunities

Social democracy and its model of citizenship was challenged in the 1960s by both the
development of rights movements and political struggles which sought a more radical,
egalitarian redistribution of power, wealth and resources, and the capacity for the welfare
state to continue to meet social demands through an increasing tax burden. Egalitarianism
and its extension of the idea of social justice brought the idea of equal opportunities to
the fore of disability politics and policy in the late 1960s and early 1970s. Two models

emerged, one that reflected both the power of liberalism in egalitarian thinking, and one the growth of a radical rejection of social democratic ideas of social justice and egalitarianism. These models – reforming and transforming – are nowhere better illustrated than in Jewson and Mason's (1986) dichotomous model of equal opportunities policies, represented below (Table 6.1).

The elements of the two different approaches to equal opportunities they identified were:

1. *Principles* -ingrained notions of fairness and justice.
2. *Implementation* social mechanisms or devices which translate principle into practice.
3. *Effectiveness* consequences of implementation in bringing about outcomes congruent with principles.
4. *Perceptions* extent to which these processes are believed to be fair and just, have been implemented and proven to be effective.

Table 6.1 Elements of liberal and radical conceptions of equal opportunities policies (Jewson and Mason 1986: 312)

Elements of equal opportunities policies	Conceptions of equal opportunities	
	Liberal	Radical
Principles	Fair procedures	Fair distributions of rewards
Implementation	Bureaucratisation of decision making (e.g. training)	Politicisation of decision making
Effectiveness	Positive action	Positive discrimination
Perceptions	Justice seen to be done	Consciousness raising (e.g. training)

The subject of Jewson and Mason's (1986) work was racism and inequality, but their general concern was to point out the conflict and contradictions of these two models and underline how both models did not of necessity produce the outcomes intended – radical policies did not, for example, guarantee radical outcomes.

The central weakness of the liberal model is that it focuses on the individual, offering individual redress through legislation rather than institutional reform where equal opportunities are transgressed. The focus remains on disabled individuals, and equality offered to individuals going through processes with no sense of the disabling nature of the wider social contexts of inequality, prejudice and impediment. It also operates only within the institutional processes through which bureaucratic processes can be put in place, and has little more than a principled rhetoric outside institutional processes. Hence, recruitment and promotion procedures may change, but social ideologies do not. It has, nevertheless, dominated the development of equal opportunities legislation and policy in Britain.

The radical model of equal opportunities does provide a framework for discussion of disabled people's experiences, needs and wants as a 'minority' suffering inequality. It focuses on what disabled people want – for example, stressing the importance of advocacy and empowerment as a basis for a society with greater 'life chances' for disabled people. Its problem is that the politicisation and positive discrimination it advocates is against the interests of able-bodied society and alien to the liberal culture of society. Radicalism looks to social change through transforming social structures and institutions, which challenges the existing powerful interests and so draws their opposition. This is demonstrable in looking at employment recruitment. The liberal 'justice' of equal competition for employment is opposed by the radical argument that society has ingrained social prejudices that can only be countered by political intervention – so the bureaucratisation of an employment recruitment form might not alleviate prejudice. Political action, such as legislation that requires companies to employ more than marginal proportions of disabled people in all occupations in their workforce is seen as more effective. This moves beyond the liberal positive action of taking prejudice out of the recruitment process by establishing social justice through advantage towards disabled people – positive discrimination. The aim becomes not just to be seen as just in the individual recruitment process, but to change social consciousness by ensuring disabled people and their achievements are visible in society. For the individual able-bodied person, this advantaging of disabled people might disadvantage them – and liberals reject this – but radicals see the social outcomes as more just.

Liberal equal opportunities focus on individual rights and redress and radical equal opportunities focus on social inequalities and transformation. The weakness of the liberal model is its failure to address the societal and structural penetration of pathologies of disability in society. The constraint to the radical model is the extent to which it challenges fundamental principles of individualism that are ingrained within dominant ideologies in Britain. Both models of equal opportunities have furthered disability politics, however, in contributing to the understanding of oppression and discrimination as a social and not an individual problem, and the radical model has underlined the need for the struggle for rights to involve social change and participative politics.

The resurgence of liberalism, New Right citizenship and the duty to disabled people

The second challenge to social democracy was the problem of balancing capitalist profit alongside social spending, which brought social democratic politics and Marshall's model of citizenship into crisis. The New Right, led by Thatcher in the UK and Reagan in the USA returned to liberal and conservative values and rejected welfarism, egalitarianism and state intervention in the 1980s. They contrasted the statist and reformist ethos of Marshall's citizenship with a market-oriented model of 'active citizenship'. This model focused on the rights and responsibilities of the individual and replaced the State with the market as access point and enabler of rights and responsibilities. As such, it returned to the liberal representation of disabled people – the 'deserving poor'. Need was measured against the inherent undesirability of welfare through the public purse, which narrows definitions of what 'need' is and allocates reduced resources to that need. The expectation was that family or charity will play a greater role in service provision. State disability service provision was seen as driven by professionals and client groups for their purposes rather than for disabled people – and as increasingly contracted out to the market, at reduced public cost. More critically, the new right rejected the 'dependency culture' of welfarism with repercussions for even the 'deserving poor' – such as increasingly stringent assessments of qualification for disability benefits rather than more time-limited employment and social benefits.

This model, which was prevalent up to the 1997 election and is still influential on policy, has the same weaknesses of liberal and conservative ideologies. Its terms of inclusion are the capacity to enter into and consume and contract in the market in 'able-bodied' society – a site of prejudice, discrimination and disadvantage. Disabled people cannot meet the ideal of the active citizen – an 'able-bodied' ideal – and so suffer reduced public funding and services and the persistent blockage of rights legislation which might reverse those reductions or enforce responsibilities upon the State. To social democrats and those who argued for equal opportunities it was a step backwards, but it enabled them to reflect on the weaknesses of State-directed or equal opportunities-led politics. For others, the movement away from the limited politics of disability offered by social democracy and equal opportunities provided a radical critique that those in power in society benefited from, and preferred, prejudicial views of disabled people.

The radical retort: Marxism and radical democracy as paths to empowerment

Radical theories – Marxism, feminism (as examples) and the like – offer a more constructive model for disabled politics because they seek to transform society and conceive liberty, rights and freedoms as socially constructed – rather than individually based – and socially denied by the exercise of power and oppression. They have not traditionally, however, focused at the issue of disability – Marxists focus on capitalist production and class, feminists on male power and patriarchy. This is not to say that they do not have something to offer disabled people – the Marxist axiom 'to each according to their needs, from each according to their abilities' clearly does. They argue an intrinsic but poorly defined expectation that Marxist or feminist change will inevitably extend equality to disabled people, but do not address disability directly as an issue with its own pathologies and politics. Indeed, the presumptions of these perspectives are of 'able-bodiedness' as the 'normal' condition in society. Radical theories offer social transformation, but within an 'able-bodied' norm.

The work of Mike Oliver is particularly striking here. Oliver (1990, 1996a) has used the Marxist idea of hegemony as a key concept in his understanding of the politics of disablement, citing Harbert (1988) in Oliver (1990):

> It is not necessary to be a Marxist to recognise that economic conditions have a significant impact on social behaviour and on relationships between different groups of individuals in society.
>
> (p.25)

Hegemony is, in simple terms, the balance of the use of coercion and manufacture of consent through ideology by which the State defends the status quo of class rule in capitalist societies. Oliver (1990) sets the terms of the capitalist, able-bodied hegemony succinctly:

> The hegemony that defines disability in capitalist society is constituted by the organic ideology of individualism, the arbitary ideologies of medicalisation underpinning medical intervention and personal tragedy theory underpinning much social policy. Incorporated also are ideologies related to concepts of normality, able bodiedness and able-mindedness.
>
> (Oliver 1990: 44)

Oliver (1996a: 126–44) argues for the need to develop a 'counter-hegemony' that retrieves the concept of disability from its present pejorative meaning, and builds a positive meaning for and by disabled people, which would form the basis of a politics of disability. This counter-hegemony would be a challenge to capitalist 'able-bodied' society, with the politics of disability becoming a strategic deployment of agitation and ideology in order to transform society from an oppressive site of disablement towards an egalitarian society which transcended the able-bodied/disabled divide (Oliver 1990: 127–33).

For Oliver (1996a, b) political struggle leads to empowerment, which is a collective process – individual empowerment is a process of negotiating individually experienced constraints, whereas collective empowerment is a political process of agitating for change in a prejudiced society. It does not imply that all disabled people undergo the same process of a shifting consciousness of their oppression and pathology in a society that ostensibly 'cares' in the provision of disabled services, but it does locate disabled people within a *social* process where the negotiation of their individual constraints leads to an awareness of socially constructed pathologies and constraints. Shakespeare (1993) shares this view in seeing the act of participating in political struggle as enabling in itself, as well as displacing statist bureaucracies in setting the agenda for provision and legislation for disabled people.

Marxism has been the principal form of radicalism to influence disability politics. It has also contributed to recent explorations into the concept of citizenship that has influenced left academics and activists in developing an alternate radicalism that might better suit disability politics – radical democracy.

Radical democracy emerged from disillusionment with the grand movements of labour and socialist politics to develop a politics that enabled a diverse of communities within society – women, ethnicities, sexualities, etc. It was also influenced by the challenge to statist and organised political systems and processes of modernity by participative and diverse movement politics. The central ideas behind radical democracy are its inclusiveness of plural and diverse interests, brought together by a commitment to egalitarianism and social justice and a participation and adherence to democratic processes. This democracy involves empowering all communities, encouraging their participation in a decentred, more localised politics, and developing their civic spirit through a more direct relation to political decision making. The essence of citizenship becomes what citizens determine for it, provided it does not exclude or disempower the communities who participate in and adhere to democratic politics. This concept of citizenship and of radical democracy itself is formed and reformed by those who live it, through continuous democratic dialogue.

The model is appealing and does offer a focus on reshaping society, on rights and empowerment and on participation by all minorities. It might, therefore, be an attractive form of disability politics. It is, however, not without its weaknesses. It lacks of theory of power and an analysis of how democratic dialogue will avoid inequalities developing from differentials in power between different groups. If people with disabilities are relatively powerless in contemporary society, by what means will they gain social and political power and in what sense will they be able to exercise that power against interests whose agendas clash with a disabilities agenda? The assumption that power will be dispersed across the democratic community is arguably optimistic. Further, there is the question of how far a society or community can embrace diversity. At what point will common ideas and ideologies that promote social solidarity surface and what will their impact be on minorities such as those with disability? Will baseline assumptions of ability still lead to pathologies of disability? A constantly redefining democracy might be subject to exaggerated public reactions such as the need to contain and constrain those with mental illness after some unfortunate episode of violence by someone with mental illness. Without a benchmark code of rights, such a model leaves itself open to rule by mass mobilisation. This model, while attractive, is still very much an abstract alternative.

Towards a politics of disability

Since the 1960s, the politics of disability has been characterised by a critical focus on able-bodied society, a participative politics that empowers disabled people and a focus on rights and social equality. It has been reinforced by more legislative and policy-oriented debates around equal opportunities, against a backdrop of traditional ideologies that render disabled people dependent and invisible politically.

The development of a politics of disability into the 21st century is likely to continue to be associated with the idea of citizenship. Oliver (1996a: 44) noted the importance of the concept in two senses, in his discussion of how disability groups have focused on citizenship and anti-discrimination law as central to their empowerment:

> ... disabled people have begun to redefine disability not as personal tragedy requiring therapy but as collective oppression requiring political action. Thus, for the former group, the history of citizenship can be seen as the achievement of certain political, social and civil rights for everyone. For the latter, disability is nothing less than the denial of basic human rights to certain groups in society.
>
> (1996a: 44)

While citizenship as a concept deals with concerns of social inclusion – the relationship of disabled people with other segments of society and the relationship between disabled people and the political world – it has often applied to disability with a focus on welfare rights that is perhaps a weakness. Discussions of welfare rights and services inevitably direct themselves towards politics within the context of an able-bodied society rather than the terms of social transformation. Fagan and Lee (1997) take this point further when they note that citizenship models do give disabled people *formal* rights, but in the *substantive* experience of their everyday lives their impairment excludes them from an equal participation in society. Thus society *disables* them because it does not move beyond presumptions of 'able-bodiedness' as a basic attribute of the individual in society. The concept of citizenship remains, however, a central element for a politics of disability, and a site for radical criticism of the present rights afforded disabled people.

Insofar as the politics of disability is transformative, it is also hegemonic. Oliver (1990: 2) identifies a key element of the politics of disablement as understanding the politics of social meanings, citing W. I. Thomas – 'if men define situations as real, they are real in their consequences' – in arguing the need for a shift in the meaning of disablement in society from an individual to a social context. The shift in focus from individual to social frames of reference is neatly summed up by Shakespeare:

> Our real enemy is not individuals, but the system which divides us, which creates our disability, which makes it possible for others to profit from our exclusion: it's convenient and easy to highlight people, but the focus of our rage and our action should be the structures.
>
> (1993: 32)

Disability politics for the 21st century

Until the beginning of the 1990s, disability politics had been principally informed by liberal values with the benefits of post-war social democratic equal opportunities impeded by the ideology of the New Right in the 1980s. It developed in a piecemeal fashion with no overarching view of the issue of disability in society. Policy principally focused on issues of accessibility to the non-disabled world, income maintenance and welfare bene-fits and health and community support provision. Drake (1999) describes policy prior to the 1995 Disability Discrimination Act (DDA) as having the overarching aims of contain-ment, compensation and the growth of forms of welfare.

In its focus on welfare service provision, it reinforced the construction of a discreet and different minority of disabled people who required special treatment and care to be ministered to them. It segregated disabled people from the wider community, providing state benefit on the basis of disability as personal tragedy and looking at rehabilitation or normalisation as legitimate goals for therapy or support and care. Policy concentrated on changing the conditions of impairment of disabled people and not the nature and condi-tion of 'able-bodied' society. As Drake (1999) observed, there was a close relationship between the ways in which power is distributed, disability is defined and social values and norms are created.

The road to the 1995 DDA as the foundation of a significant shift in the politics of disability was the Committee on Restrictions Against Disabled People (CORAD), set up in 1979. It was a product of pressure from disabled groups on the outgoing Labour government, and its 1982 report found substantial evidence of prejudice, discrimination and lack of access and rights in public institutions. The Conservatives did not accept its report, but its wholesale condemnation of piecemeal attempts to improve the lives of disabled people influenced subsequent thinking about how state provision could be directed to disabled people. The 1986 Disabled Persons (Services, Consultation and Representation Act) formally accepted the need to consult disabled people on service provision, though it did little else. The 1991 Disability Living Allowance and Disability Working Allowance Act and the 1993 Disability Grants Act, which launched the Inde-pendent Living Fund, shifted funding from service providers to disabled people them-selves. These modest changes opened up the space for a greater voicing of the grievances of disabled people and encouraged their mobilisation around a more substantial claim for rights. Inspired by the 1990 Americans with Disabilities Act and the influence of Human Rights law from the European Union, pressure for a bill of rights for disabled people grew. In 1994 a Labour-sponsored private members bill, the Civil Rights (Disabled People) Bill, offered the prospect of a substantial recognition of disability as a social problem. It was around the 1994 Bill that a range of groups from the British Council for Disabled People (BCODP) to Right Now demonstrated the development of a substantial grassroots and mobilised disability movement (Campbell and Oliver 1996).

The 1995 DDA was the highly unsatisfactory response of the Conservative govern-ment to this political pressure, anxious to allay public concern and disabled peoples' hostility and public protests while avoiding the economic cost and considerable social burden of enacting a comprehensive bill of rights. The DDA promised rights, protections and individual redress to disabled people in the areas of employment and access to goods and services. Zarb (1995) summarised it as a combination of education and persuasion, self-regulation, and limited and closely targeted legislation (p. 5). It quite specifically protected disabled people from less-favourable treatment on the basis of disability and did not offer non-disabled people legal means of challenging preferential treatment to disabled people (Gooding 1994). This made it distinct from similar legislation on the basis of race and gender. It still, however, focused on disability as characteristic of the individual and individual redress, and the National Disability Council, created to administer the Act, had relatively little power or resources for its enforcement.

What the DDA did was to provide a framework for strengthening rights for disabled people in Britain. It was undoubtedly weak in itself. It required another piece of legislation – the 1995 Carers (Recognition and Services) Act – to ensure the needs of carers were incorporated into assessments of the needs of disabled people. Subsequent legislation was also ambiguous in its benefit to disabled people. The 1996 Community Care (Direct Payments) Act, which enabled local authorities to make payments direct to service users, is often seen as a progressive step towards user control and autonomy over resources allocated for services to disabled people. As Pearson (2000) has countered, however, it can equally be seen as an imposition of market logic, representing a liberal approach to welfare provision. This places individual care over a social conception of disability, and provides a limited scope for any substantial political transformation of the way service provision is organised. It also leaves open the possibility that market-based payments will be less defensible in times of economic crisis than resources embedded in state and policy processes.

The Labour government, elected in 1997, has to some extent met its promises to give the DDA 'teeth'. Its introduction of a Disability Rights Commission (DRC) in April 2000 has created a stronger body to take on the enforcement of the DDA and allowed a forum for the development of a more empowering approach to disability as a social process and not individual possession. The DRC moves policy farther towards an intermediary step between individual redress and social restructuring aimed at changing organisational and social behaviour – what Oliver and Barnes (1993) refer to as institutional discrimination. In a sense, this is also farther along the counter-hegemonic strategy of Oliver (1990) and Oliver and Zarb (1989), which sees the need for disabled politics to both engage with the state, legislation and policy, while building movement politics in civil society. That said, it is too early to assess whether the DRC will operate to the expectations of disabled activists.

At the same time, as Drake (2000) and Barnes (2000) have observed, the centrality of work as an agent of social cohesion as well as economic distribution in Labour's policy-making and 'third-way' philosophy itself provides a barrier to social inclusion for disabled people. While economic production is structured and organised around the 'able-bodied' notion of the utility of labour, work will always be a struggle to access and perform equally for disabled people. As Drake (2000) notes, the shift in policy emphasis from benefits to work requires an equal shift from public service monitoring to monitoring private sector employment practices in order to ensure compliance with the DDA. Hitherto, governments have felt on safer ground reforming public services and show reluctance to be seen to compel business to follow social legislation.

Further, the DDA still involves enforcement through individual redress, and retains the legal notion of what is 'reasonable' in assessing claims of discrimination or prejudice. This 'reasonableness' is an 'able-bodied' construction of reason. Thus, as Gooding (2000) observes, the DDA provides some evidence of legal enforcement, particularly in service provision. It does have a number of problems, however, such as who is defined as disabled, what is constituted as prejudicial or reasonable and the focus on individual cases of direct discrimination and not group or indirect issues of discrimination. This is perhaps indicative of a desire not to regulate business but to express rights through service consumption in a way that reflects the liberal character of New Labour politics.

While it is probably too early to evaluate the DDA, and policy that promotes change in social attitudes requires time to change social beliefs and practice, it is possible to identify distinct limitations in its political scope. Gooding (2000), in her evaluation of the DDA, observes: 'Perhaps what is required, above all, is a broader change to the cultural value attached to disabled people – a paradigm shift in the way in which disability is understood' (p. 549). Gooding acknowledges that the DDA and DRC are considerable steps forward in the development of disabled politics, not least in the self-perceptions of disabled people as members of the wider community. Nevertheless, legislative, legal and policy oriented politics remain limited in their purchase on problems of social pathology and discrimination, and more radical change at structural and ideological levels remains the longer term aim of a politics of disability.

Increasingly, for academics and disability activists, disability politics is a radical politics. The Blair government, with its concept of stakeholding as a mechanism of social inclusion, offers little of specific value to disabled people. There may be marginally more resources and marginally wider services, and a culture of listening to what disabled people want. There may even be both legislation and an institutional framework that promotes the formal recognition of equality. The struggle to change able-bodied society, however, will be barely begun by such developments. Further, there are still those who feel that equal opportunities, or social democratic citizenship, or indeed the New Right, offer the most practicable models of policy provision, and reject the agenda of social transformation.

What is clear is that the academic writings and political activism that have formed Disability Studies and disability politics in the last 30 years have begun to define a distinct and specific politics of disability around which disabled people can mobilise. It draws chiefly from a radical critique of structural and cultural determinations of disability in society and the focus of political responses upon the individual. It criticises the focus of law and policy upon individual experience as a means of addressing societal division, pathology and discrimination. It recognises the need to transform rather than simply reform, and to do so at ideological, social and cultural levels, beyond the more narrow definitions of political change offered by present policy.

For the future, it is uncertain as to whether this disability politics will grow as a consequence of the effects or deficiencies of current policy. Over and above this development of a counter-hegemonic politics of disability, there is evidence of four distinct strands in disability politics that both broaden and develop the critique of 'able-boded' normality (Fagan and Reynolds, forthcoming):

- Within the politics of sexuality, disability and ethnicity, there is a growing sense in which the need to develop a concept of appreciation for difference, rather than criticise the construction of pathologies of difference. This creates difficulties for theorists of disability, who are less clear on how to valorise impairment than they are in criticising disabling processes in society. This construction of an appreciation of impairment within a disabling society offers the prospects of joining the concerns of theorists and activists with the wider domain of disabled people through the revaluing of their subjective experience.

- There is scope for developing the insights of Marxism, feminism, radical democracy and other political theories critical of 'able-bodiedness', through a re-evaluation of the specificity of 'able-bodied modernity'. This, in turn may lead to the development of a quite specific understanding of the necessity for 'able-bodiedness' in modern society, and reinforce the need for its equally specific rejection, in theorising a more equal society. This again joins the concerns of disabled people and non-disabled people, as it emphasises the oppressiveness of 'able-bodiedness' upon all people and encourages an analysis that entrenches 'able-bodiedness. with class, racism and other pathologies. This invites a politics of disability that engages with other radical politics but does not lose its specificity. Rather, it influences other forms of radicalism in their formulation of a more equal society.

- Critiques of disability have begun to focus more on the meaning of the idea of ability. In doing so, their shift from a concept predicated on difference as constraint and deficiency to a concept constructed on the basis of contingency and capacity changes the nature of debate. By focusing on ability, it is possible to join the concerns of disabled people with others disadvantaged or constrained by definitions of what we *should* be able to do in society. The deficiency of the concept of ability as describing the life experience, opportunities and freedoms available in society raises questions for everyone, and contributes to critiques of the assumption that disability is defined by addressing what cannot be experienced and enjoyed by those with impairments.

- Critiques of disability are progressively engaging with broader critical studies of the body and the mind. Again, these join the concerns of disabled people with others such as feminists, anti-racists and theorists of sexuality or mental illness. It questions the meaning of normality, the construction of ideals and models of normal behaviour and the construction of the un-normal as deviant or abnormal. In doing so it questions the pathology of difference, challenges what we understand by ideas of, for example, healthy body and healthy mind, and provides a space for seeking diversity differently.

Summary

The politics of disability is currently organised around the notion of a counter-hegemonic strategy against 'able-bodied' prejudice. This involves the development of a concept of citizenship that breaks down the able/disabled dichotomy, the development of strategic alliances for radical change and the empowerment of disabled people by political struggle and challenges to the pathologies of disability as impairment. Equally, the politics of disability is still contested by proponents of the different models outlined in Chapter 1, and this analysis is part of the debate. The radical critique has been attractive to academics and activists but many disabled people still work within established interest groups and have a more passive and limited idea of what they want in service provision, legislative change and representation. The politics of disability is still *emerging*, and has still to move from minority activism and political discourse to the hearts and minds of disabled people more generally, as well as all those who aspire to a more equal society in the 21st century.

CHAPTER 7

Disability research

Questions

- What ethical questions does disability research raise for non-disabled people?
- Is the point of research to directly improve the circumstances of disabled people?
- How might it be possible to develop emancipatory research with all groups of disabled people?
- How do you interpret the term participant observation, in relation to disability research?
- If it is true that 'you have to be disabled to understand disability', what do you think this says about the values placed upon disability research?

Introduction

Research in relation to the lives of disabled people has developed in recent years and auto-biographical accounts serve as a useful foundation for a fuller understanding of the study of disability. Research into disability has also been questioned for a variety of reasons. To some extent, this criticism has emerged as a result of the way in which the battle lines of research production have been drawn. People with disabilities and learning difficulties in particular, have tended to be treated as objects to be studied and a problem for other people rather than as individuals with the ability to participate in a research exchange. There is also a tendency to see the purpose of research in the traditional terms of either being for or against the quantification of data. Quantitative data, in the form of scientific experiments or surveys, are associated with a relative 'hardness' of results; this contrasts with the so-called 'soft' data gathered from qualitative approaches more commonly associated with investigations that try to interpret people's lives.

Virtually all social science research is an attempt to reinterpret experience and to seek explanation through increased 'depth of understanding'. Thus, the distinction between quantitative and qualitative research styles is somewhat artificial. For example, if you were to try to explain what you are doing at this moment (i.e. reading this paragraph), then you would find yourself drawn towards describing conscious decisions, meanings and intentions. These interpretations are extremely important, but they are not sufficient, by themselves, as an explanation of your actions. It is the interpretation of these various meanings that brings understanding and distinguishes the social sciences from the so-called natural sciences, such as mathematics or physics. The need to understand intentions and how the past influences the present lies at the heart of the distinct research methodology of the social sciences. The intention is to 'get inside' the situation being studied and attempt to interpret the intentions, purposes and habits of the participants.

If disability is perceived as an individual tragedy and medicalised, it lends itself to data collections that reinforce images of impairment and loss of function. This in itself can lead to a mechanistic quantification of results and it has shaped the interpretive value of survey data such as the OPCS census (e.g. Martin *et al.* 1988). On the other hand, any qualitative research which attempts to interpret and describe disability as a relative concept is also problematic, particularly for non-disabled participants. Until recently, there has been a tendency to shy away from discussions of the subjective experiences of disabled people. As has been suggested by Shakespeare *et al.* (1996), Disability Studies has tended to downplay the personal and focused instead on the structural, thereby tending to reproduce and shape the split between public and private discourses with which students of the social sciences are familiar. Indeed, one of the features that has emphasised the limited self-esteem of people with disabilities has been the reluctance to assume that disabled people have personal stories to tell of their private lives. As a consequence they have been denied access to the experiences that 'normal' society take for granted. The work of Morris (1991, 1996), Scope (1994) and Campbell and Oliver (1996) confirms that this is an erroneous assumption. As Shakespeare *et al.* (1996: 208) have observed, the narratives of disabled people can be a cathartic experience. The resolution of conflicts for disabled people may result in stories with different emphases. Things that are taken for granted by non-disabled people may create obstacles for disabled people. The environmental, political and emotional restrictions that create disability (and how these can be positively overcome) form the basis of most research in Disability Studies.

Disability research in the community

The paradigm for disability research that emerges from the social model (which acknowledges that social barriers are imposed by society) views the person with the disability as the decision maker and at the centre of any research encounter. This paradigm has developed as a reaction to research into disability as sickness and tragedy. The primacy of the person with a disability is at the forefront, with emphasis on the shared identity of oppression with other marginalised groups. This poses questions for non-disabled researchers who form the majority of the research-active community. Stone (1996: 223) has urged that 'the researcher should not be a slave to outsider theories or socio-political movements. Definitions need to begin with individuals, families and communities at the grassroots and not with outsiders.' Wiseman (1978: 317) has memorably described the role of the qualitative researcher as that of a detective in a murder mystery and the issue of objectivity is as 'the combination of nearness and remoteness, concern and indifference' is alluded to by Harding (1991: 124). In thinking through the implications for disability research the idea of the researcher as 'stranger' inadvertently, reinforces the dilemma of whose side you are on in the research relationship and the social setting in which it takes place:

> The role of the obligatory cup of tea and affable enquiries about families and weekends should not be underestimated for establishing some ongoing commitment in a new research enterprise. While this may seem a superficial practicality to raise, it is important for researchers to be aware of the dilemma posed by trying to match research and social roles and also separate out the two parts.
>
> (Moore *et al.* 1998: 44)

It can be argued that if such an approach is adopted it lays itself open to accusations of a number of abuses, misunderstandings and miscarriages of justice (Stone 1996). However, this would deny the place of sensitivity and interpretation in the creative reconstruction that is the research process. The qualitative researcher who is seeking narrative accounts is, necessarily, an investigator who moves into the private circumstances of people's lives and has the potential to, either deliberately or unintentionally, turn informants' lives upside down. In relation to research into the lives of disabled people, the approach emphasises the need to remain aware that an informant is neither simply a 'research subject', nor a metaphor for generalised oppression. For many disabled people, research into their lives has become an activity that is undertaken by those who have power and is imposed upon those who do not (e.g. Oliver 1996b). Research in such circumstances, reinforces a sense of further oppression and the violation of personal experience. Booth (1996), however, has more recently argued that the narrative or storytelling method of research is about to make a legitimate resurgence. The personal experiences and perspectives of people within oppressed groups have been excluded, for too long, from the traditional forms of academic discourse. Disabled people have until recently lacked the power to make their voices heard and conventional scholarship has tended to subordinate the reality of people's lives as anecdotal rather than serious scholarship. There is a power and energy that such cathartic research narratives from disabled people manage to articulate. Some examples from different life experiences are included in the appendix.

In qualitative research the researcher is attempting to make valid sense of the social world, and of the people being studied. In their attempt to re-interpret what some people would describe as their everyday lives, researchers are also reconstructing and exposing often unacknowledged truths. As such, concerns arise for the validity and reliability of data. There should also be a sense of responsibility towards informants (which should be at the heart of any research). These considerations are of paramount importance in the development of analytic insights.

There are a number of pointers that the researcher in Disability Studies may use to help retain this sense of empathy:

- assume, at least at first, that no one is lying in the information you receive;
- acknowledge that there is no such thing as absolute truth – there are a variety of perspectives and room for a range of insights;
- nothing that you see or hear is completely irrelevant to your study – it may serve to enrich a direction that you are already pursuing, or set you onto another topic;
- if you must choose between an official story and that of an individual (that is institution v individual) it is likely that an individual is telling the more unblemished truth and that the institution is not being totally honest;
- recognise that there is nothing that happens or that people tell you about that 'doesn't make any sense'. It is part of their lives and they think it makes sense;
- assume that human beings may not be very sophisticated, or smart, in the decisions they make, but they are doing the very best they can under the circumstances.

The ethics of disability research

It is anticipated that all research is guided by sound theoretical principles and this is particularly the case in relation to investigation in connection with the circumstances of people with disabilities. Furthermore, both local and national government policy in relation to disability is anticipated to be informed and underpinned by sound research. Unfortunately, this is not always the case. French (1994a: 136) encapsulates the problems associated with disability research when she indicates that the way disability is defined sets the tone for any research project. The majority of large-scale research activity is quantitative in its nature and this reflects the level of funding allocated to such activity. This in turn tends to reinforce the notion that disability is something contained within the individual; that it can be estimated, quantified and extrapolated from survey data (e.g. OPCS surveys, Martin *et al.* 1988). Such surveys imply that people with disabilities have to compare their levels of difficulty in, for example, reading a newspaper, or walking a hundred metres, with non-disabled people. Not only will this vary between the levels and types of impairment experienced, but it also suffers from the lack of a normal baseline against which to measure their efforts:

Even basic facts such as the number of disabled people residing in a given place, are based upon the criteria used to define disability which, in turn, may reflect the interests of the researchers or their funders.

(French 1994a: 138)

Social science research is presented as a neutral, value-free exercise which is expected to result in the acquisition of factual data. The research that has emerged in relation to Disability Studies has tended to follow in this direction too. In reality, this independence and balance is a myth. The majority of research is carried out in university departments, or in association with universities and the influence of the body funding the research is often fundamental to the direction of the outcomes; frequently these are directed towards policy that is itself ambivalent and demands further research. In relation to disability research, in particular, the more radical proponents of a politics of disability would suggest that it is impossible, if not irresponsible, to remain neutral; either you are on the side of the oppressor, or on the side of disabled people. Research in this context should be assisting disabled people in their struggles (Barnes 1996). In such a climate it is important to realise that if a researcher tries to present an honest account of what is happening, it will often mean upsetting at least one of the parties involved:

there must always be room for argument and counter argument and crucially for researchers, to reveal matters that may be uncomfortable, for specific interest groups and even those funding the research.

(Bury 1996a: 112)

Representation

Representing the views of disabled people has often been difficult. Information and data on disabled people have formed the basis for numerous statistical reports. Indeed they have become the very stuff of acres of newsprint related to the caring services and more occasionally they have been the subjects of best-selling books and films. Sometimes too disabled people have reached national attention through 'brave deeds' (such as pushing a wheelchair from John o' Groats to Land's End or as a result of some frequently painful but always 'miraculous' intervention of a medical nature.

These stories and reports have been influential in generating a collective recognition of disabled people as victims of both internalised and externally generated oppressions; but they have not been told by disabled people themselves. Their lives have been interpreted, retold and packaged for the consumption of a society that still sees disability as a kind of personal tragedy, in which the able-bodied majority have custody of the lives of the people with disabilities. Until very recently, in effect, disabled people had very little opportunity to tell their own stories within the political and cultural contexts of their personal circumstances. This profusion of able-bodied anthropology has prompted an inevitable reaction from disabled researchers:

> The glut of this one-way attitude research prompted one of my friends (a disabled woman), while we were sitting in the audience at a conference presentation to whisper to me 'I'm tired of hearing how they feel about us. Why doesn't anybody ask how we feel about them?'
>
> (Linton 1998: 101–2)

There cannot be any effective research into people's lives that is not to a greater or lesser extent autobiographical. Hevey (1992) and more recently Campbell and Oliver (1996) have reinforced this point, suggesting that it is ridiculous to believe that 'objectivity' can only exist outside personal consciousness. In other words, attempts to be objective have only served to hide the personal and distance the person from the text of their experiences. Oliver (1992; 1996b) has commented, more distressingly, that scientific, 'hard' social research has done little to change the status quo; neither improving the quality of life of disabled people nor having much effect on policy, legislation or social change:

> The problem is that most social research has tended to privilege methodology above experience and, as a consequence does not have a very good track record in faithfully documenting that experience; whether it be the black experience, the experience of women, the experience of disability and so on. (Oliver 1996b: 45)

Oliver (1992, 1996a), Campbell and Oliver (1996) and Bury (1996a, 1996b), have all argued that research in the area of Disability Studies should be seeking to break away from the shackles that restrict research paradigms to a simple dichotomy between survey and more qualitative methods. Research should instead attempt its own emancipation in both form and content. If disability research becomes confined by the definitions of disability as 'social oppression', with its inevitable distinctions between insider and outsider accounts, there is the danger of a number of unwanted consequences. There is the central concern of alienation and cynicism – across both the broad constituency of disabled people and within society in general. This, in turn, demands the formation of new alliances between researchers and their research subjects:

> the idea that research should become a site for 'struggle' suggests a politicisation of research that may have a number of unintended consequences. While it may be taken as axiomatic that individuals have a unique insight into their own experiences, it does not logically follow that they are qualified or able to undertake research. Moreover, such a view also runs the risk that the status of being disabled should be the main criteria for carrying out research on the subject. This sits uneasily in an argument in which the very idea of 'disability' as a defining characteristic of individuals, is being challenged.
>
> (Bury 1996a: 35)

The research conducted by Campbell and Oliver (1996) is powerfully instructive in light of this discourse. As researchers and as disabled people they not only expose the inherent tensions between insider and outsider accounts, but also reveal the connections between disability research and research around other related movements, like the marginalisation experienced by gay rights campaigning groups.

Research that shows a connection between the dual oppressions that mask the real experience of disability has not often been undertaken. Shakespeare *et al.* (1996) have researched and explored some of the more hidden sexual experiences in the lives of disabled people and in this way innovative research also acts as a liberation which tells of shared oppressions and can reveal the extent of disabled people's anger and protestation. But such research is still in its infancy. Nevertheless, the ethnographic, collective and private oral biographies that disability groups have begun to assemble provide an opportunity for disabled people to trace the history of their political consciousness, define their own issues and understand their own experiences (e.g. Berrington *et al.* 1996; Cartwright *et al.* 1996; Morris 1996, Bloemers and Wisch 2001). For such accounts to be included in the realms of research, they need to be publicly accessible and available. This often calls for funds for dissemination that is not always sufficiently considered when the original research proposal is first put forward. The vested interests of the researchers also need to be open to scrutiny and debate. For those who are interested in disability-related issues as an area of research but who remain as outsiders and allies, collaborative research would seem to be a way to withstand some of the suspicion that is associated with research and researchers in this area of the social sciences.

Conducting and writing up research in Disability Studies

Researchers in the social sciences have taken considerable interest in discovering which factors have the most influence in shaping the ways in which the members of different social groups interpret their situations. Ethnographic accounts, in particular, seek the opportunity to find out how different people conceptualise the social world in which they live. They also seek to respect the cultural and ethical values integral to the lives of their informants. Thus, students in the area of Disability Studies can usefully learn from the ethnographic traditions of research in the development of a life-history approach to disability awareness. This includes the perceptions of disabled informants, carers, service providers and so on. The development of a life history anticipates that students will find out about people's images of themselves and of their social world. Since it requires that informants discuss and describe their perceptions in their own terms, it requires the researcher to interpret rather than to predetermine the agenda or structure of an interaction.

Tom Shakespeare (1996) gives an insight into the rules by which he conducts qualitative research. These generally coincide with aspirations that all researchers into disability issues might learn to put into operation. The aim is to give an accurate representation of the views of those involved in the research process, providing a sufficient and adequate explanation of the purpose of the research and providing the opportunity for participants to ask questions and to revise their statements. Any research interviews undertaken need not be rigidly structured – giving participants some say in the direction that is taken during a research exchange is important. In the writing-up phase and the development of a reflective account of disability research there is potentially some tension in that what has been uncovered should be presented in a form that is accessible to all; but it must also be able to withstand the rigours of academic criticism.

When carrying out any piece of research there can be pitfalls. In the social sciences, and Disability Studies in particular, the method chosen can affect the findings. The presence of the researcher can affect how people behave and the answers they give. For these reasons it is advisable to seek opportunities to carry out follow-up interviews with informants, in the hope that given the regularity of contact respondents will become more relaxed and feel more confident in expressing themselves freely.

The writing of biographies and autobiography is of course an ancient practice, but the life history – the elicitation of semi-structured autobiographies for the purposes of social research – is of rather more recent origin. Life histories were originally carried out by anthropologists studying the vanishing lifestyles of American Indian tribes (e.g. Benedict 1934) and the technique was made famous by the Chicago School of Sociology. More recently the life-history approach to research has been encouraged in the form of oral history with disabled people as a group and with individuals; e.g. Zarb (1993b) with older people, Shakespeare *et al.* (1996), on the sexual experiences of disabled people, Campbell and Oliver (1996) on the development of a politics of disability, Cartwright *et al.* (1996) with physically disabled people in the north-west of England.

In ethnographic or life-history research, the interviewer rarely comes to the interview with a detailed agenda or questionnaire since the primary aim is to encourage informants to talk about their lives on their own terms. The fundamental point is to reduce the danger of the interviewer imposing his or her own opinions on their informants through the form of the questions posed. It is, nevertheless, impossible to take an entirely passive role when carrying out interview research. Informants are inevitably expecting to be guided by the interviewer, at least in the initial stages of any interview, and whenever there is a break in the talk it will be expected that it is the interviewer who 'will make the next move'. It is also the case that it is often in the best interests of the researcher to gently steer informants towards those areas of their lives which are considered most relevant to the research purposes. It is consequently useful to have decided beforehand on the general 'shape' of the information/topical exchange and to have some questions prepared, both to get things started and to stimulate further relevant talk when things begin to flag.

Reflection

The imposition of ablist views on disability research is a concern that can both cause offence and prevent a proper understanding of disability being brought to a wider audience. While a shared understandings of disablement is often better informed and more sensitive as a consequence of research it is really only possible to briefly touch people's lives and not enter them. Only a disabled person can claim to have anything near to a similar experience to other disabled informants (e.g. knowing how important it is to plan a journey away from home around the availability of accessible public lavatories, which as many research reports indicate are often far from accessible and thus far from public).

The development of a research study involves all concerned in a range of experiences. From the outset, the intention should be to make use of the voice of the interviewee and to explore their perceptions of their daily lives. At the same time it has to be anticipated that as consumers of services, the views expressed by disabled people may indicate varying levels of dissatisfaction. Non-disabled researchers may anticipate concern to be expressed by disabled people about being overlooked, made 'invisible' in a world that regards 'normal circumstances' as the ability to walk, remain ambulant, be articulate and aware. It can come as a shock to find this is not always the case. For some, the response to conflicts around provision and the meeting of need may simply result in acceptance, even gratitude, for the professional services that are offered and available.

A certain level of incomprehension about disablement can begin to establish itself at certain points for a researcher or research team. This tends to occur when researchers are unprepared for encounters and conversations emerge that are not in accord with their own theoretical views. Some informants may perceive researchers as extensions of the very services that they either welcome or criticise, while others may assume that researchers are part of an advocacy service who are able to bring about instant change. There is sometimes the expectation of a *quid pro quo* or a quick research 'bargain' that can be negotiated by way of a swap – the individual 'story' of any one person's circumstances in return for advocacy, advancement or immediate practical help. This can be both unexpected and unwelcome, involving the researcher in issues that go beyond dispassionate academic enquiry that can sometimes be distressing.

From the outset, disability research has to acknowledge the fundamental principle that the people who really know best about the experience of disability are disabled people themselves. It is evident, after a number of years as an ally, that this is not necessarily the same as being able to articulate a case for disabled people. What people know best is their own circumstances, and this does not have to include (or even acknowledge) impairment, handicap or disability. Thus, some people who appear to be living with a great deal of dependency on medical support may have little understanding of the cause of their functional impairment or its prognosis. Some who have been promised services may have been waiting for months or years to receive them. To a researcher, disabled informants in these circumstances should by now be getting angry, militant and calling service providers to book. But the purpose of the researcher is not to appear to criticise, but to attempt to understand. If an informant appears to be disorganised, or in some cases lacking the will and initiative to take on 'authority', they may have consciously chosen not to! The function of the researcher into the life-histories of people is to record and interpret not to prejudge.

The inclination to set about advocating for the individual rights and entitlements of informants is understandable, but out of keeping with the proper purpose of the research exercise. These are the frustrations that can be felt by the researcher with a theoretical knowledge of disability awareness and equality of opportunity. But this awareness of injustice may often be far more keenly honed than the levels of dissatisfaction or frustration expressed by those who are participating as research informants.

Case-study research based on the social model of disability has suggested that disability arises as a consequence of a more complex process than being physically, sensorily or mentally impaired and marginalised. Disablement is a process which results from a sequence, or combination, of circumstances and attitudinal judgements. It is suggested that these judgements and opinions come together to form the key features that create a 'lifestyle' and a subjective assessment of one's 'place' in the locality. No one dimension by itself is necessarily deliberate or singly capable of creating marginalisation, but as a total package, or combination, they contribute to an individual's comprehension of his or her place in society. Research activity around the social model also reminds us that it is never possible to completely identify with research informants. While some researchers may became friends with informants, these friendships remain peripheral to the researchers' own lives. Differences of gender, life experience, class and educational background, as well as physical and/or sensory impairment, influence and shape the structure of interviews, responses and interpretations.

While it may be possible to empathise with an interviewee, informant or research subject, it is impossible to fully comprehend the intricacies and complex psychology of another person's experience. Just as important to consider is the inevitable discomforture of temporarily 'passing through' another person's life experience. The need to reconcile two worlds is part of the skill of the developing researcher in Disability Studies. Knowing how to move in, however sensitively or intensively, for a brief period and then return to a different series of relationships and affiliations, in a different social world, is both a personal skill to be developed and an issue to be reflected upon.

Part of the intention of disability research is to go beyond exposing the differentials in provision and resource allocation. It is also required to better understand, inform and feed into the exercise of democratic participation around the outcomes of community care. Developing researchers have to become aware of the consultative exercises that have to go on between services and disabled people, e.g. local health authorities and social services. However, for the majority of people research does not touch their lives. The voices that are heard and the people who tend to attend meetings are those from official organisations, and those individuals used to speaking in public. If for no other reason, therefore, research that sets out to report on the circumstances of people's lives continues to be valuable. It restores the balance somewhat; back to the people themselves, their views and their concerns.

Summary

Research in the area of disability has tended to be dominated by quantitative surveys and questionnaires that estimate and measure the functional limitations of people in their day-to-day lives. Such research has served to confirm disability as an individual deficit. It has often been conducted by non-disabled researchers in a fashion that places them outside the circumstances of disabled people and their families. The growing interest in 'emancip-atory research' (Oliver 1992, Stone 1997) and the development of qualitative, case study research conducted by disabled people themselves, or in cooperation with non-disabled people, has shifted investigations of disability towards an exploration of the lived experiences of disabled people within the developing policies and practices of inclusive communities.

CHAPTER 8
Medical health and disability

Questions

- What are the implications of health care for people with learning difficulties?
- How can training programmes for health-care professionals respond to the particular risk factors associated with the poor health of people with disabilities?
- What would need to be included in a proposal for the development of a 'healthy lifestyle' for people with learning difficulties in your district?
- What are the links between symptoms of illness, isolation and attitudes towards disablement?
- How might the *Health of the Nation* strategies improve the circumstances of people with learning difficulties?

Introduction

We live in a society that values good health, physical fitness and well-being as 'wholeness'. As a society we link ability with physical fitness, power, money and sexuality. Such values tend to sustain and reinforce some fundamental and negative judgements about the value of disabled people. The promotion of the right of people with disabilities to enjoy appropriate health and opportunities for personal relationships is still not universally acclaimed. People are respected more for doing things, for being active rather than being passive and dependent. The idea that those with disabilities might also wish to enjoy sexual relationships as part of a healthy lifestyle has taken even longer to be accepted.

One of the most striking features of the history of disability rights is the nature and prevalence of impairments and handicapping conditions that are linked to inequalities in health. 'People's experiences of disability and of socially constructed illness have a simultaneous and compounding impact, and in doing so, extends analysis of the impact of unequal social relations' (McLeod and Bywaters 2000: 10–11). The comparatively recent understanding of the social construction of disability issues has been complemented by a similar shift in medical practice, towards a realisation that orthodox medical care is not capable of regulating areas of human life, as societies develop community care and embrace de-institutionalisation. The site of medical regulation 'is no longer restricted to specific institutional settings such as the clinic or the hospital, nor is it restricted to the treatment of a particularly dangerous illness by a narrow group of professionals caring for a passive patient' (Marks 1998: 73). This move into community health promotion has focused attention on the need to monitor a range of inequalities that link disability and illness:

- the unjust, socially constructed distribution of disease which may lead to impairment;
- the social disadvantages that occur in the course of relatively short-term experiences such as acute illness, childbirth or surgical intervention;
- the actual experience of physical impairment, not just disablist responses to it; Crow (1996 p. 7), for example, argues for recognition that, through the suffering it represents, 'impairment in itself can be a negative, painful experience'. We would go further and argue that impairment as a physical state is permeated by the impact of unequal social relations, quite apart from any disablist social responses

(McLeod and Bywaters 2000: 11).

And yet one of the dramatic indicators of the improvement in the health and well-being of people has been the greater life expectancy compared to 100 years ago. Diseases such as polio are now virtually non-existent in the United Kingdom and tuberculosis, which killed more than 3,000 people a year at the beginning of the century is now both rare and easily treatable. Advances in the efficacy of drugs and medicines, combined with improvements in surgical skills, have significantly reduced the incidence of certain health conditions linked to impairments and disablement. These changes are not only reflected in the improved survival rates, but recovery from many conditions can now be complete, whereas in the past it was only partial. Nevertheless, it is a paradox that while medical skill has significantly reduced the incidence and prevalence of certain deformities, the same skill has enabled increasing numbers of children with severe and profound disabling conditions to survive.

The link between health, social acceptance and the image of the body has always been dangerously ambiguous. To be healthy implies a positive relationship between physical, social and mental states of well-being. This inter-relationship between 'healthy lifestyle', environmental factors, exercise and diet has become increasingly relevant in the development of health for all of us. However, for disabled people the 'biological clock' of disablement particularly highlights the link between the medicalisation of impairment, increased longevity and changing patterns of living. Advanced medical knowledge means many people are surviving illnesses that previously would have proved fatal, but which leave them severely disabled. This in turn has a number of implications for the development of rehabilitation and care services and for the training of staff. Similar considerations apply to the effective development of multi-agency services in order to mitigate psychological and emotional distress.

Disability and health

Most ill-health is dealt with by people living in their own homes and away from the attention of health professionals. Though brief stays in hospital, consultations in surgeries, day hospitals or outpatients clinics and prescribed treatment are highly significant events, much of the management of illness, including looking after yourself or others, working for recovery, putting up with symptoms, taking home and commercial remedies and potions, is undertaken without requiring medical advice or intervention. Even when people rate their symptoms as severe it has been indicated that 25 per cent do not seek medical treatments. Repeatedly it has been reported that it is not the frequency or length of attendance in hospital which determines any sense of well-being in patients or their carers, but a range of material, environmental and social resources which are not equally distributed.(Rowntree 1997, 1998). 'Differences in income and wealth between patients and carers of different socio-economic groups are compounded by assumptions based on gender, racial, disablist and heterosexist stereotypes – for example, that women are "natural" carers; black people "look after their own"; disabled people are necessarily dependent on others' (McLeod and Bywaters 2000: 68).

It has been argued that there are parallels between the treatment of the female body, and the treatment of the health needs of disabled people of both sexes:

> A disabled person's body is one which is acted upon, one which has things done to it because it doesn't function properly. We may experience surgery, tests that involve taking blood or other substances from us, or drug treatment with their side effects. ... Our ill bodies, like women's bodies are therefore more animal, less sublime, and everyday we are surrounded by images of thin, well, active bodies, with their implicit negative messages about our own bodies, our limited energy levels or physical limitations.
>
> (Marris 1996: 20)

One of the major mistakes so often made in relation to disability is to associate an illness label with an impairment and then to generalise that label. For example, the labels of a 'heart-defect' or cerebral palsy are open to a range of interpretations and responses. One person diagnosed with a heart condition may be able to lead a perfectly normal life, another person may be bed-ridden, while a third may be only capable of limited exercise. The effects of cerebral palsy may be so mild in one person as to be only recognisable to an experienced observer, another person may have enormous difficulty in speaking, eating or walking.

Research also suggests that the health risks faced by people with disabilities are greater than had previously been believed, e.g. cardiovascular disease and cancers appear to be more common and a high proportion of people with disabilities (and particularly learning disabilities) 'carry one or more risk factors associated with morbidity and mortality from these causes' (Turner and Moss 1995: 2).

The planning of the delivery of health and medical care for someone who has a disability is also a major issue, particularly as they move from child to adult services. A person with an impairment such as spina bifida or cerebral palsy, whose legs are affected but who has a good mental capacity, may be able to respond better to physiotherapy than another person with cerebral palsy or spina bifida who also has a learning disability and who cannot understand the directions given by the physiotherapist. For the majority of people, the general practitioner is often the first port of call when someone is ill. Nevertheless, the disablist impact of stigma associated with illness can lead to different forms of discrimination. The doctor may be unaware of how to interact with a physically disabled, or learning disabled person; or may believe that more specialised care is required. Thus a disabled person's, or their family's chances of receiving the appropriate support for their accompanying emotional, social, material and care requirements are jeopardised. In relation to particular health conditions, such as HIV/AIDS, it is interesting to note that although downright bigoted public attitudes have shifted in the UK there is still a stigma 'fanned by the tabloid press').

It is probable that everyone is born with some kind of health defect. Some people may be slightly pigeon-toed, others may have a mole or birth mark of some kind. These are minor blemishes, non-disabling and normally overlooked until some of them re-emerge as more problematic health issues in later life. However, in the past, birth deformities have been considered both an ancient curse and a mark of status. Images of deformity appear in surviving records of the oldest civilisations. It has been noted that achondroplasia (dwarfism) is illustrated in Egyptian tomb paintings more than 5,000 years old and is documented in Greek and Roman annals (Garland 1995).

> Clubfoot was known in the XIth and XIIth dynasties; a cleft palate has been discovered in an Egyptian mummy, and cases of harelip and congenital amputations are recorded in pre-historic Peruvian pottery. Using clay tablets the Babylonians catalogued more than sixty deformities of the ear, nose, mouth and limbs.
>
> (Marshall 1976: 2)

Birth defects are mistakes in body formation, or function, that can be caused by heredity, disease, or by environmental influences. Heredity and environment may work together to produce a child with a health defect. Such is the extent of human variation that it is impossible to give a precise definition of a birth defect. However, it is generally accepted to be anything that is present at birth that will deprive the child of physical or mental health. Some dysfunction is so slight that it may be classed as inconveniences, e.g. left-handedness or colour blindness. On the other hand there are birth defects involving many organs, which result in rapid and premature death within hours after birth. Between these extremes there are a range of conditions that are medically well known. Diabetes and muscular dystrophy are examples of abnormalities in body chemistry, while limb deformities and cleft palates are associated with errors in the anatomical structure of the body. All these conditions are congenital defects, as are some blood disorders such as haemophilia.

Many birth defects are caused by a combination of heredity and environmental factors working together. Nevertheless, just as heredity can make some individuals and not others react to allergens in the environment (like pollen and some drugs), so a particular unborn child's inherited predisposition in the womb may be influenced while another baby may show no environmental reaction at all. For example, not every woman who has rubella in early pregnancy will give birth to a child with an impairment and not all women in the 1960s who took the drug thalidomide, early in their pregnancy, gave birth to malformed infants. Subtle genetic influences have probably had a greater impact on us all.

A healthy lifestyle

Health promotion agendas around exercise, diet and alcohol consumption are often considered as part of a healthy lifestyle. This contrasts with the perception of disabled people as 'sick' and unhealthy which has already been commented upon and rejected. Paradoxically, however, ill-health and sickness brings with it some elements of comfort to those who feel uneasy about disability: 'It offers an avoidance which is ideal, because it is not only "humane", but a symbol of caring. It is a solution to the problems posed by "eternal children" in adult form …' (Shearer 1981: 90).

The health of both populations and individuals is inextricably bound up with economic development. While it is by no means clear that health status automatically improves with rising levels of development, there is a clear correlation. Using the UN population statistics for 1990 it is possible to identify a global estimate of the prevalence of people with moderate and severe disability of 5.2 per cent (Helander 1993: 22). Nevertheless, when it is realised that these estimates refer to prevalence of disability and 'need for rehabilitation' this can be considered to be a global underestimate. The often cited estimate made by the WHO in 1976, of 10 per cent of the world population, may in fact be nearer to the truth. This estimate was based on a number of calculations of disability rates resulting from diseases, trauma, malnutrition, genetic causes, etc. These calculations included a high proportion of people with slight and reversible disabilities, such as those caused by malnutrition. In any given country, the more it is possible to feed all inhabitants, to provide regular water supply and basic preventative medicine, the less likely is the incidence of severe and long-term disablement.

The prevalence of disablement in the world is estimated to be close to 300 million people. However, this figure does not include temporary or short-term disabilities caused by curable diseases or reversible conditions. Disability has come to be linked with a range of conditions and defects other than purely physical ones. In many cases the main causes of disablement arise from illnesses and diseases which have a damaging effect on the body. Diabetes, kidney failure and severe asthma are examples. As has already been noted, disablement also arises from wider social factors in a person's life and environment. Cosmetic and prosthetic surgery is dedicated to both physical normalisation and bodily enhancement. It is offered as a solution to a vast range of physical 'problems' and blemishes. Prostheses, organ transplants and replacements offer technological solutions to biological damage and the whims of fashion. As part of lifestyle, the 'presentational self' has become an important marker of social status and lies at the core of aesthetic discrimination. This 'centrality of the beauty myth in contemporary western culture has made 'aesthetic stratification as powerful as class, gender or ethnic stratification' (Synnott 1993: 101) and aesthetic relationships have become a significant factor in the oppression of disabled people. (Hughes 2000: 560)

Genetic diseases and disability

Since the dawn of time the human race has been suffering from the consequences of genetic disease. Even now, most of the four thousand or so of the conditions which result from mutations in a single gene remain incurable, blighting the hopes of whole families and casting the long shadow of inherited disorders across generations (Kent 1996: 5).

Biotechnology and genetic medicine hold the keys that may radically transform our concepts of health and disease in the foreseeable future. It is the responsibility of politicians and regulators to create the framework that will facilitate and encourage this in response to the entirely legitimate demands of millions of people in families whose lives are affected by the uncertainties of genetic diseases. Prenatal screening is arguably a 'form of quality control for fetuses' (Sinclair and Griffiths 1994: 206) and has associations with eugenic invalidation and elimination of disabilities *in utero*. The new genetics establishes a framework for distinguishing health and human potential 'on the basis of the amount of "genetic capital" that can be identified in a given sample of DNA' (Hughes 2000: 564). The potential for this technology to be a new form for invalidating the lives of disabled people suggests that disabled people 'need more than bland assurances from the scientific community that the new genetics is not a repackaged version of the old eugenics' (Hughes 2000: 565).

It has been reliably estimated that across the European nations that make up the European Union, as many as 30,000 children die each year as a direct result of genetic disorders. Possibly ten times this number are born with significant impairments or long-term health problems (Kent 1996: 73). As examples, both cystic fibrosis and haemophilia are inherited recessive gene disorders. However, as scientific knowledge of human genetics advances, it is clear that more common diseases such as breast cancer, osteoporosis and diabetes have been discovered to have a genetic component. The main characteristics of cystic fibrosis are chronic lung infection, poor digestion due to pancreatic insufficiency and the possibility of liver malfunction in some people. As people with cystic fibrosis grow older they tend to develop a specific form of diabetes. Despite the ever-improving survival rates, and intensive research, it is still the case that cystic fibrosis leads to premature death. Haemophilia, the blood-clotting disease that mainly causes internal bleeding of the knees, elbows and other joints is also a genetically predetermined condition, although it is probably now best known in relation to the publicity arising from the HIV/blood transfusion scandals of the 1980s.

Where families are at a known risk of carrying, or are affected by, a genetic disorder the recent rapid advances in scientific understanding of the human genome carry the potential for effective intervention. Research also carries with it the ethical risks associated with any biomedical enquiry into genetic disease (see Chapter 5)

Chromosomal abnormality

There are a number of syndromes associated with disabling conditions that are a result of chromosomal abnormalities. Down's Syndrome is the most common condition that results from a chromosomal disorder. The condition is characterised by a flatness of the face and thick epicanthal folds around the corners of the eyes, making them appear to slant upwards. Other features include a protruding tongue, defective heart, webbing of the skin folds between fingers and toes, short height and a tendency to obesity. There are basically three types of Down's Syndrome. By far the most common is trisomy 21, where there is an extra chromosome on the 21st pair of chromosomes in the nucleus that becomes a human embryo. In effect, the 21st set of chromosomes is in reality a triplet rather than a pair, causing a condition called trisomy. Mosaicism in cell structure arises because of faulty cell development as a consequence of chromosomal disorders. Some of an individual's cells may have an extra chromosome while others do not and this leads to the condition of Down's Syndrome.

The likelihood of having a child with Down's Syndrome is dependent to a great extent on maternal age. More Down's Syndrome infants tend to be born to women over the age of 40. The medical procedure of amniocentesis, involving examination of the amniotic fluid around the foetus in the uterus, is sometimes recommended to older women in the 18th to 20th week of pregnancy in order to determine whether or not the child will be born with Down's, or other chromosomal abnormality.

Metabolism or nutrition

Most genetically determined impairments are attributed to metabolic disorders. Two such conditions caused by a combination of defective recessive genes are phenylketonuria (PKU) and galactosaemia. Phenylketonuria involves the inability of the body to convert phenylalanine, a common dietary substance, into tyrosine. The accumulation of phenylalanine results in abnormal brain development and can lead to mental impairment. The condition can be detected by a screening test shortly after birth and controlled by dietary measures throughout childhood. Galactosaemia, another metabolic disorder, is a disease that involves the inability to metabolise galactose and can again be controlled through dietary regulation, e.g. by following a regime of a milk-free diet.

As the interest in nutrition and healthy eating has grown, so the manufacturers of food and dietary supplements have begun to claim that food supplements can act as medicines providing cures or treatment for certain diseases. The Food Commission in surveying over 300 products and their promotional literature has found many claims appearing to border on illegality:

> ... dozens of cases where manufacturers are making claims which imply the products have a medicinal effect contrary to the Medicines Act. Others are making carefully worded claims which imply a health benefit without expressly making a medical claim.
>
> (*The Food Magazine* 1997: 1)

Infection and intoxication

There are a number of infections that have a serious effect on foetal development; some affect the mother while others are particular to the developing baby. Rubella, syphilis and herpes simplex in pregnant mothers are all conditions that can cross the placental barrier and lead to impairments and disabilities in the unborn foetus. Rubella can be controlled through preventive vaccination but is most dangerous in the first three months of pregnancy (trimester). The venereal diseases of syphilis and herpes simplex, on the other hand, present a greater risk at later stages of foetal development. Examples of infection in the child rather than the mother are meningitis and encephalitis. Meningitis is an infection of the covering of the brain which may be caused by a variety of bacterial or viral agents. The condition can lead to mental retardation and or sensory impairment. The more serious infection of encephalitis is an inflammation of the brain. It can lead to immediate trauma and mental dysfunction, or the effects may not occur until years later.

Like infections, poisoning can occur in the expectant mother or the unborn child. During the past 20 years there has been a growing awareness of the harmful effects of a variety of substances, e.g. the toxic effects of tobacco, alcohol and even food additives, as well as the more well-known hazards of hard drugs such as heroin. The more subtle effects of prescribed drugs have also been implicated as having a harmful effect on the development of the foetus. Less well understood are the potential hazards of environmental pollutants in exhaust fumes, lead-based paint and toxic agents which effect organisms at the lower levels of the food chain. The problems of drug abuse are disturbingly widespread in their effect when it is recognised that drug availability is more common than one might at first believe and that drug poisoning can come in a variety of forms, e.g. cigarettes, alcohol, glue, paint, cold remedies, amphetamines and valium-based products.

Just as drug misuse may have consequences that can lead to impairments, so too can the use of drugs be used as a method of therapy and intervention. The treatment of Attention Deficit Hyperactive Disorder (ADHD) is commonly through prescribed drugs. Attention Deficit Hyperactive Disorder is a condition in children and young people, typically characterised by distraction, short memory and physical over-activity. Sufferers are often talkative, have poor concentration and are low in achievement and work output. While there is no consensus on the causes of ADHD, recent theoretical considerations suggest that 'more than 80% of cases are caused by a malfunction within the inner ear system' (Jensen 1995: 286). This is the area that affects vision, regulates balance and sensory motor responses. It is a feature of hyperactivity that the most successful treatment for overcoming the learning disabilities arising from the condition is through a prescription of activity-inducing amphetamine-based drugs, such as Ritalin.

Trauma or physical agents

The brain of the developing foetus and young child is relatively vulnerable to a variety of accidents. Damage to the brain can occur before, during or after birth and can lead to impairments. Before birth high levels of X-ray can result in brain dysfunction. Injury can also occur during delivery if the child is not positioned properly in the uterus. A difficulty that can sometimes occur during delivery is anoxia (deprivation of oxygen). After birth, a blow to the head can, of course, cause damage to a child's brain and lead to impaired development of the nervous system.

The health needs of people with disabilities

Studies of the health and lifestyle of people with disabilities have tended to concentrate on the concerns for primary health care of populations in institutions. There is now an accumulation of evidence that changes in longevity and lifestyle as a result of the closures of long-stay hospitals is altering the health-related disorders of people living in non-institutional settings and these changes are being reflected in the death rates of disabled people. Ironically, people with greater independence, living in the community may now be more likely to follow lifestyles which place a higher risk on their health, resulting in more health-risk related deaths, e.g. from smoking, poor nutrition and cardiovascular disorders.

There are a number of ways in which living in the community may bring higher health risks. People with disabilities in the United Kingdom are now exposed to many of the increased risk factors relating to cardiovascular disease, cancers, mental illness, sexual health and accidents that affect the rest of society. In addition they face increased risks of obesity and fitness-related factors. These are particular threats for people who may already face a range of other health-related impairments, such as visual and hearing disorders and poor dental health. Obesity has been linked to increased mortality from cancer of the colon, rectum and of the prostate in men. In women it is associated with cancer of the gall bladder, breast, cervix and ovaries (Garrow 1988). These risks affect people equally and apply to the general population at large as well as people with disabilities. However, opportunistic screening would identify more cases at an earlier age and help to prevent the onset of obesity-related disablement.

Screening for osteoporosis, as another example, would benefit not simply older people who suffer from inadequate and discriminatory health care, but more specifically women (who statistically outlive men anyway) who have gone beyond the menopause. Henwood (1990) indicates that there are more than 46,000 people in England and Wales who suffer hip fractures each year and 60 per cent of them are women over the age of 75.

The impact of discrimination in relation to health screening in old age suggests that there are a number of hard decisions to be made. The efficacy of health screening in old age may be more limited than using resources to improve lifestyle rather than for disease detection. There are a number of erroneous assumptions made about the nature of diseases in older people and response to treatment. There is a relatively high proportion of cancers, gastro-intestinal disorders, foot disorders, balance disorders, incontinence and obesity associated with disabled people in old age. However, the relative under-treatment of, for example, cancer in older people means that tumours which could be controlled or cured are not (Henwood 1990). In addition to Alzheimer's disease and dementia, other conditions associated with early ageing have also been identified among adults with Down's syndrome. Musculo-skeletal weakness and particular conditions such as osteoporosis have been observed as preventable risk factors: '… osteoporosis fractures in the elderly present a major healthcare and social problem which is largely preventable. The consequences of these fractures are enormous both socio-economically and as regards morbidity and mortality' (Office of Health Economics 1990: 19).

The Health of the Nation

The *Health of the Nation* initiative was established by central government in 1992. It established five key national priority areas for improving understanding of the health needs of the population:

- coronary heart disease and stroke;
- cancer;
- mental illness;
- HIV, AIDS and sexual health;
- accidents.

In 1995 it was also established that the sub-population of people with learning disabilities should be considered a priority group for considerations of preventative health care (HMSO 1995). It has been particularly evident that the risk factors related to these five areas are at least as prevalent among people with learning difficulties as among the general population. Research into the healthy lifestyles of this sub-population suggests that while strategies for health promotion among learning-disabled people are encouraged, the most common initiatives tend to be around weight loss/maintenance and healthy eating, There is less consideration given to areas such as fitness or anti-smoking education (Turner 1996).

Coronary heart disease and stroke

There is evidence that the risk factors associated with cardiovascular disease are at least as prevalent among people with learning difficulties as in the general population (Turner and Moss 1995). Increased risks of cardiovascular disease have been linked with obesity, higher cholesterol levels and hypertension. Studies in both the UK and the USA suggest that obesity is higher among people with learning difficulties than among the general population. Bell and Bhate (1992), in a survey report, indicated that 19 per cent of males and 35 per cent of females living in a community for people with disabilities were found to be obese. These figures compare with 6 per cent and 8 per cent respectively of the general population.

Poor cardiovascular fitness is indicative of a sedentary lifestyle and this tends to be confirmed by the limited number of studies that have been conducted in this area in the United Kingdom. Flynn and Hirst (1992) found that a low proportion of a sample of young people with learning disabilities aged between 14 and 22 took part in sport compared with a matched sample of young people in the general population and that much of their time was spent in passive activities such as watching television.

Cancer

Cancers are the most common causes of death in the UK, after heart disease, and account for approximately 25 per cent of deaths (HMSO 1992).There is some evidence that cancer-related deaths are beginning to increase among the population of people with disabilities. Jancar (1990) found that death rates from cancer in an institution in the UK increased from 10 per cent in the period 1931 to 1980, to 17 per cent of all deaths in the period 1976 to 1985. Jancar concluded that this may indeed be due to increased longevity, but the findings also indicate a significant increase in certain gastro-intestinal cancers, which may be a reflection of certain unexplained changes in lifestyle. As with heart disease, deaths due to cancer appear more prevalent among people with moderate and mild learning disorders, compared to those with more profound and multiple disabilities (O'Brien *et al.* 1991). There has been a long and well-established link between death from leukaemia and Down's syndrome. This is estimated at between 10 and 20 times greater than in the general population (Fong and Brodeur 1987).

Mental illness

Mental illness is the third of the *Health of the Nation* key areas. Evidence from a number of large-scale studies suggest that the prevalence of mental ill-health among disabled people is somewhat different compared with the general population. The evidence indicates that the prevalence of mental illness in people with learning disabilities is at least as high as in the general population (Moss 1995; Turner and Moss 1995). For a person with a learning disability, whose adaptive skills may already be limited, an additional mental illness is likely to lead to the need for considerable levels of support and a seriously impaired quality of life.

Sexual health

The promotion of the rights of people with learning difficulties to enjoy appropriate health and sex education and opportunities for personal and sexual relationships has been established as a key theme of the *Health of the Nation*. It recommends a strategy that seeks to reduce the incidence of HIV and other sexually transmitted diseases and encourages the development of effective family planning services. There is a huge range of information available concerning the need for 'safe sex' to prevent sexually transmitted diseases. Unfortunately, this information is not always easily accessible to people with disabilities (Shakespeare *et al.* 1996: 17). There is an assumption that disabled people, particularly those with a learning difficulty, have limited sexual activity. In fact, the idea that people with learning difficulties might wish to enjoy permanent sexual relationships and marriage is still treated as a taboo subject which is both unclear and contradictory in its messages for disabled people. For example, while it is not illegal to carry out a sexual act with a woman who is learning disabled, provided she has given consent, two people with learning difficulties wishing to marry are still expected to seek consent for their actions from a professional member of the caring services.

An important aspect of sexual health, particularly for people with learning difficulties, is the detection and prevention of sexual abuse. This applies to people living in the community as much as to those remaining in institutions. In recent years the extent of physical and sexual abuse experienced by people with disabilities has become more widely known and discussed. Harassment and abuse is offensive and an obscene violation of anyone who is a victim. However, for people with disabilities the offence is amplified by their relative powerlessness as victims of attack. In order to counter this, a number of strategies have been developed. For example, British Telecom have established a separate specialised mini-com (text phone) line to monitor harassment arising from sexually obscene or malicious telephone messages to deaf people (*Disability Now* Feb. 1996: 6).

Nowadays the risk of people with learning difficulties being sexually abused is an acknowledged if sad fact of life. The issue of sexual abuse with its additional hazards of HIV and other sexually transmitted diseases or psychological damage, has been studied by Turk and Brown (1993) in residential settings in the UK. They indicate that the risk of abuse comes almost equally from other residents, from staff, family members and others. Turk and Brown also report that 55 per cent of the 119 cases studied allegedly resulted in emotional trauma for the victim.

Accidents

Accidents are the most common cause of death among people under 30 in the general population. The majority of these occur on the roads or in the home. An aim to reduce the incidence of accidents is the fifth of the *Health of the Nation* key areas.

Although the use of a car is likely to be much lower among disabled people, there is some evidence that fatal accidents may be more common among people with learning difficulties. The *Health of the Nation* refers to people with disabilities having an increased vulnerability to accidents and, thereby, requiring the involvement of carers and services, including the provision of safety items and adaptations (HMSO 1992: 113–14). This increased risk relates to the high prevalence of certain conditions (e.g. dementia among older people with Down's syndrome, vision loss, movement disorders and skeletal abnormalities). It has been speculated that particular conditions that are vulnerable to accident, such as the high prevalence of atlantoaxial vertebra instability among children with Down's Syndrome, may be linked to the high incidence of degenerative arthritis of the neck among adults (Howells 1989).

The need for recreation, pastimes and relaxation

There has been very little published research in relation to exercise fitness, diet and weight loss among disabled people in the United Kingdom. Research evaluating weight loss programmes among people with disabilities in the United States generally reveals patchy results. Studies concerned with the maintenance of weight loss are particularly unconvincing, reporting that some subjects in a small-scale study actually gained weight in the 12 months following the baseline measurement (Fox *et al.* 1984). It is probable that neither diet nor exercise, by themselves, will be sufficient for long-term maintenance of weight loss and what will be required are intervention programmes that can be sustained and monitored at regular intervals.

Access to recreational facilities and to recreation itself is, literally, a vital component for everyone. Recreation embraces a complete range of different pastimes. It is a way friendships are formed outside the workplace or home environment; it can also be a way to keep fit. The physiological and emotional needs that can be met from recreational pursuits are vital to a balanced, healthy lifestyle and include enjoyment, competition and satisfaction.

Alternative and complementary medicine

The oppresive desire for perfection in evertything and modern consumer culture suggests that there are no excuses for not looking good in contemporary society. Modern health care suggests that there is a choice of 'solution' for every bodily burden, blemish, bulge or imperfection. However, many disabled people who may have experienced years of surgery in childhood feel that the health profession creates as many difficulties as it cures.

As market economics have begun to create internalised competition within state-run health services in a number of countries, the funding of provision formerly freely available to all people is coming under threat. Changes in the funding of the National Health Service are particularly worrying for people whose impairment is also a serious illness. As the long-term costs for care and medical provision become increasingly the responsibility of individuals, the additional expenses of people with impairments and disabilities compared to non-disabled people places upon them a disproportionate financial burden.

For some disabled people, therapies such as acupuncture, homeopathy, aromatherapy and diet have provided an alternative or antidote to conventional medicine. As Marris (1996) has suggested, a holistic approach is fundamental to most complementary therapies. The emphasis is on treating the whole person rather than individual organs or parts of the body. A holistic philosophy also guides the spirit of anthroposophy that underlies the teaching of Rudolf Steiner, whose first requirement is that those who follow his principles should turn their attention to the improvement of their physical and mental or spiritual health (Steiner 1994).

Marris (1996) argues that complementary medicine can offer a radical challenge to the inclination for victim blaming. The holistic approach offers the possibility of a more equal relationship between practitioner and patient; it recognises and appreciates that health care involves an appreciation of the multiple stresses on both individuals, their sense of selfhood and the environment in which they live. Complementary and holistic medicine does, nevertheless, have its own limitations, the most obvious being availability and expense. She also raises other criticisms:

Just as with conventional preventive medicine, we are given a set of rules to live by, such as avoiding alcohol, cigarettes and various kinds of food. Once again the blame for illness can be laid on our shoulders if we do not do the right things. The much clearer understanding that exists within complementary medicine of the links between physical and mental well-being can also lead to undue pressure to think positively all the time. It becomes a duty to have our emotional house completely in order.

(Marris 1996: 201)

Summary

Illness can be a solitary experience. Something as minor as a cold or a toothache can make people feel excluded and cut off. The experience of living with an illness in a culture which does not have high regard for people who are ill or disabled has influenced the way in which people think about their world, their politics and their health. The health of people with disabilities is particularly linked to strategies for prevention and rehabilitation. Thus, the *Health of the Nation* has identified five key areas that have reference to people with learning difficulties. They also suggest that the whole population is, increasingly, being expected to take more responsibility for their own health and exercise needs and the preventative strategies which can help to ward off ill-health. It is no longer sufficient to believe that the State will meet the costs of treatment. Research findings also suggest that people with learning difficulties, who are now living in the community, are more vulnerable to the health risks associated with daily living (e.g. heart attack, stress, obesity) than their counterparts in institutions. This is a marker of an inclusive lifestyle that is perhaps more unintended than anticipated.

The marginalisation of disabled people both in health maintenance, disease prevention, lifestyle and in their interaction with wider society has a variety of causes. Urban areas, housing, sports, leisure and health facilities are designed by people with an idealised imagination that unintentionally tends to preclude the participation of all. The majority of the population are bound by the designs and convictions of a minority. Some of these issues serve as the basis for Chapter 9.

CHAPTER 9

The enabling environment

Questions

- Consider the environmental barriers for people with physical impairments in the normal household. How might they be overcome?
- What are the limitations of technology in overcoming communication difficulties?
- Explore the practical implications of microelectronics for assisting disabled people.
- Contact your local or regional resource centre for adaptive aids. How do they assess and match people with the equipment available?

Introduction

There are a variety of personal, environmental and architectural barriers that can prevent the full participation of disabled people in society. There is still a great deal of work to be done if disabled people are to become central to the removal of these obstacles. This chapter will focus upon three key areas:

- physical and technological environments (housing, transport systems and access to public amenities and information technology);
- social and recreational environments (including opportunities for participation in the planning and delivery of services by disabled people);
- economic environments (which includes employment, and access to income and financial benefits).

Census surveys (Martin *et al.* 1988) suggest that some 4.3 million people in the United Kingdom cannot walk for a quarter of a mile without stopping and/or without severe discomfort, and that 2.3 million people cannot stand alone without severe discomfort. These are two of the bald facts that maintain the image of dependency that is associated with impairment and disability. And from behind these utilitarian statistics has emerged a growing industry of technological aids and equipment intended to facilitate the lives and circumstances of disabled people. The rehabilitation industry of care management includes access to increasingly sophisticated prostheses, mobility aids and other items of equipment intended to provide a more enabling experience.

The socio-political structures that have shaped both the practical and aesthetic space of the built environment have remained largely under-researched in relation to disabled people. However, creating barrier-free environments for people with a range of impairments is about more than examining the physical dimensions of buildings. Doors, ramps and lifts are all undeniably important in making the built environment more accessible, but as Napolitano (1996) has indicated, good inclusive design is also about psychological dimensions of change. Disabled people can be given positive messages when the front entrances of buildings are ramped, or transport systems and the signing on notices are sensitively worded, at the right height and clearly visible:

> The element of struggle so often present in daily life fades, confidence and the ability to function is enhanced and a relaxed and open attitude is more likely to prevail. When making access arrangements this psychological element needs to be considered carefully: if the way that disabled people are expected to get into buildings is round the back, past the bins and through the kitchens, what message does that communicate?
>
> (Napolitano 1996: 33)

Physical, social and recreational environments

Discrimination against disabled people is most noticeably visible and blatant when related to access to buildings and transport. There are numerous studies which have highlighted the combination of patronisation and discrimination that maintains the physical exclusion of the majority of disabled people (e.g. Flynn 1989; Gooding 1994; Morris 1991, 1996; PSI 1995; Imrie 1996). Most modernist architectural ideals continue to be fundamentally ableist:

> In particular, it is popularly assumed that because the built environment seems to facilitate access for the majority of the population (which is a contestable notion), it is the responsibility of the minority to cope by overcoming their handicaps and/or compensating for them.
>
> (Imrie 1996: 12)

By promoting the social model of disablement, people with disabilities have started to reconceptualise and transform the worlds that we all share and inhabit, 'the emergence of direct action is, in part, premised on an assertion of their differences and on critiques of state welfarism and the paternalism of the wider structures of the "caring" industries' (Imrie 1996: 166). This politicisation of the distinctions between 'ablist' space and 'disablist' space, mainly as a result of action by disabled people and their organisations, has begun to highlight the often blatant discrimination and oppression that has subordinated disabled people. Morris (1993) has, for example, illustrated the way in which choice in housing patterns for disabled people has been restricted both in terms of geographical location and architectural design.

Legislation relating to the built environment and disabled people tends to still be more adequately met in the conditions of the Chronically Sick and Disabled Person's Act (1970), than the Disability Discrimination Act (1995). This latter piece of enabling legislation has no powers to enforce compliance and carries a substantial number of clauses that permit avoidance of full legal compliance. The main regulatory provision with regards to disabled people that reflects government policy for the pursuit of merely utilitarian ideals is Part M of Schedule 1 of the Building Regulations. This is a piece of building law that requires access and facilities for disabled people to be provided in certain classes of new buildings (see Imrie 1996: 101 and 117–18 for further details). The DDA legislation on employment now requires more consideration from small employers, but these changes are still little understood by the majority of Britain's employers who do not feel affected by the new law when it comes to the requirement to make adaptations to access in the workplace.

Much of the built environment – housing, transport, public buildings and amenities, including places of worship – remain inaccessible to disabled people. There is a general view among the leisure industry, as Barnes (1996) points out, that the presence of disabled people in cinemas, pubs, clubs, restaurants and other places of public togetherness is bad for business. Images of disabled people in the communication media also continue to present a particularly horrid and distorted view of the experiences of disability and impairment.

One of the ways in which attempts to create enabling environments goes badly wrong is when in removing one barrier another is created. This is a common dilemma for people with mobility impairments who wish to have access to the few adapted toilets that exist for disabled people. Often the lavatories are kept permanently locked or are inaccessible without assistance. One author highlights the issue:

Whether the mobility impaired person is stopping off at a motorway service station or a public convenience they will be confronted by the same thing. While non-disabled people can simply walk into a lavatory, or get in for a small price, people with mobility impairments have to send off search parties for someone who has a key....

(Napolitano 1996: 31)

Another concern emerges when good and reasonable access has been developed and incorporated into an existing building, but non-disabled people simply abuse or use the facility insensitively. For example, think of the number of lavatories for disabled people that are misused as store cupboards, with mops and buckets, light bulbs removed or furniture placed too close to the doors for the facility to be accessible to somebody in a wheelchair; think too of the vehicles parked across ramped entrances to buildings, preventing people with mobility impairments from leaving or entering.

For everyone there is the need to relax from life's everyday responsibilities and roles – for example to drop in to the local pub for a drink with friends at Sunday lunchtime, to go for a walk in the country, to share an intimate meal or play a game of football. These are but a few examples of the ways in which people relax and spend their leisure time. Recreation embraces a complete range of different pastimes. It is a way friendships are formed outside the workplace or home environment; it can also be a way to keep fit. The physiological and emotional needs that can be met from recreational pursuits are vital to a balanced, healthy lifestyle and include enjoyment, competition and satisfaction.

As Chapter 8 indicated, access to recreational facilities and to recreation itself is a vital component of everyone's health. It should be remembered that while our concentration is upon the demands for accessible recreation from disabled people, there are many others who are unable to take advantage of sport and recreation. For a variety of reasons the single parent on welfare benefits is isolated from recreation as a consequence of his/her poverty and environmental conditions; the solitary individual who feels that they cannot participate in social activities becomes the social isolate; and the executives who leave no time in their lives for activities other that their work lead themselves to stress and isolation within their families.

If access to relaxation is denied or made difficult then access to the complete satisfaction of a whole range of human needs is also denied. Exclusion can emerge from the physical limitations of a venue (such as a cinema with limited wheelchair access). It can also emerge as a result of ignorance/prejudice, e.g. the belief that someone with a disability is not interested in many recreational activities, or is unable to participate in them. There is also a long-standing belief presuming that people with disabilities should go to special clubs/venues and be offered activities like tray making or wicker basket weaving. Worthy pastimes as they are, they should not remain the sole means of relaxation available to disabled people!

There is a convenient tradition of service-dependency and a consequent limitation of choice offered to disabled people. This has tended to allow non-disabled people in society to feel 'comfortable' with the issue of disability and at the same time allowed them to ignore the full range of human diversity and potential in relation to the rights of disabled people to take part in recreational activity. Whether organised or informal. Ironically, the comparative lack of competitive success of British athletes in the 1996 Olympic Games has escalated the profile of British success in the para-olympic movement and has made disabled sport more visible. These top-class athletes are seen increasingly as top-class athletes who have a disability and not as disabled athletes. The role that these athletes play is of great importance as they are grabbing the attention of a society that admires competition and forcing the issue of disability to be heard. Disabled people are seen as not only capable of enjoying sport but as extremely competitive, excellent sports people. This can only have a positive effect for the development of a fuller range of recreational activity for all people who have a disability.

Housing

Having a decent home, possessions and comforts is important to our physical and material well-being and to our planning for the future. However, where we live depends on a number of factors, not least of which is level of income. It is difficult to measure, but not difficult to imagine the impact of inappropriately adapted housing on the lives of physically impaired people. There are over 4 million people with mobility impairments in the United Kingdom and there are only 80,000 accessible homes.

It is transparently obvious that the majority of housing stock is unsuitable for people with mobility impairments. However, the main area of social inequality in relation to housing arises from social divisions. The housing inequalities of disabled people are evident from the incidence of homelessness among disabled people in the population. This arises as a consequence of low earnings potential and as a consequence of the heavy reliance placed upon the rented sector of the housing market at a time when there are fewer houses available for rent. The lack of purpose-built or adapted housing for disabled people has also helped to increase the numbers of disabled people who are homeless (Morris and Winn 1993).

The concept of accessible housing would mean that thresholds would be level, doorways sufficiently wide and electric sockets at reasonable heights. The essential features within kitchens, bathrooms and toilets would be placed with more thought and consideration for everybody's needs. Thus, they would be within the reach of independent access. At the moment, equipment and fittings are not immediately suitable for the majority of people (e.g. the elderly, children and certainly not for people with mobility impairments).

As access groups throughout the United Kingdom have observed, houses are used by a succession of occupants over different periods of their life cycles and should be more suited to these changing circumstances. Gooding (1994, 2000) has made the fundamental point that more adaptable housing would not only help to break the mould of the ghettoised selfishness of 'special needs' housing for the disabled minority. It would also help to build a friendlier environment that benefits a wide variety of people. This would encourage more chances to create more humane spaces in which disabled people can entertain others or accommodate friends.

Technology and its limitations

It is evident from the rapid growth in technological aids in every phase of modern living that information technology (ICT) is one of the major influences for improving access as well as employment and education for disabled people. Participation in community involvement by disabled people has also been assisted by micro-electronic prosthetics, or artificial technical aids. By the beginning of the next century, ICT is likely to be at the heart of the development of independent living and learning.

Having to make do is a common problem for disabled people. Media designed for non-disabled people cannot always be adapted for those with disabilities. An illustration of this can be made with reference to people who are visually impaired and the development of software from Microsoft. Although Microsoft Windows software accounts for 80 per cent of the software market, the system was originally inaccessible to visually impaired people. In similar fashion, disabled people who use computer speech output systems to provide them with textual information may find it uncomfortable to read from their computer screens for long periods of time. The flexibility of a book or a paper text is unavailable to them, replaced instead by the linear time-based format of a computerised speech output. No matter what sort of electronic or technological equipment is available, it is only ever as good as the human support that lies behind it. Technology, of itself, is only one piece of the jigsaw.

Enabling technology has a number of applications for disabled people and focuses on four main areas:

- facilitating communication, e.g. this can be through word processing, voice output communication aids, text to braille;
- easing the pressure, e.g. having easy access to a computer and relevant software can help to improve opportunities for accessing libraries, meeting deadlines, paying bills, etc.;
- access to mainstream electronic resources, e.g. finding information and communicating with people at the computer, the internet, CD ROMs and multimedia;
- it can be used in a diagnostic, restorative or remedial role.

Access to a vast range of information can be achieved through the power of the computer. Just as software packages can be purchased to aid speech development or improve literacy difficulties, access to the Internet can help disabled people participate in discussion groups without having to physically visit them. For example by using the world wide web, or e-mail, people with disabilities can obtain information in exactly the same fashion as any other user, but in an environment which is suited to their physical needs and by using whatever enabling technologies they require.

In relation to the increased independence of disabled people, innovative adaptations and developments are exploiting the power of ICT (e.g micro-electronics are already being used to help to overcome the handicapping effects of physical and sensory impairments). Opportunities for the development of physical mobility are also enhanced by advances in the improved design of aids and equipment in both the workplace and community settings. These can include such environmental items as remote control devices for opening and shutting doors and improvements in overall standards of access to buildings and work spaces.

The development of micro-electronic technology plays a significant role in the education of children and students with learning difficulties (Warwick *et al.* 1997):

- at a *micro level* the support provided can take the form of advising individuals. ICT can give instructions, coach teachers, provide advice about software and hardware;
- at a *meso level* the ICT can provide opportunities for the exchange of ideas, consultation and developing policy for particular strategies and or techniques (e.g. working groups for the development of ICT for discrete handicaps, such as CONVIG for the visually handicapped in the Netherlands and the Marconi Project in the Bologna district of Italy);
- at a *macro level* there are opportunities for national consultation (e.g. in the United Kingdom there is the National Federation of Access Centres which can provide consultancy and diagnostic screening).

Advances in communication technology have begun to make it easier for people with sensory disabilities to attend ordinary social and work settings. Visual display units attached to voice sensitive switches have begun to revolutionise communication for those who are physically disabled with a speech defect, with partial hearing or who are deaf. Optical scanning devices such as the Arkenstone Scanner or the Kurtzweil Reading Edge, linked to Braille printers and voice synthesisers, and software have begun to benefit readers who are partially sighted. Moreover, where once such equipment was considered prohibitively expensive, it has now fallen to a price that makes the purchase not only viable but an important dimension of any support strategy.

Johnstone (1995) has pointed out that the past decade has shown that people with disabilities and children with special needs now expect to have a right to access both the curriculum and opportunities for social independence as a result of advances in micro-electronics and information technology. Difficulties in note taking, personal record keeping and drafting written work can now be surmounted through the use of new technology. These advances have played their part in the development of access to equality of educational opportunities.

Although many disabled people have benefited from using information technology, these benefits are neither universal nor fully realised. Vincent (1993) has suggested that this is due to lack of appropriate support beyond the mere provision of equipment and devices. The first line of development for this appropriate support is in assessment of individual needs in relation to the technology available. Simply having access to a computer does not guarantee the development of independent learning or of educational opportunity. Other frustrations with the use of micro-computers have emerged as a result of the limitations in available software. Where the hardware of machinery, speed of loading and amounts of memory have improved dramatically '… much of the available software is, for all its quantity, educationally inadequate' (Hegarty 1993: 194). Many of the available programs seem to offer little that could not be achieved as well by other means and without the accompanying frustrations. In other words, much of the available resource material is packaged in a fashion that fails to exploit the potential of the micro-computer or take into account theories of learning.

Support for the development of ICT skills

Interesting examples of the use of computer technology in the United Kingdom are cited in Hawkridge and Vincent (1992) and Vincent (1990). Their studies indicate the value of developing expertise and experience in conjunction with research organisations (e.g. the National Federation of Access Centres), in order to develop both wider networks and disabled people's self-confidence. They indicate how, through the use of appropriate programs, schools and colleges of FE have facilitated the mastery of social and life skills with young learners who have specific learning difficulties. It is clear that this collaboration with regional and national resource centres for the development of both software and hardware (e.g. tracker balls and adapted keyboards) has enabled learners to engage in activities which they not only consider to be appropriate for their age but also on a par with those activities they see being done by 'mainstream' learners.

The study by Hawkridge and Vincent (1992) reporting their research within the OECD programme for 'Supporting Active Life for Young People with Disabilities' has, nevertheless, pointed to some important reminders about the strengths and limitations of computers for staff and students alike. They suggest that new technology can give students and young people with disabilities and special educational needs both a wider choice of courses and enhanced educational and employment opportunities. While this is broadly true for all aspects of disability and special educational needs, the new technology cannot provide enablement, access or opportunities without a proper assessment and re-assessment of an individual's needs, or the appropriate training for students and their teachers and carers, information, advice and technical services.

The wider implications of assistive technology, assessing and training people to use it, are complex. Schools, college and community education centres and employers need to play a role in the development of work with disabled people and to provide advice, experience and good practice. People will then have opportunities that, in turn, can increase their independence. Assistive technology can enable people with disabilities and special needs to acquire skills that match current and future requirements in employment and daily activity. The speed of advance means that many people are still unaware of this

advent. Coaxing the neurones of quadriplegic patients to gain control of computer technology has already been achieved and even as this book goes to print researchers in the
USA have harnessed the means to link computer technology to the brain stem of a living
organism (*Guardian* 18 April 2001: 1). Researchers at North-western University, currently
experimenting with simple organisms, ultimately hope to create advanced brain-
controlled prostheses for people whose normal ability to control their limbs has been
disrupted by a stroke or Parkinson's disease.

It may be considered impressive that a severely disabled person can learn to operate a
switch with the blink of an eyelid and as a result communicate through a computer, but it
requires the sensitive involvement of specialist assessors to determine if this is all that is
required to sustain or improve their quality of life. It may be that the interface with a
keyboard could be improved by using another part of the body to operate a switch, or that
a speech synthesiser could improve communication or even that the position of the
equipment could be determined in a more ergonomically efficient fashion:

> The difference between non-assessment and assessment can be the difference between
> frustration and the benefits of an enabling technology that opens up new opportunities.
>
> (Vincent 1993: 2)

The immense storage and interactive power of CD-ROM technology, the portability of
computers and the growing panoply of technical aids suggests that it is only a matter of
time before they can be used by people who wish to study in their own time and yet
remain in regular touch with a 'home base'. Electronic tutorials, advice and consultancy
via the Internet and arrangements with a specialist tutor or advisor working from a
modem-linked computer terminal some distance away in a college, school or resource
centre are clearly worth consideration.

The rapidly developing power of ICT emphasises the importance of the personnel
who manage it. At present there is no clear professional profile for these professionals
who are leading the way. The hardware will be only as effective as the strengths of those
who manage its use. Their skills will have to be recognised and rewarded. This potential
of ICT also gives rise to an ethical question, concerning the relationship between an 'independent consultant' and the commercial companies with which he or she is in regular
contact. Whether it is possible for a consultant to remain completely independent is a
matter for debate. It may be more appropriate to establish some professional regulations
and set conditions for collaboration.

Benefits and finance as enabling factors

The poor financial circumstances of many disabled people can often be significantly more
problematic than the actual impairment that contributes to disablement. The additional

costs associated with being disabled can cause a range of competing and contradictory emotions. As the emphasis for long-term care has shifted relentlessly from the responsibility of state and more towards the individual, benefits may have begun to be considered as a privilege, or charity handout. However, the specific benefits available to disabled people are there as a right, to meet the costs of living with a disability, costs such as heating, transport, clothing and personal assistance.

The Social Security system is notoriously complex and for this reason it is best to seek more detailed and specific advice from specialist sources such as a local Benefits Agency or the national welfare handbooks provided by the Child Poverty Action Group (e.g. CPAG 2001). A well-known and regularly updated directory of information and opportunities for disabled people is provided in conjunction with the Royal Association for Disability and Rehabilitation (Darnborough and Kinrade, 7th edn 1996). Benefits paid out to people with disabilities can be either means-tested or non-means-tested benefits. Means-tested benefits are only paid out if people have limited income and capital; they are only awarded following a thorough investigation into people's financial circumstances. The most important means-tested sources of benefit are:

Income Support

This is the main benefit for people with a low income. For people with a disability the general rules for entitlement to income support, among them being available for work, may not apply as a direct result of illness or a physical/mental impairment.

Housing Benefit

Payable to people on a low income and living in rented property. This can include private and local authority accommodation, including sheltered accommodation. It is not, however, usually eligible to people in residential care or a nursing home. The amount of benefit received depends on a person's level of income, the number of people in the 'family' and the amount calculated as 'eligible' rent for the purposes of a rebate or allowance. It is paid by local authorities but is a national scheme.

Health benefits

Although the National Health Service generally provides free health care, there are charges for prescriptions. Exemptions from these charges on a number of grounds including low income, physical disablement or other health conditions can apply.

Tax credits

A relatively new system of allowances in the form of tax credits has also been introduced to supplement the finances of low-paid workers. These top up the wages of low-paid workers with disabilities. To qualify for tax credits an individual must have a physical or mental disability that puts them at a disadvantage in getting a job. They must also fulfil one of the disability conditions of the disability and disadvantage test (CPAG 2001: 146–7).

Families' Tax Credit

This has replaced Family Credit and is unavailable if the level of capital a person has is above a certain amount. It is a weekly payment, normally payable for a period of up to 26 weeks, and it is only payable if a claimant has at least one dependent child. If a disabled person or his/her partner is in receipt of the Disabled Working Allowance they will not be entitled to claim Working Families' Tax Credit.

Disabled Person's Tax Credit

This is a benefit paid to people who are in work but have a disability which puts them at a disadvantage in the labour market. It tops up a claimant's wages if they are in full-time work. Part-time workers can claim Income Support instead. To qualify for DPTC a person must have a disability that puts them at a disadvantage in getting a job.

Non-means Tested Benefits

Non-means-tested benefits do not involve a detailed examination of personal finances. So long as a person meets certain basic conditions, called 'conditions of entitlement' (such as being disabled, widowed or available for work), the benefits are payable. Non-means-tested benefits are intended to supplement or compensate for inability to work or any loss of earnings. Thus, for people with disabilities the most significant long-term non-contributory benefits are:

Severe Disablement Allowance

This tax-free benefit was abolished for first time claimants on 6 April 2001. People entitled to the SDA prior to this date will continue to receive it. To qualify people must have been incapable of work for 28 weeks. It was a particularly significant allowance for people who had not paid enough National Insurance contributions to claim either sickness or invalidity benefits. The lowest age limit was 16 and it was not income related. People who become disabled after the age of 65 could not normally claim this benefit.

Disability Living Allowance

A tax-free benefit for people who need help with personal care and/or getting around. The claimant must be under 66 when an application is made and have become disabled before their 65th birthday. The allowance is made up from two parts: a mobility component, which has two rates; and a care component which has three. In 1992 this benefit replaced Mobility Allowance and Attendance Allowance for people under the age of 65

Attendance Allowance

A tax-free allowance that is available to adults who are 65 or over with severe physical or mental disabilities and who require a lot of care or supervision either by day or by night, or both. If a person qualifies for Attendance Allowance or Disability Living Allowance and has a carer who is not otherwise 'gainfully employed', they may also be eligible for Invalid Care Allowance, for their services.

Other sources of help can come from special funds and from local and national charities. The best known is perhaps the Family Fund, administered by the Joseph Rowntree Memorial Trust. It exists to provide help in the form of goods, services or a grant of money to the families of children under the age of 16 with severe disabilities. The fund has wide discretion to provide help that will relieve stress arising from the day-to-day care of the child. In general, it can only help with certain needs which are not met by statutory services. The following are some examples of the kind of help it has been able to provide:

- hire cars, taxi fares, cars and driving lessons so that a family can go on outings;
- washing machines and dryers;
- clothing, bedding and furnishings;
- in certain circumstances, aids and adaptations;
- family holidays;
- recreation equipment.

A special trust established and financed by the government – the Independent Living Fund – still operates to provide assistance to people with very severe physical or mental disabilities who are on a low income. In 1993 a more restrictive set of rules were set down as criteria for accessing the fund. People who are eligible must be aged between 16 and 65, in receipt of the highest rate of Disability Living Allowance, be living alone or with people who cannot meet the claimant's care needs in full, and be on a low income. The fund is operated through contact and assessment from local social services.

Services at home

Social services departments have a duty to provide certain services to disabled people and to inform disabled people about these services. The Chronically Sick and Disabled Person's Act (1973) set out the following key services as fundamental, although all are dependent upon a needs assessment from the social services.

Home carers

Formerly home helps would visit on a reasonably regular basis to carry out certain tasks. Previously these were domestic tasks, such as cleaning and shopping, but now priority is given to people who need help with personal care such as dressing, toileting and washing.

Meals on wheels

This is a delivery service bringing meals to older and disabled people who cannot leave the house. Vegetarian and special dietary and religious requirements should usually be catered for.

Day centre and respite care

These facilities differ from area to area, but local authorities have a duty to provide or arrange these if a disabled person has been assessed as needing them.

It is becoming increasingly common to find that local authorities are either making a charge for some or all of the above services, or challenging the ruling that they have the responsibility. Although there is still a legal duty to provide services it is also recognised that the level of service provision is dependent upon the funds available to provide them.

Health services

The family doctor is normally the first point of contact with the health services. GPs can give direct treatment or refer on to other parts of the service (e.g. hospital specialists or district nurse). Getting to hospital, for example, can be considered an entitlement for ambulance transportation if a GP considers a patient to be medically unfit to travel to hospital by other means. The costs of travelling to hospital can also be subsidised if someone is in receipt of Income Support or Family Credit.

Other NHS services include district nurses, community occupational therapists, chiropody and special beds for disabled people at home. The NHS also provides an incontinence supply service on referral from a GP or the social services department.

Summary

Attempts to ensure that environmental conditions are accessible to disabled people can often produce adaptations that are insensitive. Architectural aesthetics and health conditions have long been associated with psychological well-being and this is exacerbated by fears of disability and loss. What has been more widely overlooked are other environmental considerations, including levels of disability-related benefits, adaptations in the home and means of assisted communication. Ultimately, students of Disability Studies must develop improved awareness of computer-assisted prosthetics and information technology (ICT). This can include updating on the use of the technology for meeting individual needs and the organisation of the brain. However, ICT has exciting possibilities for innovative access to medical advances and staff development as a whole. This should include the expertise and experience of all participants including disabled people themselves.

CHAPTER 10

Future directions

Questions

- How can society respond to freedom as power and freedom as right in relation to disabled people?
- Will the search for individual self-determination and choice by disabled people simply reduce diversity and narrow the options available?
- Will the development of Disability Studies, as an academic discipline, prevent the development of inclusive communities?
- How far does the study of disability issues provide an opportunity for the relocation of the professional management of services for disabled people by disabled people?
- How can non-disabled people begin to look at the special oppressions experienced by disabled people without appearing to be tokenistic?

Introduction

In this chapter the issues of rights and entitlements forms the backdrop for a final critical reflection on the advancing acceptance of Disability Studies as an academic discipline. The understanding that disablement, as opposed to impairment, is a cultural phenomenon is now well established and the strength of a Disability 'Movement' and disabled people themselves as the engine for change is also beginning to be understood. However, what has not yet been clearly articulated is the direction that the Disability Movement is taking. While the relationship between disability politics and the power brokers in the rest of the world is becoming more clearly established, the silent majority of disabled people remain isolated and uninformed. Proposals for the recognition of the rights of disabled people now need to be matched with policies for ensuring that the hard-fought battles for disability awareness are sustained and articulated on behalf of all people with a disability or impairment. There are emerging tensions between independent living, the right to be born and the right to be different. Disability Studies as an academic programme has a responsibility to track and evaluate these developments. However, if the study of disability issues remains esoteric and academic, safely placed within higher education, it is in danger of losing some of its essence, an understanding that the lives of disabled people are quantitatively and qualitatively different from the lives of non-disabled people.

As this book has set out to explore, 'Disability is a fact of life. The human population is different in all sorts of ways; we should preserve diversity and recognise the moral value of every individual' (Shakespeare 2001: 4). Nevertheless, the location of Disability Studies within the wider dimensions of community action may help to shape and develop an understanding of a disability perspective and by so doing it affects the lives of disabled and non-disabled people alike. The study of disability as a theoretical concept combined with an understanding of its practical, 'hands on' consequences in relation to welfare services (e.g. the way in which bureaucratic procedures can control both claimants and officers in the distribution of benefits) can be a way to developing a true understanding of power and oppression. For Coleridge, the use and abuse of power in the development of alternative service provisions is fundamental to the development of social justice for disabled people: 'the question of how power is handled once it is acquired is as important for the disability movement as for any other liberation movement' (Coleridge 1993: 212). The same sentiment is echoed a decade later, 'only an analysis and exposure of the discrimination, prejudice and abuse that we face will get us our rights' (Hurst 2000a: 1087).

The central task of Disability Studies is to promote the exploration of community values using the perspectives of disabled people. As such, the shape of the discipline is closely aligned to the work of the radical politics of the Disability Movement and the examination of society through an exploration of groups and individuals who are placed at the margins. Through highlighting the denial of citizenship rights and social justice for individuals with disabilities the Disability Movement has offered a valuable starting point for a critical evaluation of society. However, such an ideological framing of Disability Studies is only properly located within British disability politics, 'the movement in other countries, while adopting a social minority group approach, have not built their campaign and self-definition around the social model' (Shakespeare and Watson 1997: 293).

Over the last two decades working parties consisting of individuals and groups working on behalf of disabled people have produced reports which have attempted to establish structural social changes that are intended to remove the final vestiges of those physical, economic or social restrictions that have acted as barriers to the full inclusion of disabled people into mainstream society (e.g. The Snowdon Report 1979; The Warnock Report 1978; and The Griffiths Report 1988) However, the recommendations of these reports have tended to reinforce and perpetuate the tradition of marking out disabled people as individually different and special. The establishment of a Disability Rights Commission in the United Kingdom has the potential to provide disabled people with a collective opportunity to challenge this form of sanctimonious oppression. However, an officially mandated body also carries with it the seeds of the very patronage it seeks to challenge. Challenging the disablism in society is not about special pleading. It is more about acknowledging and asserting the real differences that exist between disabled and non-disabled people. Disability Studies provides a cross-disciplinary context in which these, sometimes false and oppressive, explanations for the origins of disability can be addressed. As this text has attempted to explain: 'Special is usually synonymous with segregated. Disabled people do not have special needs. We have the same needs as anyone else: basic needs such as information, housing, transport. Disabled people are only abnormal because our ordinary needs are not normally met' (Shakespeare 1997: 9).

Approaches to the care and education of disabled people have had the effect of reminding us all that barriers and restrictions are not new and that their removal has been addressed before. The real starting point for their removal lies not solely in legislative change but in the recognition that disability is not simply a personal or individual problem. It is also a collective concern that challenges the underlying structures and principles of social justice, equality, inclusion and autonomous decision making.

Equal rights and entitlements

An important characteristic of the change that has taken place in the Disability Movement has been the shift towards self-organisation and the taking of control by disabled people themselves in the organisations representing their interests. This has been argued by Oliver (1990), Fagan and Lee (1997) and Fagan and Reynolds (forthcoming) who remind us that an organisation *of* disabled people (e.g. the BCODP – British Council of Disabled People) has a very different relationship to the State and the political system from organisations *for* disabled people (e.g. the Royal Association for Disability and Rehabilitation – RADAR). At a wider level, there is a growing recognition in British society that disability is not a matter of certain individuals being unable to meet the demands of society, but of the failure of society to recognise its own disabling potential and our collective failure to address the specific needs that arise from this.

The history of the development of Disability Studies is littered with expressions and descriptions of the public appetite for exhibitions of human freaks and oddities. This theme has been most widely explored by Thomson (1996, 1998, 2001). Haffter (1968) researching the literature into European folklore concerning disabled people reminds us that in Tudor and Stuart England a considerable element of popular humour was directed at the eccentric and the deviant, but as middle-class values and Puritan reticence brought changes in public attitudes to 'unavoidable misfortune' it came to be considered inappropriate that disabled people and disability issues should be seen as subjects for humour outside the circuses and travelling freak shows. For some commentators, these accounts arouse conflicting emotions which are illustrative of the revolution in public attitudes towards disabled people. For Thomas (1978: 145) there is 'revulsion at the Roman Holiday mentality that could turn deformity into a commercial venture, and admiration for the human curiosities that fashioned a worthwhile life for themselves in the tolerant and accepting community of the circus'. The status of disabled people has thus altered – from that of despised and discriminated individuals to derogation through custodial and philanthropic concern and on towards inclusion and self-confidence.

Legislation may have begun to force change in the health, housing employment and care of disabled people. At the same time this has been accompanied by a growing involvement in the expression of concern from those wishing to help disabled people, either as individuals or through voluntary groups. Much of this help comes from non-disabled men and women and the philanthropic motive still drives many people into volunteering to help:

> They do not wish to play the out-dated Lady Bountiful, but find in their involvement an opportunity to express a concern for human values. Disablement allows some of them to be politically active in an area untouched by ideologies of the extreme right or left.
>
> (Thomas1978: 146)

This may still be true, but what is certain, is that the study of disability has become both more radical and political and that disabled people themselves have become more self-confident in asserting their own interests. This is encapsulated in an ascerbic correspondence from one of the 'founding fathers' of the Disability Movement, commenting on the growing interest in disability by non-disabled people:

> There's something beautifully ironical about an able-bodied person residing in a Western industrial society, who has not contributed to the ideological development of the disabled people's democratic movement for emancipation in this world, setting himself up as the ideological conscience of disabled people in non-Western rural areas.
>
> (Finkelstein 29 November 1996 Internet *Centre for Disability Studies*)

The emergence of rights as entitlement has influenced much of the discourse in relation to disability issues. This is closely linked to the emergence of Disability Studies as the examination of the social consequences of a disabling environment, rather than any exploration of individual biological inferiority. In the last ten years the recognition of the rights of women and black people has not only become accepted but discrimination on such grounds is deemed to be offensive to an educated mind. It is troublesome to see that for a number of reasons such equality is still not granted to disabled people. It leaves a number of questions to be addressed, e.g. are rights attributes to which we are all entitled or do they have to be earned? Are they entitlements that are to be received or fought for? From the perspective of disabled people who are emerging as a recognised political movement, equality means the acceptance that disabled people are equal citizens and that social barriers, discrimination and prejudice which are associated with an impairment have to be removed:

> … the main way to change structures is to enable disabled people to exercise agency as direct action protesters, self-organised groups, lobbying groups etc. – which is only likely where disabled people have self-esteem, pride etc. I have yet to see a research report which directly changed structures….
>
> (Shakespeare, *Disability-Studies Research* 16 December 1996)

Inclusion – celebrating difference

The discussion about rights and entitlements has been linked to a range of attempts to counter differences and inequality in society. Equality in its turn assumes that similarly situated people are prepared to treat each other in a similar fashion. However, it overlooks or more particularly fails to indicate the element of responsibility that is anticipated as a consequence of rights. As Gooding (1994, 2000) reminds us, this formal model of equality suggests that rights are being perceived as achievements that are gained as a consequence of struggle and are an end in themselves, rather than a shared, collaborative part of human endeavour to morally improve as a society. Equality can only operate in the absence of any relevant differences between members of protected cultural groups and the rest of society. However, any discourse around inclusion and the equality of disabled people has to recognise that this issue of differences is fundamental. The assertion of difference between dominant groups and disabled people meant that early attempts to counter discrimination tended to reinforce stereotypes, i.e. of a white, able-bodied and essentially male 'norm'. Not only does this tend to perpetuate superiority, manifested in a hierarchy of status, but it forces oppressed groups to attempt to counteract, or even deny the presence of, differences in the belief that to be 'normal' is to have to conform and to be assimilated.

French (1994a) has suggested the pressure to be 'normal' in society is often conducted at the expense of disabled peoples' needs and rights. Morris (1993) also believes that the assumption that disabled people want to be normal, rather than as they are, is one of the most oppressive experiences to which disabled people are subjected. Morris rejects the view that it is progressive and liberating to ignore differences. She maintains that disabled people have the right to be both equal and different:

> I do not want to have to try to emulate what a non-disabled woman looks like in order to assert positive things about myself. I want to be able to celebrate my difference, not hide from it.
>
> (Morris 1991: 184)

Social acceptance is ever more tightly constrained in ideologies of 'getting on'; succeeding in education and in market-led values of personal competitiveness. These expectations can lead many disabled people to try and become superhuman, in order to avoid the negative connotations of helplessness and personal incompetence. French (1994a) gives the examples of deaf people who learn to talk, blind people who are taught to use facial expressions appropriately and people with Down's syndrome having cosmetic plastic surgery, as some of the more doubtful opportunities offered to people with impairments. These interventions have been offered in the belief that they will help to overcome lack of social acceptability, reduce isolation and improve chances to compete with non-disabled people.

The emphasis on inclusion without sensitivity to its consequences may, however, lead non-disabled people to deny or fail to believe that a person's impairment or disability exists. There are a number of implications – one is the denial to the right to be disabled and to identify with and be proud of engaging in the struggle for the acceptance of disablement as a political identity. This is particularly the case with those who have relatively hidden impairments who manage to 'pass' as normal. This gives rise to the erroneous assumption that disabled people are just like everyone else. This is one of the messages that can be inferred from some of the more poorly considered first attempts at writing equal opportunities statements. The 'lack of acceptance by non-disabled people of the reality of disability, can lead disabled people to deny and minimise the oppression and difficulties they face' (French 1994a: 53).

The concepts of autonomy and social justice

While it is impossible to provide a complete and definitive explanation of social justice, the idea fits with any discussion of rights, fairness and choice in relation to policy and practices concerning the lives of disabled people. This book has indicated many examples of the ways in which people with disabilities, as a group, have been subject to treatment that is fundamentally unjust. Policy and practices in education, the medical service and employment all demonstrate examples of the discrimination that is still shown towards disabled people. It is nevertheless, a feature of the changing nature of society that the fragmentation of group action as a method of realising change has been replaced by the demands for individual autonomy, choice and justice. Disabled people are beginning to operate with a collective voice and setting out to claim social justice as a rights issue. At the same time there are clear indications that there have been shifts in the perceptions and meaning of equal opportunities. Other interpretations of social justice are emerging, all of which focus upon the juxtaposition between collective and private responsibility. At one level equal opportunity is being redefined within a framework of individualism, entitlement and power. At another the focus is upon shared responsibility, the redistribution of wealth and reward. The latter focus places people who feel marginalised through economic circumstances and simple prejudice at a further disadvantage as the agenda of social justice is altered. The concept of social justice as a mutual consensus and coopera-tion in equal shares of any collective surplus managed by the state, is changed – to a perception of social justice as individual entitlement. This view, drawn primarily from right-wing political thinkers in the United States (e.g. Rawls 1971), is predicated on the belief that justice emerges from self-interest rather than collective endeavour and depends upon what individuals bring to a relationship or exchange for their mutual interest, rather than to distribute any collective surplus that emerges from collective or group activity. Thus, social justice is the entitlement to exercise power, particularly by individuals rather than groups. Such free-market thinking suggests that the only basis for helping the less fortunate is through the voluntary transfer of goods and benefits from those who have more, to those who have less. This raises the question of whether a fair society is possible without the means of some control from an executive authority that determines the manner by which it is to be paid for. A society consisting solely of uncontrolled individ-uals raises spectres of at best charity handouts, benign neglect and a further marginalisa-tion for groups considered to be economically redundant or 'unfit' (Mithaug 1996).

Many of the early reformers who had advocated for more humane treatment of people with disabilities had argued that disabled people should have access to the same rights and social resources as 'normal' people. This philosophy lies at the heart of Wolfensberger's constructs of 'normalisation' and 'social role valorisation' and assumes that social justice resides in equality of access to treatment, welfare services and the physical environment.

Wolfensberger's contentious view of human value is consistent with a theory of justice that focuses on individual rights rather than group identity. His analytical framework deliberately focused on improving the circumstances of people with severe learning diffi-culties. It has served to shift the thinking of welfare service providers but has arguably done little to empower and politicise end users. The equally contested term 'social justice' is more broadly based, focusing on the tension between market- and state-oriented ideas of a fair and just distribution of 'social goods'. Rawls (1971) argues that there are two basic principles in maintaining socially just practices. First, that each person should 'have the most extensive basic liberty compatible with similar liberty for others'. Secondly he suggests that primary social goods should be distributed equally, with the exception of an unequal distribution which favours those who are socially disadvantaged. The distributive view of social justice regards it as a responsibility of the State to provide for the needs of disabled people. As Rizvi and Christensen (1996) and Ardilles (2000) have pointed out, this perception of social justice as distributive efficiency has influenced initial policy reforms of services for disabled people. For example, in relation to the education of students with disabilities social justice was originally perceived as fairer educational oppor-tunity and was based on the assessment of individual needs. Fairness of distribution was nevertheless, still focused around problematic and narrow assumptions of 'normal' indi-vidual behaviour, rather than a fundamental reappraisal of the ideologies, attitudes and assumptions inherent in society as a whole.

The notion that social injustice towards disabled people can be overcome by a distributive state welfare system that equates with social justice is clearly insufficient in the current economic, political and cultural climate. The case has been made succinctly:

> … distributive solutions to social injustice fail to recognise power relationships which shape and sustain injustice. People with disabilities continue to be culturally oppressed and socially marginalised while their interests are still defined by advocates acting on their behalf. People with disabilities continue to demand the right to define what is in their best interests.
>
> (Rizvi and Christensen 1996: 4)

The analysis of what constitutes the 'best interests' of disabled people seems to lie at the heart of the purpose and future of Disability Studies. Commentators who strongly identify themselves with the needs and rights of disabled people advocate a radical policy of inclusion, or alternatively a more affirmative model of disability. They demand and define equality of opportunity in terms of location in the political process and in particular in the definition of disability rights (Hurst 2000b). Critics of inclusion suggest that disabled people require services to be managed on their behalf, as they will continue to face serious and chronic barriers to achievements over their lifespan and will not be able to compete successfully with non-disabled people.

Since the 1950s the costs of the welfare state in the United Kingdom have risen with structural changes in employment patterns and shifts in the demographic trends of the population. People are living longer and the workforce is declining. Changes in the labour market have seen a decline in manufacturing industry, an increase in part-time work and the 'feminisation of labour', with the consequent growth in service industries, de-regulation of working practices and the demands for flexibility from employers. Long-term unemployment and changes from a passive welfare state to a more active and judgmental benefits system has caused many people to become ineligible for benefit payments. For example, in the United Kingdom, a deliberate strategy of requiring people to be active and earning their benefit, rather than remaining legitimate but passive recipients of welfare has affected the philosophy and response to both unemployed people and other marginalised groups in society, including those who are disabled. It has been suggested that society is in transition – from modernity to post-modernity – and that 'this change is so radical that it represents nothing less than a decoupling of the economic from the social, at least at the level of the nation state' (Oliver 2000: 14). While Oliver was warning with particular reference to special education, his analysis also has resonance for a redefinition of social policy in relation to disability and disadvantage.

Some warning shots

Legislation is in place that is designed to determine equality of opportunity for disabled people. However, the outcome of any legislation depends on what people do at local level and the relative newness of anti-discriminatory legislation means that it is vulnerable to the 'watering-down' effects of compromise as disabled people are expected 'to be reasonable' in the face of public expenditure cuts. A backlash against the costs of addressing disability issues has begun to be identified in the USA (Johnstone 1996c); the notion of the deserving and the undeserving is beginning to once more emerge and prompt moves to exclude or ration health and social care to some people with certain types of disabilities, e.g. those with HIV/AIDS or mental health considerations.

The Disability Movement across the Western world is experiencing 'establishment backlash' and a 'greying of the leadership' as the original firebrands of the disability-rights movement grows older or are sucked into the bureaucracy of mainstream provision of services and care. To some extent this illuminates the very success of the case for disability rights and legitimates the study of disability as an academic discipline. At the same time it suggests that Disability Studies, like the Disabled People's Movement, has to be prepared to fend off attacks from more-established groups and forms of academic enquiry. When a backlash occurs against any cause, it emerges because the movement is perceived as a threat. In previous times, disabled people and the study of disability issues was viewed as merely a charity case deserving of sympathy. The disability movement is now demanding that disabled people be treated as equal citizens and disabled people are beginning to experience 'establishment backlash' (e.g. this may be a withdrawal of the preferential treatment associated with parking places for disabled people, or the refusal to allow car use in pedestrianised town centres). It is the role of Disability Studies to encourage the evaluation and critical appraisal of these developments.

Disability Studies provides an opportunity to develop the analysis of a number of strands that have tended to remain separate. Psychological explanations of impairment or the interpretations of disability as individual loss need to be addressed, as do the social influences that tend to stigmatise disabled people. The voice of disabled people themselves has seldom been taken completely seriously. However, the discourses in Disability Studies encourage disabled people to speak out and be listened to. Moreover, the discipline brings the two constituencies of disabled and non-disabled people together and allows people to speak of how disability impacts on and affects their own lives.

The realisation that most disabled people are essentially non-political takes some time to dawn for many students of Disability Studies. However, perhaps this is not altogether surprising. Disabled people grow to affirm the experience of disability. This may emerge initially as a biological/medically determined and socially stigmatised impairment, without appreciating the political associations of the status 'Disabled Person' as a form of social, cultural and patriarchal oppression. It might be argued that the course of most people's lives is built around a tacit and unconscious acknowledgement of patriarchy and paternalism. For example, our personal agendas or day-to-day circumstances are modelled and/or determined by the interests of parents, carers or the state. Thus, in these circumstances, it is easier to relinquish responsibility to others in the belief that, in general, they are setting out to 'do good'. The outcomes achieved are effectively theirs to control and resolve (e.g. all parents to a greater or lesser extent take on board some responsibility towards their own children. Most of us break away from these ties in our adolescence and early adulthood. For these very reasons, it takes an act of conscious will for disabled people to remove themselves from this form of patriarchy, be it from a parent or the state).

Disability from this point of view is both deliberately created and perpetuated; it is part of the defining relationship between the impairment of an individual and the material environment within which the individual functions. It is socially created barriers that attach the precise meanings and boundaries of the disability for the individual with impairment and it is the environmental context that defines the person as disabled. As a consequence, it is the disabled person and their carers who then face the task of making sense of this relationship and, who struggle to transform this construction. These struggles may take place in terms of either an individual or the actions of a group. It is through such action that disability takes on the mantle of political action.

For disabled people, life circumstances appear to be determined far more significantly by issues that are beyond impairment. Physical or sensory dysfunction is a factor, but it is a constant. The less certain features of a lifestyle, such as income or day-to-day health are perceived as separate and more pressing than the known, enduring considerations of physical loss or pain. In other words, for many people and particularly those with low incomes daily living is embedded in wider aspects of impoverishment and oppression. This aspect of disability research is not directly associated with the discrimination and exclusion experienced by disabled people. However, it emphasises how any two people may experience their impairments in different ways and construct differing identities for themselves. And this link between disability and wider disadvantage is important too for the future of Disability Studies. The personal experience of impairment is a critical element in the construction of personal identity and therefore disability research but it does not negate the fact that people of difference may also be discriminated against collectively and that these acts of shared discrimination require exposure and explanation.

Changes in definition

The discussion of definition brings the debate around disability and Disability Studies back to some of the issues first raised in Chapter 1. During 1997 the World Health Organisation had begun debating the need to revise the international classification of Impairments, Disabilities and Handicaps (ICIDH), as originally promoted in 1980. The proposed new classification of conditions has undergone a significant revision and the title of the ICIDH has been changed from Impairment, Disability and Handicap to ICIDH-2 International Classification of Impairments, Activities and Participation. Thus, the twin terms 'handicap' and 'disability', are to be expunged, in the belief that they are no longer usefully descriptive of people's circumstances.

This new classification has undergone systematic field trials and consultation with a final version now expected sometime in 2001/2002. The rationale for this change is 'to avoid the negative connotations of certain of the terms previously used' (WHO 1997: 1). The WHO has, thus, retained the descriptor 'impairment', but replaced the term 'disability' with what is considered a more neutral term 'activity' and any negative associations in this dimension are described as 'activity limitations'. The term 'handicap' has been replaced by the alternative 'participation' and the negative associations in this dimension are described as 'participation restrictions'.

The original ICIDH classifications of impairment, disablement and handicap as functional difficulties were intended to call attention to the variations of difference within individual health conditions, which may apply to everybody. However, inevitably the classification has tended to become a shorthand, associating an individual with a category of medical loss or disadvantage. In the 1980s the creation of the three dimensions was considered by some disabled people as a step forward in developing the recognition that society has the potential to be oppressive. However, as political awareness of disability has grown and the social model of disability has become better understood, the framework of the ICIDH has, itself, come to be considered oppressive (Pfieffer 1998, 2000; Hurst 2000a). Its use as a classification, operating at a level of individual need for the treatment for specific conditions, is still fundamental but it is now anticipated that ICIDH-2 will have relevance for broader areas of social policy. The compilers of the ICIDH did not intend to characterise the relationships of the three original terms as a rigid linear progression, but now in ICIDH-2 they explicitly acknowledge that disablement is a process that operates at broadly two levels: the environmental and the personal. Environmental factors are considered extrinsic to and outside the individual (these may include social attitudes, the legal system and architecture) while the personal factors may include fitness, health conditions, age, gender, psychological well-being and other characteristics. These personal factors differ from the environmental but have an impact on how disablement is experienced. 'In examining the relationship between these planes of experiences the revised scheme suggests that "participation" (handicaps) may cause impairments, and thus create a causal "loop" back to the beginning' (Bury 2000: 1075). At present no personal factors are listed in the classification and their assessment is left to the discretion of the users.

This revision of the WHO classification suggests that the term 'disability' be dropped. This has a number of implications for both disabled people and the shaping of attitudes in society towards the concept that has become known as 'disablement'. It is difficult to believe that those who have developed a political awareness and pride in the status of being a 'disabled person' will be altered by the semantic change to activity limitations; but there is the potential for inconsistency in both the construction and the experience of disability, confusing the label with particular individual health conditions and personal experiences. The ICIDH-2 classification continues to emphasise individual pathology and what people cannot do, rather than celebrating what they can, arising from a health condition. For disability activists the classification, thereby, continues to undermine the collective voice of disabled people in their attempts to seek out an alternative terminology of their own choosing. For others 'the problems associated with the ICIDH have stemmed from criticism which has often been ideologically motivated, and has not always been in the best interests of disabled people' (Bury 2000: 1077).

It is also evident from the WHO deliberations on classifications that the European perspective on disablement, which emphasises the imposition of a disability on a person by society, is at odds with the approach adopted in other countries, where disablement is associated more with an acquired pathology or condition (see Hurst 2000b). This suggests that the political consciousness of disabled people in Europe, and in particular the United Kingdom, is still, more radical and assertive than elsewhere in the world.

Summary

Social justice and its political consequences is a particular concern for the study of disability issues in the UK. Nevertheless, most disabled people are not politically active and their experience of disability is initially a consequence of accident or a biologically/medically determined and socially stigmatising health condition. The political associations of disablement as a form of social, cultural and patriarchal oppression only emerge slowly. The chapter argues that the course of most people's lives is built around a tacit and unconscious acknowledgement of patriarchy and paternalism and that in these circumstances, it is easier to relinquish responsibility to others in the belief that, in general, they are setting out to 'do good'. Finally, the chapter briefly explores some of the strengths and weaknesses in the proposed changes in the WHO classifications of impairment, disability and handicaps.

Conclusion

Since the first edition of this book was published in 1998 the study of disability and the political circumstances of disabled people has become even more firmly established as an area of study. In England the degree programmes and research outputs from universities such as Coventry, Leeds, Sheffield, Northumbria and Edge Hill are testament to the growing interest in this area. These courses run alongside interdisciplinary programmes and research enquiries that have been developed in other parts of the world. Through the influence of the 'social model' these enquiries have focused students on radical critiques of structural and cultural determinations of difference, rather than explorations of individual difference. Students of Disability Studies should, nevertheless, be questioning the sufficiency of the social model in a post-modern era that is seeking to redefine the direction of social movements.

That disablement is a socially constructed concept in the service and shaping of power is now a generally accepted orthodoxy. The challenge to these discriminations has begun to be addressed through legislation and the establishment of a Disability Rights Commission – akin to the Equal Opportunities Commission. However, it is important to remember that the life circumstances of disabled people are determined far more significantly by issues that are beyond physical loss or impairment. The less certain features of a lifestyle, such as income, or day-to-day health, are perceived as separate and sometimes more pressing than the known, enduring considerations of physical loss or pain. There are also inequalities among disabled people, for example those people labelled with severe impairments and/or learning difficulties still face boundaries, when it comes to achieving equal citizenship, even in relation to other groups of disabled people.

Disability Studies has developed its own critical terminology to address these concerns and offers an epistemology that can run counter to standard scientific practices and explanations. As an emerging discipline it promises not only the opportunity for emancipation through critique and research, but also suggests new insights and frameworks for understanding human behaviour and interaction. Nevertheless, like all new areas of scholarship, Disability Studies must beware of generating its own set of stereotypical assumptions (e.g. that the social model of disablement offers a sufficient explanation of causation). In similar fashion, students setting out on a programme of Disability Studies must not become too defensive, or apologetic, when challenged in their attempts to establish the social critique of disablement as a legitimate area of academic discourse. While academic analysis does not immediately help to explain to the individual with a severed spinal column how they can regain bladder and bowel control, it does something that is, ultimately, more important – it brings understanding through a variety of interpretations, and links the circumstances of disablement to the totality of human experience. This allows a point of entry to understanding via one of the most powerful but often disregarded areas of all our academic lives; the imagination. Disability Studies helps students to connect scholarship with imagination and links the abstract claims of sociology and medical science with the concrete realities of people's lived experiences. Students of Disability Studies are setting out on an investigation that touches the boundaries of human dignity. As such, they confront rather than hide from the collective responsibility that we have towards each other.

Appendix

Two interviews made by students as part of a course assignment on the circumstances of disabled people, quality of life and life history are included in this appendix. They are intended to supplement the ideas outlined in Chapters 4 and 7

Read the extracts and in small group discussions, consider the following issues:

- Are the life stories that emerge from these interviews similar? What are the key themes of the two informants?
- How far do you consider that the people interviewed think of themselves as disabled people rather than people with impairment?
- Using the model outlined in Chapter 4 (Figure 4.1) as a basis, critically consider and discuss the main factors that are central to the informants' perceptions of quality of life.
- Do you identify any differences between the interviewer/informant relationships in the two extracts? Note these differences and compare them with your colleagues.
- Using the knowledge gained in Chapter 7 consider how you would approach an interview.
  - How might you encourage informants to speak to you?
  - What are the ethical and confidentiality issues to be addressed?
  - In your opinion have the interviewers in these two extracts been successful in framing their conversations?
  - What questions would you have asked these informants?
  - Simulate an interview situation with a partner. Change places after about ten minutes and compare the difference between asking and responding to questions.
- As an additional task consider how you would set about establishing links with potential informants. Would it be important to include them or their organisations in the eventual analysis and evaluation of the data? What do you consider to be 'yours'? What might be considered 'theirs'? Is it ethical to write about people's circumstances without involving them in any evaluation and reflection?

Interviewee A

INTERVIEWERS	Q1 and Q2
INFORMANT	Anonymous
AGE	62
GENDER	Female
OCCUPATION	Retired
DISABILITY	Spinal paralysis
PLACE OF INTERVIEW	Home address
DATE OF INTERVIEW	September 2000
LENGTH OF INTERVIEW	50 minutes
METHOD	Tape recorder and notes

Q1   How's things?

A1.   Oh, fine.

Q1   Do you actually get up earlier than you used to?

A2.   I do on a Monday, half past seven. Mind you, I like being up. I don't like lying around being in bed, but its just on a Monday. The home helps have a meeting at nine o'clock so if they don't come before the meeting they have to come about half past ten so I persuaded them to come earlier.

Q1   Did you have any problems persuading them?

A3.   No, well the one who comes every day, she sometimes comes a bit earlier and does a few jobs so she doesn't mind, but it was in case the other one couldn't fit it in, but she's managed to work around it.

Q2   Does that make it a longer day for you?

A4.   Yes, I suppose it does really. You see every other night I go in my easy chair so it means I stay up till about ten o'clock, but tonight I go to bed around eight so it's not so bad. I've got used to sitting up, some of my friends they go to bed in the afternoon.

Q2   I must admit I like a bit of a nap.

A5.   Well I did that once and it was when Stuart's nan and grandad were having a party, so I thought, I'll go to bed for the afternoon, so I got in for about half past two and I didn't want to get up.

Q2   Did you not? Down for the day!

A6.   But it would be finding someone to get me back up. Mind you, the children are in at half past three, you can't stay awake when they are around.

Q1   Are you still managing to go to school, last time I came you said you'd stopped because of the taxi?

A7.   No, we've still not worked anything out because my neighbour next door, she said about using the van, well she's started college, she's there on Wednesday, Thursday and Friday. So the only other thing would be to find somebody else who'd drive it but then it would mean insuring it for them and Stuart rang them up and they said it would be about 14 pound a month extra to have another named driver on the thing.

Q1 Even if they are an experienced driver?

A8. Yes, it's just because of all the adaptations. I think they are a bit wary. So unless I knew I was going to use it a lot, it wouldn't really be worth doing.

Q1 I think that this is one of the things, did you see that Scope is doing a survey, it used to be the Spastic Society, it's one of the things they are looking at, insurance and the idea that disabled people are being discriminated against by insurers, because they get them always. I mean if someone is experienced, I don't really see that it should matter putting them on the insurance. So do you miss going to school?

A9. I don't know, I liked it but I found the lunchtimes were strange because the staff rooms were upstairs, so I ended up sitting in the hall in my lunch hour and nobody else was there.

Q1 Did nobody else bring their lunch down to come and sit with you?

A10. Not really. I think they all had jobs to do. I suppose they just thought, 'Oh, she won't want us mothering her.' I don't think they were being funny or anything, because they're not like that there.

Q1 No, they just thought they were giving you a bit of space.

A11. The children are really good.

Q1 Do you miss their company more than the actual going out?

A12. Yes, because I used to like that.

Q1 Is there any way you could go back to teaching yourself, if you had an assistant …? Or is it not something you've thought about?

A13. Er … I don't know. I don't know if I'd be able to do it or not because I find my concentration goes, even if I'm reading something I find I don't concentrate as much – or whether that's just old age. No, but before I could read a book straight through and not bother and now I find even reading an article, I lose track of where I'm up to, but whether that is solely because I haven't done anything for so long.

Q1 Do you have any problems holding books?

A14. Yes, I have to put them on the table to read them.

Q1 Perhaps the position you are in doesn't help …

A15. It might be, yes. And also turning over pages in paperbacks I find difficult. But yes, position could have something to do with it, like normally you'd lie full length on the settee. I'd look well if I tried to do that, I might get there but I'd never get back up again! Mind you, if you do that and you land in a funny position, like when I fell out of the chair one time in the lift, somebody got me a pillow to put my head on in the lift shaft and I just said, 'Oh, this is nice', because it was a change, they must have all thought I was completely barmy but I said, 'Oh, it's lovely this.' It was a change to actually lie down in the middle of the day. They all kept coming to look at me and they all said, 'Have you banged your head?' I said 'No.'

Q1   Don't know if you've heard but there's been some publicity lately that the county is short of money, you know for social services. A few people said they've had their services reduced, have you been affected at all?

A36.   Did you know I'd been on the television for that?

Q1   Oh, you should have told us you were going on!

A37.   Well I didn't know. What happened was on the Friday morning I got this phone call, my friend had called which was unusual because she doesn't usually call on a Friday morning and it was the head of social services in the county, saying that my name had been put forward, because the home helps had been to ask if they could interview somebody about this thing they were doing about cuts in to the county council. I said, 'Oh no, that's fine' because I'd always said if anybody wanted to know anything … so they came on Saturday night.

Q1   What about shopping for clothes?

A60.   Well, I tend to go to Evans in Bxxxxxx though at other times I have owned catalogues. But Bxxxxxx I usually tend to go to. In fact, I've just rung my mum now because she was in Evans and they've got some good trousers on the sale rail, so I've sent my mother on a scouting trip but I don't know whether I find I need them high at the back and you can't get them.

Q1   Oh?

Q2   It's because you're sitting all the time, you know, they ride down.

A61.   Yes, and I find also with Evans, the seams on them are hard. When I was in the spinal unit I used to wear trousers from M&S and Littlewoods, well they're really tough seams which is good for wear and tear, but they used to leave lines on my legs, so now I just stick with these.

Q1   So tough seams could damage your skin?

A62.   Yes. My mum keeps saying, 'You should buy the Marks' because they last longer' and I say, 'Yes, and I could end up spending weeks in bed and that's no use'. That's another thing I've found, you know that catalogue, you know the…? We went to this place, it was like an exhibition full of disabled vans, cars, clothing, all sorts of disabled aids at the G-Mex Centre in Manchester, this is going back about two years. And Stuart had a look at the trousers, he's my tester for things, and he found the seams really stiff, he said that if I wore them all day, I would be in trouble and yet they're supposed to be …

Q2   Catering for the disabled …

A63.   Yes, perhaps they'd be OK for a paraplegic who is moving around more …

Q2   So you can't actually lift yourself?

A64.   No, well what I do is, I keep moving my legs, I've found that if I just sat stiff all day, I can't do anything, so I sometimes pull myself back in my chair (demonstrates) like that. But I find I haven't got a lot of strength in this arm, because when I was in the accident I got a scar at the top so I don't know whether that affects the strength or not.

Interview B

INTERVIEWERS	Joan and Ann
INFORMANT	Wayne
AGE	49
GENDER	Male
OCCUPATION	Volunteer
DISABILITY	Arthritis
DATE OF INTERVIEW	March 2000
LENGTH OF INTERVIEW	50 minutes
LOCATION OF INTERVIEW	Edge Hill University College
INTERVIEW FORMAT	Field notes and tape recorder

Ann: Are your circumstances different to say ten years ago?

Wayne: Mmm ten years ago. Let me see that brings us back to 1990. Mmm … generally similar actually. Ah no let me think. No I finished, I finished work in mmm … yes they are different then because I went into paid employment at that time. I was working for an educational charity. I had this supported placement scheme to help me but now I'm on benefits so I suppose in that way things have changed.

Joan: So have your families attitudes changed and yours have changed all over the years?

Wayne: They have but I don't think they have kept up with mine.

Joan: Right so yours have.

Wayne: Yes. I mean my attitudes have changed dramatically but my family, I can't make them go on one of the disability awareness training courses but I do so. Mmm they are good in terms of home and support and stuff. But I don't think their views are as liberal as mine are in terms of disabled people should be, you know. Mmm given access to all areas of society.

Ann: Do you feel included in society?

Wayne: Mmm I do and I don't. I mean in a sense, I've made a decision that approaching the age of 50 I would probably not get paid employment now and I'm reasonably happy with that because of the things I'm doing in the voluntary sector. I feel that I'm doing useful things within society. But a lot of people with attitudes as such they would see me as inverted comma's 'a failure' because I'm not in paid employment. Mmm so where I am included its pretty much because I've decided I'm included not because other people have decided I'm included. If you know what I mean because I'm fairly self-confident and I've made that decision. Then as far as I'm concerned yes I am included but a lot of people might have other feelings.

Joan: Mmm. Do you know anything about the European Union?

Wayne: Very little idea.

Joan: Does it make a difference whenever you are making … with your access matter group does it make any difference whenever you are going out to organisations to audit them?

Wayne:	The European Union.
Joan:	Yes.
Wayne:	I don't think so.
Joan:	No.
Wayne:	No.
Joan:	Just local ones.
Wayne:	Well I think most people I speak to would listen to British regulation and British law they don't seem to know any European code of civil rights or any draft of declaration about the rights of disabled people.
Ann:	Do you have any disabled friends?
Wayne:	Yes.
Joan:	Are you restricted by the environment, which you live in?
Wayne:	Aaa to some extent yes. I mean I use the stair lift just to give you an example. I use the stair lift to get up to the first floor of my house but my house has a converted attic as well and I can't go up there because you know you couldn't get social services stair lift, two stair lifts basically, so to some extent I am restricted mmm although we have spent money and had various amounts of money spent to make it more accessible but aaa. Were you just talking about the home environment or were you …
Joan:	Yeap.
Wayne:	Yes.
Joan:	Well everywhere even transport, access to other buildings that you would visit frequently?
Wayne:	Right. I've just had mmm a very long campaign to make a big community hall that I use quite regularly more accessible and it has taken me years but finally its getting there. I mean in a sense its easier to fight for other people than it is to fight for yourself, you know. Aa but gradually we got there. But certainly I can use public transport even trains you know I have to arrange it 48 hours in advance to get assistance to do every thing getting on and off trains and so on. Buses I never consider it because I just assume they are inaccessible. So I'm lucky I can drive.
Ann:	You said before that mmm you didn't view yourself in comparison to other disabled people.
Wayne:	Mmm.
Ann:	So how do you think other people treat you?
Wayne:	Well these days now I do. I do. I'm quite happy to see myself as a disabled person but that doesn't make any difference you know because I believe disabled people should be included in all aspects of society and being disabled is just on the line of parameters you know. One of you has blonde hair and one of you hasn't you know. I just view I'm disabled and some people aren't. It's the same sort of comparison. Mmm but in the past you know I definitely had a feeling that I wanted to be associated with non-disabled

people rather than disabled people. These days I don't mind if they're nice people I'll associate myself with them.

Ann: Is that because of the social model?

Wayne: Yes, I think so partly the social model but partly just you know sitting with a lot of people with arthritis and realising that they had very similar experiences to me and actually the first time I went away on the course with other people with arthritis there was a fantastic degree of empathy because you know you will get up having a rough night. Which one regularly does with arthritis you find that 70 per cent of the people in the room have had a rough night as well you know. So you're just sympathetic just understanding you know, whereas you know if I walked into a room full of non-disabled people or people who haven't got arthritis even, even if they were disabled people there wouldn't be the same degree of understanding and tolerance. Recently I was at an international conference, which started at 9.30 in the morning. I turned up at 10.15 because I was very tired from travelling the day before and I wasn't ready at 9.30. Now one or two people sniped a little bit at me but most people knew exactly why and just didn't mind. That would be very difficult to deal with in some situations.

Joan: Mmm your disability, your impairment has been a major influence then in all aspects of your life?

Wayne: Yes, definitely, yes.

Joan: Yes cause you had it since you were …

Wayne: 3 (Three).

Joan: 3 (Three).

Wayne: Mmm.

Ann: Have you had to make any difficult or challenging decisions?

Wayne: Mmm.

Ann: In your life that stand out.

Wayne: Mmm, to do with my disability.

Ann: Well that's up to you.

Wayne: Yes, yes. Mmm well yea I've made one decision well to have nothing to do with the NHS. (Everyone laughs)

Wayne: Which was quite interesting. Mmm well I will tell you this because you have asked me. I wouldn't necessarily volunteered it as its not directly related to my arthritis. When I was at university I learnt something called transendental meditation, which was a stress management technique, and I don't want people to get confused and think it's a coltish thing or some new religion. As a result of that within three years I was able to stop my medication and cope as I was coping before because so how there is a lot of stress associated with arthritis and if I can get rid of stress then I don't need so much medication so, and I began to use my wheelchair less. And I realised when I went back to my doctor and I explained the situation he said he was very annoyed with me, and he said he give me permission to vary the dosage of the medication because you're an intelligent person but I never give you permission to stop it. And I said that I had consulted another doctor who meditates and he told me what to do if I was going to try to stop and I have succeeded very well thank you. And I'm much happier not being on this medication. And this guy blew his lid. So for 20 years I've had nothing to do with the NHS. I just pulled away I just modified my diet and my lifestyle and meditated regularly and was able to cope with the arthritis. In a way that the previous 20 years I hadn't been able to.

Ann: Coped better.

Wayne: Yes and I worked out that within the first 20 years of my arthritis I took 40000 dispirin, 20–30000 other tablets and when I've made after I had been meditating for three years, I was able to stop and I made a decision not to take any more and I didn't need to and I've coped pretty well without them. Mmm but you know that's meant to have made some decisions about not having operations perhaps I should have had conventionally speaking, not taking medication and so on. Distancing myself from the NHS, it's a big risk actually as I may need at some stage to go back. Mmm, relevantly, recently I registered with another consultant and I just see him once a year you know, again I don't take any medication or anything but I'm happy keeping my foot in the door as it were. So that was quite a big decision and also I said about not been in paid employment. I mean in a sense that was a personal decision because I could probably have found some really boring job sort of tucked away somewhere doing something I didn't like much with some nice supportive employer who you know would let me have some extra time off when I needed it. I could have probably have found a job like that and managed but that's not what I wanted to do you know once I got interested in campaigning this is what I wanted to do. If someone will pay me to do this and provide me with an environment where I can do it then I do it. But I'm not prepared to do something that I won't enjoy doing which is probably then going to have a bad effect on my arthritis anyway and I'm not prepared to do that.

Joan: Are you satisfied with your life?

Wayne: Recently I mean you know.

Joan: Is it well balanced?

Wayne: It is now. It is now because I'm confident enough to make decisions about what suits me and balance external influences on my internal requirements you know. Aaa for instance this week three committees that I'm on I just decided not to go because I was completely. I've done too much in the last week. I was completely exhausted at the beginning of the week and I know that yes I could push myself a bit further and go to that meeting but the chances are that would have a very negative long-term effect on my health. So I've just had to make the decisions to do less for this week and then I'll do some more next week. Mmm but yea that's the situation.

Ann: What has been the most difficult criticism that you have received?

Wayne: Other people criticising me you mean.

Ann: Yaa what are the most difficult.

Wayne: Mmm, although my parents don't say it before, I mean anymore I think my father in particular regards me as a failure because I'm not in paid employment. And I mean that's hard but he doesn't say it any more as he is in his 80s but I think that's his attitude. And in the disability community well not everywhere in the disability community but in the disability community there is a perception that if one parent that it rises and causes pain and it causes fatigue and so on and then if you opt to be in voluntary work rather than paid work everyone should have the right to do that and they should be facilitated to be as effective in voluntary work as they want to be. Mmm society in general I don't think understands that yet or you should work, you should work that's they attitude. Mmm even if its going to make you worst even if its going to cost money for the NHS in the future because of work making you worse and then you have to have more operations and go on medication. And I've made that decision that I don't want to do that.

Joan: Have you ever felt annoyed or angry with anybody, you know over your disability whether they were looking at you when you were in a wheelchair or what?

Wayne: Mmm. Yes but I mean unless I'm every tired I'm usually aware that showing my anger is not the best way to deal with it, not to let myself my anger you know go. That the best way to deal with things is to be diplomatic and rather than to confront people, or to hint at things or to lobby to make your point quietly and politely. Mmm its best to channel anger rather than just letting it go.

Joan: When you were younger at university did you, did … were you ever hurt by anything?

Wayne: Physically or emotionally?

Joan: Emotional.

Wayne: Mmm. I can remember you know getting a bit drunk and being at a disco and trying to bop around just the same as everyone else and being in real pain. And you know being really upset not being able to participate, do things other students did, mmm I've not paid for it, I mean everyone if you have a late night and you drink too much you pay for it, but that's reasonable but in my situation I was having to spend several days in bed afterwards you know or something like that.

Ann: So would you say that mmm, that being disabled has affected your self-confidence? How would you rate that on a scale of 0–10?

Waynet: Mmm. My disability would have had a very profound effect on my self-confidence and it did, it did initially but when I learnt to meditate I became more confident, it got rid of the stress and became more confident in myself. I mean I think I've compensated for the disability now. I think I've got as much self-confidence as I would have had even without the disability. Mmm because I've learnt to live with it and to actually mmm … Compensate I suppose really.

Joan: Is there anything in your life that you really want to do? Like now at this stage.

Wayne: Mmm. Good question. I mean my main aim which I thought I would never fulfil I achieved it last year. I always thought it would be very hard to fulfil, I went round the world last year. I got a xxxxxxxx scholarship, travel scholarship and went to study disability in New Zealand; I had to take a PA with me. They paid for the PA to come with me as part of the deal, so I took six weeks and went round the world. I went to

New Zealand via California, Hawaii and come back via Bali, Australia. I didn't do too badly. Mmm that sort of thing I wanted to do since about the age of nine, I wanted to go around the world and despite almost because of my disability maybe I wouldn't have had that opportunity to have it paid for if I hadn't had my disability.

Ann: Would you say you were happy?

Wayne: Oh yea, yes definitely. Probably happier than a lot of people who are you know who are stuck in hum drum jobs not doing things that they feel they are useful in society for. I feel that the campaigning that I do is very useful.

Ann: Would you say that you are creative in any way?

Wayne: Mmm see this is interesting, see when I was younger I used to always think I wasn't because I wasn't very artistic or musical or anything but I realised I am actually quite creative in for instants in chairing meetings. You know in handling people, being in situations, in lobbying situations. I see opportunities and I put people together to create their works and so I am creative, but in a way that I didn't think I was. But I realise I am.

Joan: We were going to ask you about your spiritual well-being but you have already said that you were happy and …

Wayne: Mmm.

Ann: The last question is how can your quality of life be increased, if at all how could it be?

Wayne: Yea, I think there are a number of financial issues, which if they were addressed would make a significant difference. I mean one is that I think we need to have a benefit system, which is more flexible to disabled people. Mmm I'm very keen on this, in Norway for instance there is a thing called partial capacity benefit and basically if you initially pass the criteria for needing that benefit because of your impairment, you can still earn; you can be on the maximum level of benefit and still earn £5000 a year without it affecting your benefit. So that gives you a flexibility to considerably add to … you know … your lifestyle and so on without coming off the benefit, without losing all the protection.

You also have the option if your condition improves or, alternatively, if your situation improves … you find the possibility of some work you can do, which won't affect your condition. You can choose to go from 100 per cent benefit to 75 per cent benefit. You personally, as the disabled person can opt to have that change, you can also opt to go down to 50 per cent benefit or 25 per cent benefit, its always you the person who makes that decision its not some doctor choosing on your behalf. Now if I had that sort of … or something similar in the British benefit system. Occasionally sometimes the work I do for charities that I charge for I could actually be getting a percentage of that for myself as my own income and that would be fair because very often it's me who does the disability awareness training session but I earn £300 and it goes to 'Access Matters'. Now really I should to be earning that £300. Mmm … but I can only do a few days a year because of my disability. Now if we had a flexible benefit system, which would allow me to, for instances earn ten days a year that would be an extra £3000 without knocking up my benefits I would be happy. I would be happy to pay tax on it, the same way everyone else does, that would give me the flexibility and self-confidence to do this work, not just because I enjoy doing it but actually to get some benefit from it as well.

So that would make a huge difference ... a scheme like that to allow someone with a long-term physical condition to opt in and out of work when it's appropriate, when it suits them, that would make a huge difference, to your self-esteem, to your standard of living.

The other thing is that we are talking in an educational environment, I think there should be a similar sort of funding for postgraduate part-time students that there is for full-time undergraduate students because I missed the opportunity not only in a MSc. (Master of Science Degree) here but a MA (Master of Arts) which I started somewhere else. I could not get the funding. I was offered the course but I couldn't get the funding for the course fees, travelling expenses and accommodation expenses or anything and I think that's wrong ... because I think, you know, you've suffered. You're academically qualified to do a course, they should be given the funding to allow them to do it. Especially if they are in the situation where they can't go out and earn money. It's because there isn't specific funding for disabled people, once you're in a postgraduate situation or you are not in full-time employment. You know there is often funding for those who are in full-time employment but if you are in part-time employment sorry in full-time education but part time count so much ...... (trails off)

Now I think that part-time one would extend over also to ... for instances ... Mmm ..... single parents and parent with kids who can't work full time or study full time, who would actually like to do a course, I think there should be more flexibility with getting funding for education, you know for people who can't afford it but would like to do it. Now I've given you two specific ones there.

Ann: Thank you for that.

Wayne: Oh I'll give you one more thing actually. I'm a tremendous benefit from complementary therapy, a way of dealing with stress, it's not dealing with my disability specifically but after I learnt that (complementary therapy) I became very aware of things like chiropractic therapy and different things and a number of those have had substantial help for me. I mean none of them has cured me; none's had such an ongoing benefit as the meditation. But I do believe that, ... you know ... that many people with long-term chronic conditions and impairments would benefit dramatically from complementary therapy and I really think that we should get it of the NHS (National Health Service). I think that it would save a whole country a lot of money if a lot of these therapists were to make peoples lives more comfortable. You know they're not as dramatic sometimes as more of the conventional therapies you know, chemotherapy, it either cures you or it kills your cancer one or the other. But they make some peoples lives so much more comfortable they allow them to do so much more and used as preventive therapies I think they could have dramatic impact, I think what happens today is that we tend to do everything wrong and wait for our bodies to give up on us ... then expect doctors to cure us overnight. But I think if the whole of the health system was more orientated towards prevention and using complementary therapy then I think people's lives will be better.

Joan: Thank you.

References

Allen, A. (1997) 'Policing the gene machine: can anyone control the human genome project?', *Lingua Franca* **7** (3), 28–37.

Ardilles, A. (2000) *The Inclusive Education Movement and Minority Representation in Special Education: Trends Paradoxes and Dilemmas.* Manchester: ISEC, Including the Excluded, July.

Bach, M. and Rioux, M. (1996) 'Social well-being: a framework for quality of life research', in R. Renwick, I. Brown and M. Nagler (eds) *Quality of Life in Health Promotion and Rehabilitation.* London: Sage.

Baine, D. (1988) *Handicapped Children in Developing Countries.* Edmonton: University of Alberta.

Banfelvy, C. (1996) 'The paradox of the quality of life of adults with learning difficulties', *Disability and Society* **11** (4), 569–78.

Barnes, C. (1990)*Cabbage Syndrome.* London: Falmer.

Barnes, C. (1994) *Disabled People in Britain and Discrimination.* London: Hurst and Co.

Barnes, C. (1996) 'Disability and the myth of the independent researcher', *Disability and Society* **11** (1), 107–10.

Barnes, C. (2000) 'A working social model? Disability, work ands disability politics in the 21st century'. *Critical Social Policy* **20** (4), 441–57

Barker, D. (1983) 'How to curb the fertility of the unfit: the feeble-minded in Edwardian Britain', *Oxford Review of Education* **9** (3), 197–211.

Barnes, C. and Mercer, G. (eds) (1996) *Exploring the Divide: Illness and disability.* Leeds: The Disability Press.

Bauby, D. (1997) *The Diving Bell and the Butterfly.* London: Fourth Estate.

BCODP (1994) *Access Denied: Human Rights and Disabled people.* London: Liberty.

Beardshaw, V. (1988) *Last on the List: Community Services for People with Physical Disabilities.* London: King's Fund.

Beck, U. (1995) *Ecological Politics in an Age of Risk.* Cambridge: Polity Press.

Bell, A. and Bhate, M. (1992) 'Prevalence of overweight and obesity in Down's syndrome and other mentally handicapped adults living in the community', *Journal of Intellectual Disability Research* 36, 359–64.

Benedict, R. (1934) *Patterns of Culture.* Boston: Houghton-Mifflin.

Berrington, E. and Johnstone, D. (1994) *Disability and Health: The Concerns of Disabled People in West Lancashire.* Ormsirk: Edge Hill University College/West Lancashire Association of Disabled People.

Beresford, P. and Harding, T. (eds) (1993) *A Challenge to Change: Practical Experiences of Building User-Led Services.* London: National Institute for Social Work.

Berrington, E. *et al.* (1996) *The Life of the People.* Ormskirk: Edge Hill University College/WLAD.

Blanch, D. (1994) 'Employment integration, economic opportunity and the Americans with Disabilities Act: empirical study from 1990–1993', *Iowa Law Review* (79) 4, 854–923.

Bloemers and Wisch (eds) (2001) *The Voices of Europe.* Oxford: Peter Lang.

Blunkett, D. (2000) *Letter of Guidance* to the Disability Rights Commission, February

Booth, T. (1992) *Making Connections.* Milton Keynes: Open University Press.

Booth, T. (1996) 'Sounds of still voices: issues in the use of narrative methods with people who have learning difficulties', in L. Barton (ed.) *Disability and Society: Emerging Issues and Insights.* London: Longman.

Borsay, A. (1986) 'Personal trouble or public issue? Towards a model of policy for people with physical and mental disabilities', *Disability, Handicap and Society* 1 (2).

Bottomore, T. and Marshall, T. (1992) *Citizenship and Social Class.* London: Pluto.

Bracking, S. (1993) 'An introduction to the idea of independent integrated living', in C. Barnes (ed.) *Making our Own Choices: Independent Living, Personal Assistance and Disabled People*. London: BCODP.

Brisenden, S. (1986) 'Independent living and the medical model of disability', *Disability, Handicap and Society* **1** (2), 173–8.

British Council of Organisations of Disabled People (1994) *Access Denied: Human Rights and Disabled People*. London: National Council for Civil Liberties.

Brown, R., Bayer, M. and Brown, P. (1992) *Choices and Quality of Life*. London: Chapman and Hall.

Burke, E. (1995) *The Americans with Disabilities Act: Ensuring Equal Access to the American Dream*. Washington: National Council on Disability.

Burt, C. (1925) *The Young Delinquent*. London: University of London Press.

Burt, C. (1938) *The Backward Child*. London: University of London Press.

Bury, M. (1996a) 'Defining and researching disability: challenges and responses', in C. Barnes and G. Mercer (eds) *Exploring the Divide: Illness and Disability*. Leeds: The Disability Press.

Bury, M. (1996b) 'Disability and the myth of the independent researcher: a reply', *Disability and Society* **11** (1), 111–13.

Bury, M. (2000) 'A comment on the ICIDH2', *Disability and Society* **15** (7), 1073–7.

Bynoe, I. *et al.* (1991) *Equal Rights for Disabled People*. London: IPPR.

Campbell, J. and Oliver, M. (1996) *Disability Politics: Understanding our Past, Changing our Future*. London: Routledge.

Carter, H. (2001) 'Signs of the time', *Guardian*, 2 May 2001, pp 10–11.

Cartwright, L. *et al.* (1996) *The Voice of the People*. Ormsirk: Edge Hill University College/WLAD.

Chapman, T. *et al.* (1997) *Measurements of 'Quality of Life' and Services for People with Learning Difficulties and their Carers in the North West of England*. Ormsir: Edge Hill University College.

Charlton, J. (1998) *Nothing About Us Without Us: Disability, Oppression and Empowerment*. London: University of California Press.

Child Poverty Action Group (1994a) *Rights Guide to Non-means-tested Benefits*, 17th edn. London: CPAG.

Child Poverty Action Group (1994b) *National Welfare Benefits Handbook* 24th edn. London: CPAG.

Child Poverty Action Group (2001) *Welfare Rights Handbook*, 3rd edn. London; CPAG.

Christensen, C. and Rizvi, F. (1996) *Disability and the Dilemmas of Education and Justice*. Buckingham: Open University Press.

Coleridge, P. (1993) *Disability, Liberation and Development*. Oxford: Oxfam.

Colker, R. (1998) 'Affirmative action, reasonable accommodation and capitalism: irreconcilable differences?', in G. Hauritz *et al.* (eds) *Justice for People with Disabilities: Legal and Institutional Issues*. Melbourne: The Federation Press.

Cooper, D. (1996) 'Gathering evidence in the USA', *Skill Journal* **55**, 24–28.

Corbett, J. (1996) *Badmouthing: The Language of Special Needs*. London: Falmer Press.

Corbett, J. and Barton, L. (1992) *The Struggle for Choice*. London: Routledge.

Corker, M. (1999) 'New disability discourse, the principles of optimization and social change', in M. Corker and S. French (eds) *Disability Discourse*. Milton Keynes: OU Press.

Craft, A. (1992) *Aspects of Adulthood: Sex Education in Further Education for Learners with Severe Learning Difficulties*. London: FEU.

Crawley, B. (1988) *The Growing Voice: A Survey of Self-advocacy Groups in Adult Training Centres and Hospitals in Great Britain*. London: CMH.

Crawley, B. (1989) *Independent Living for Adults with Mental Handicap*. London: Cassell.

Crow, L. (1996) 'Including all our lives: renewing the social model of disability', in C. Barnes and G. Mercer *Exploring the Divide: Illness and Disability*. Leeds: The Disability Press.

CSO (1996) *Social Trends*. London: Central Statistical Office.

Darnborough, A. and Kinrade, D. (eds) (1996) *Directory for Disabled People*. London: Woodhead-Faulkner.

Daunt, P. (1991) *Meeting Disability: A European Response*. London: Cassell.

Davis, L. (ed.)(1997) *The Disability Studies Reader*. London: Routledge.

de Crespigny, L. with Dredge, R. (1991) *Which Tests for my Unborn Baby?* Australia: Oxford University Press.

Degener T. (1992) The right to be different: implications for child protection, *Child Abuse Review*, (1) 151–155

DfEE (1994) *Code of Practice: On the Identification and Assessment of Special Educational Needs*. London: HMSO.

DfEE (1998) 'New commission to promote disabled people's rights', *Press Release* 98/373, 21 July.

DfEE (2001) *Towards Inclusion – Civil Rights for Disabled People*. London: DfEE.

DHSS (1988) *Caring for People (The Griffiths Report)*. London: HMSO.

Disability Now (1996) *The Disability Manifesto: What Has to be Done*. London: Scope, Creative Press.

DPI (1982) Proceedings of the First World Congress, Singapore, Disabled People's International.

Drake, R. (1999) *Understanding Disability Politics*. London: Macmillan.

Drake, R. (2000) 'Disabled people, New Labour, benefits and work', *Critical Social Policy* 20 (4), 421–39.

Driedger, D. (1989) *The Last Civil Rights Movement*. London: Hurst & Co.

Dugdale, R. (1877) *The Jukes, A Study in Crime, Pauperism, Disease and Heredity*. New York: New York Prison Association, 31st Annual Report.

Edinburgh Review (1865) *Idiot Asylums*, Vol 122, pp.37–72.

Ephraem, L. (1984) *Health of One Million*. New York: UNICEF.

Equal Opportunities Review (1997) 'Implementing the DDA', *Equal Opportunities Review* January.

Equal Opportunities Review (1999) 'Following up the DDA', *Equal Opportunities Review* August 86, 12.

Equal Opportunities Review (2000) 'DDA having major impact on employers', *Equal Opportunities Review* 93, 8.

Erlanger, H. and Roth, W. (1985) 'Disability policy: the parts and the whole', *American Behavioural Scientist* 28, 3.

Fagan, T. and Lee, P. (1997) 'New social movements and social policy: a case study for the disability movement', in M. Lavalette and A. Pratt (eds) *Social Policy: A Conceptual and Theoretical Introduction*. London: Sage.

Fagan, T. and Reynolds, P. (forthcoming) *The Politics of Disability: Ideology, Politics, Policy*. London: Sage.

Felce, D. and Perry, J. (1996) 'Exploring current conceptions of quality of life', in R. Renwick, I. Brown and M. Nagler (eds) *Quality of Life in Health Promotion and Rehabilitation*. London: Sage.

Finch, J. and Groves, D. (1983) *A Labour of Love: Women, Work and Caring*. London: Routledge and Kegan Paul.

Finkelstein, V. (1979) *Attitudes and Disabled People: Issues for Discussion*. New York: World Rehabilitation Fund.

Finkelstein, V. (1987) 'Disabled people and our culture development', www.leeds.ac.uk/disability-studies/archiveuk

Finkelstein, V. (1993) 'Disability – a social challenge or an administrative responsibility?', in J. Swain *et al.* (eds) *Disabling Barriers – Enabling Environments*. London: Sage/Open University.

Finkelstein, V. (1996) *Modelling Disability*, Disability Archive, www.leeds.ac.uk/disability-studies/archiveuk

Finkelstein, V. and French, S. (1993) 'Towards a psychology of disability', in J. Swain *et al.* (eds) *Disabling Barriers – Enabling Environments*. London: Sage/Open University.

Finn, D. (1987) *Training Without Jobs: New Deals and Broken Promises*. London: Macmillan.

Finn, D. (1997) Job-seeker's Allowance Conference, 14th March 1997, University of Portsmouth.

Flynn, M. (1989) *Independent Living for Adults with Mental Handicap*. London: Cassell.

Flynn, M. and Hirst, M. (1992) *This Year, Next Year, Sometime ...? Learning Disability and Adulthood*. London: National Development Team/Social Policy Research Unit.

Fong, C. and Brodeur, G. (1987) 'Down's syndrome and leukemia: epidemiology, genetics, cytogenetics and mechanisms of leukemogenesis, *Cancer, Genetics and Cytogenetics* 28, 55–76.

The Food Magazine (1997) 'Food Supplements – has the hype gone too far?', Issue 38, August p. 1.

Fox, R. *et al.* (1984) 'A streamlined weight loss program for moderately retarded adults in a sheltered workshop setting', *Applied Research in Mental Retardation* 5, 69–79.

Freeman, A. (1988) 'Who's moving the goal posts?', in L. Barton (ed.) *The Politics of Special Educational Needs*. London: Falmer.

Freedman, S. (1999) *A Critical Review of the Concept of Equality in the UK Anti-discrimination Law*. Cambridge: University of Cambridge, Centre for Public Law.

French, S. (ed.) (1992) *Physiotherapy: A Psychosocial Approach*. Oxford: Butterworth-Heinemann.

French, S. (1993) 'Disability, impairment or something in between?', in J Swain *et al.* (eds) *Disabling Barriers, Enabling Environments*. London: Sage.

French, S. (1994a) 'Researching disability', in S. French (ed.) *On Equal Terms: Working with Disabled People*. Oxford: Butterworth-Heinemann.

French, S. (1994b) 'Ageism', in S. French (ed.) *Physiotherapy: A Psychosocial Approach*. Oxford: Butterworth-Heinemann.

Garland, R. (1995) *The Eye of the Beholder: Deformity and Disability in the Graeco-Roman World*. New York: Cornell University Press.

Garrow, J. (1988) *Obesity and Related Diseases*. Edinburgh: Churchill-Livingstone.

Gillespie-Sells, K. and Campbell, J. (1991) *Disability Equality Training Trainers Guide*. London: CCETSW.

Gillott, J. (1997) 'Gene Junction', *Guardian,* 20 February 1997, p. 14.

Goddard, H. (1912) *The Kallikak Family*. New York: Macmillan.

Goffman, F. (1970) *Stigma: Notes on the Management of Spoiled Identity*. London: Penguin.

Gooding, C. (1994) *Disabling Laws, Enabling Acts*. London: Pluto.

Gooding, C (2000) 'Disability Discrimination Act: from statute to practice', *Critical Social Policy* **20** (4), 533–49.

Gould, S. J. (1996) *The Mismeasure of Man* (revised edn). London: Penguin.

Griffiths, M. (1990) *Enabled to Work, Working Together.* London: FEU.

Griffiths, R. (1988) *Community Care: Agenda for Action.* London: HMSO.

Grimley Evans, J. (1997) 'Measuring outcomes from health services for older people', in I. Philp (ed.) *Outcomes Assessment in Health Care for Elderly People.* London: Farrand Press.

Guardian (1997) 'Scientist scorn sci-fi fears over sheep clone', 24 February 1997, p. 7.

Guardian (1997) 'Scientists 'able to create human clone', 26 February 1997, p. 6.

Guardian (2001) 'More efficient killing fields', 8 March 2001, p. 8.

Guardian (2001) 'Robot with living brain created in US', 18 April 2001, p. 1.

Guardian (2001) 'I had to fight for her, she couldn't fight for herself', 26 April 2001, p. 44.

Haffter, C. (1968) 'The changeling: history and psychodynamics of attitudes to handicapped children in European folk-lore', *Journal of History of Behavioural Sciences* 4, 55–61.

Hameister, H. (1996) 'The human genome project in progress: the construction and meaning of the genetic map', in I. Wilczek (ed.) *Biomedical Research and Patenting: Ethical Social and Legal Aspects.* Baarn: European Platform for Patients' Organisations.

Harding, S. (1991) *Whose Science? Whose Knowledge? Thinking from Women's Lives.* Milton Keynes: OU Press.

Hariharan, S. (1982) 'CBR manual in practice', *One in Ten* **2** (2), 2.

Hawkridge D. and Vincent, T. (1992) *Learning Difficulties and Computers: Access to the Curriculum.* London: Jessica Kingsley.

Harbert, W. (1988) 'Dignity and Choice', *Insight* 25 March 1988.

Haydon, S. (1997) 'Sweden owns up to racial purification', *The Independent,* 25 August 1997, p. 10.

Hegarty, S. (1993) *Meeting Special Needs in Ordinary Schools.* London: Cassell.

Heise, L. (1992) *Violence, Health and Development Project.* New Brunswick, NJ: Women's Global Leadership, Rutger's University.

Helander, B. (1988) *Family Health Management in the Gansaxdheere District of the Bay Region, Somalia,* Mogadishu, Somalia: UNICEF.

Helander, E. *et al.* (1983) *Training Disabled People in the Community,* 3rd edn. Geneva: World Health Organisation.

Helander, E. (1993) *Prejudice and Dignity: An Introduction to Community Based Rehabilitation.* New York: UNDP.

Henwood, M. (1990) 'No sense of urgency: age discrimination in health care', in E. McEwen (ed.) *Age: The Unrecognised Discrimination,* 43–57. London: Age Concern.

Herrnstein, R, and Murray, C. (1994) *The Bell Curve: The re-shaping of American Life by Difference in Intelligence.* New York: Free Press.

Hevey, D. (1992) *The Creatures Time Forgot.* London: Routledge.

Hirst, J. (1996) 'People power', *Community Care* 1141, October, p. 23.

HMSO (1992) *The Health of the Nation,* Cm 1986, London, HMSO.

HMSO (1995) *The Health of the Nation: A Strategy for People with Learning Disabilities.* London: Department of Health.

HMSO (1996) *Disability Discrimination Act (1995).* London: HMSO.

Howells, G. (1989) 'Down's syndrome and the general practitioner', *Journal of the Royal College of General Practitioners* 39, 470–5.

Hughes, B.(2000) 'Medicine and the aesthetic invalidation of disabled people', *Disability and Society* **15** (4), 555–68.

Hughes, A. *et al.* (1996) 'Comparing quality of life for people with learning disabilities and people who are unemployed or retired', *British Journal of Learning Disabilities* 24, 99–104.

Hugil, B. (1997) 'Britain's Expansion Zone', *The Observer,* 13th April, 29.

Huitt, K. and Elston, R. (1991) 'Attitudes towards persons with disabilities expressed by professional counsellors', *Journal of Applied Rehabilitation Counselling* **22** (2), 42–3.

Hunt, P. (1966) *A Critical Condition,* www.leeds.ac.uk/disability-studies/archiveuk

Hurst, R. (2000a) 'To revise or not to revise?' *Disability and Society* 15 (7), 1083–8.

Hurst, R. (2000b) 'The international disability rights movement'. New Directions in Disability Studies seminar series, Centre for Disability Studies, Leeds University 11 October 2000.

Hyde, M. (2000) 'From welfare to work? Social policy for disabled people of working age in the United Kingdom in the 1990's', *Disability and Society* **15** (2), 327–42.

Imrie, R. (1996) *Disability and the City: International Perspectives.* London: Paul Chapman.

Ingstad, B. and Reynolds-Whyte, S. (eds) (1995) *Disability and Culture.* Berkeley: University of California.

Jancar, J. (1990) 'Cancer and mental handicap: a further study', *British Journal of Psychiatry* 156, 531–3.

Jensen, E. (1995) *Superteaching.* Delmar, California: Turning Point.

Jewson, N. and Mason, D. (1986) 'The theory and practice of equal opportunities: liberal and radical approaches', *Sociological Review* 34, 2.

Jackson, M. (2000) 'Introduction', in L. Brigham *et al.* (eds) *Crossing Boundaries: Change and Continuity in the History of Learning Disability.* Kidderminster: BILD.

Johnstone, D. (1995) *Further Opportunities: Learning Difficulties and Disabilities in Further Education.* London: Cassell.

Johnstone, D. (1996a) *Inclusive Education and Community: Integrating the Special Professional.* Paper given to the European Forum, Lucenec, 13–18 May 1996.

Johnstone D. (1996b) 'Transition to further education for students with learning difficulties and disabilities', *Innovation in Learning in Education: The International Journal for the Reflective Practitioner* **2** (3), 11–17.

Johnstone, D. (1996c) 'The Decline of Disability Leadership in California'. Unpublished paper, Edge Hill University College.

Johnstone, D and Warwick C. (1999) Community Solutions to Inclusion: some observations on practice in Europe and the United Kingdom, *British Journal of Learning Support,* **14** (1), 8–12 .

Kalyanpur, M. (1996) 'The influence of western special education on community based services in India', *Disability and Society* **11** (2), 249–66.

Kennedy, I. (1980) Reith Lectures, *The Listener.* London: BBC.

Kennedy, H. (Chair) (1997) *Learning Works.* Coventry; FEFC.

Kent, A. (1996) 'Patients' views of patenting', in I. Wilczek (ed.) *Biomedical Research and Patenting: Ethical Social and Legal Aspects.* Baarn: European Platform for Patients' Organisations.

Kurtz, R. (1964) 'Implications of recent sociological research in mental retardation', *American Journal of Mental Deficiency* 69, 506–10.

Levine, D. (1985) *The Flight from Ambiguity: Essays in Social and Cultural Theory.* Chicago: University of Chicago Press.

Liggett, H. (1988) 'Stars are not born: an interactive approach to the politics of disability', *Disability, Handicap and Society* **3** (3), 6–13.

Linton, S. (1998) *Claiming Disability: Knowledge and Identity.* New York: New York University Press.

Loney, M. (1983) 'The politics of self help and community care', in A. Brechin *et al.* (eds) *Handicap in a Social World.* London: Hodder & Stoughton.

Lyons, M. and Hayes, R. (1993) 'Student perceptions of persons with psychiatric and other disorders', *The American Journal of Occupational Therapy* **47** (6), 541–8.

Maglalic, R. *et al.* (2000) 'Making direct payments a choice: a report on the research findings', *Disability and Society* **15** (1), 99–114.

Malson, L. and Itard, J. (1972) *Wolf children and The Wild Boy of Aveyron.* London: NLB.

Marks, D. (1998) *Disability: Controversial Debates and Psychosocial Perspectives.* London: Routledge.

Marquis, R. and Jackson, R. (2000) 'Quality of life and quality of service relationships: experiences of people with disabilities', *Disability and Society* **15** (3), 411–26.

Marris, V. (1996) *Lives Worth Living.* London: Pandora Books.

Marshall, G. (1976) *The Challenge of a Handicap.* Coventry: Exhall Grange.

Martin, J. *et al.* (1988) *The Prevalence of Disability among Adults.* London: HMSO.

McKnight, J. (1995) *The Careless Society: Community and its Counterfeits.* New York: Basic Books.

McLeod, R. and Bywaters, S. (2000) *Social Work, Health and Equality.* London: Routledge.

Meager, N. *et al.* (1999) *Monitoring the Disability Discrimination Act (1995).* London: DfEE.

Miles, M. (1981) *Handicapped Children and their Needs in the North West Frontier Province of Pakistan.* Peshawar, Pakistan: Mental Health Centre.

Miles, M. (1985) *Where there is no Rehabilitation Plan: A Critique of the WHO Scheme and Suggestions for Future Directions.* Peshawar; Pakistan: Mental Health Centre.

Miles, M. (1990) 'The "community base" in rehabilitation planning: key or gimmick?', in M. Thorburn and K. Marfo (eds) *Practical Approaches to Childhood Disability in Developing Countries: Insights from Experience and Research.* St. John's: University of Newfoundland.

Miles, M. (1995) 'Disability in an Eastern religious context: historical perspectives', *Disability and Society* **10** (1), 49–70.

Miles, S. (1996) 'Engaging with the disability rights movement: the experience of community-based rehabilitation in Southern Africa', *Disability and Society* **11** (4), 501–17.

Miles, M. (2000) 'Disability on a different model: glimpses of the Asian heritage', *Disability and Society* **15** (4), 603–18.

Mitchell, D. and Snyder, S. (eds) (1997) *The Body and Physical Difference: Discourses of Disability in the Humanities.* Michigan: University of Michigan.

Mithaug, D. (1996) *Equal Opportunity Theory*. London: Sage.

Moniga, S. and Vianello, R. (1995) *Job Possibilities and Quality of Life for Handicapped People in Europe*. Karlsruhe: European Association for Special Education (EASE).

Moore, M. *et al.* (1998) *Researching Disability Issues*. Buckingham: Open University Press.

Morris, J. (1991) *Pride Against Prejudice*. London: The Women's Press.

Morris, J. (1993) *Independent Lives: Community Care and Disabled People*. Basingstoke: Macmillan.

Morris, J. (ed.) (1996) *Encounters with Strangers: Feminism and Disability*. London: The Women's Press.

Morris, J. and Winn, H.(1993) *Housing and Social Inequality*. London: Hilary Shipman.

Morrissey, P. (1991) *A Primer for Corporate America on Civil Rights for the Disabled*. Horsham, PA: LRP Publications.

Moss, S. (1995) 'Methodological issues in the diagnosis of psychiatric disorders in adults with learning disability', *Thornfield Journal*. University of Dublin.

Napolitano, S. (1996) 'Mobility impairment', in G. Hales (ed.) *Beyond Disability: Towards an Enabling Society*. London: Sage.

National Heart Forum (1997) *The Price of Poverty*. London: The National Heart Forum.

Nimbkar, E. (1971) 'Simple aids for handicapped children in India', *International Rehabilitation Review* 22, 6–8.

Nkabinde, Z. (1993) 'The role of special education in a changing South Africa', *The Journal of Special Education* **27** (1), 107–14.

Nirje, B. (1980) 'The normalisation principle', in R. Flynn and K. Nitsch (eds) *Normalisation, Social Integration and Community Services*. Baltimore: University Park Press.

O'Brien, J. and Tyne, A. (1981) *The Principles of Normalisation: A Foundation for Effective Services*. London: The Campaign for Mentally Handicapped People.

O'Brien, K. Tate, K. and Zaharia, E. (1991) 'Mortality in a large Southeastern facility for persons with mental retardation', *American Journal of Mental Retardation* 95, 397–403.

O'Day, B. (1996) 'Re-authorization of the rehabilitation act: comprehensive solutions or political satisficing? *Disability and Society* 11 (3), 411–27.

O'Toole, B. (1987) 'Community based rehabilitation: problems and possibilities', *European Journal of Special Needs Education* 2 (3), 177–90.

Office of Health Economics (1990) *Osteoporosis and the Risk of Fractures*. London; OHE.

Oliver, M. (1983) *Social Work with Disabled People*. Basingstoke: Macmillan.

Oliver, M. (1990) *The Politics of Disablement*. Basingstoke: Macmillan.

Oliver, M. (1992) 'Changing the social relations of research production', *Disability, Handicap and Society* **7** (2), 101–14.

Oliver, M. (1996a) *Understanding Disability: From Theory to Practice*. Basingstoke: Macmillan.

Oliver, M (1996b) 'Defining impairment and disability: issues at stake', in C. Barnes and G. Mercer (eds) *Exploring the Divide: Illness and Disability*. University of Leeds: Disability Press.

Oliver, M. (2000) 'Decoupling education policy from the economy in late capitalist societies: some implications for special education', ISEC 2000, Manchester, *Including the Excluded*.

Oliver, M. and Barnes, C. (1993) 'Discrimination, disability and welfare: from needs to rights', in J. Swain *et al.* (eds) *Disabling Barriers: Enabling Environments*. London: Sage.

Oliver, M. and Barnes, C. (1998) *Disabled people and Social Policy: from exclusion to inclusion*. London: Longman.

Oliver, M. and Zarb, G. (1989) 'The politics of disability: a new approach', in *Disability, Handicap and Society* **14** (3), 221–40.

Parmenter, T. (1992) 'Quality of life of people with developmental disabilities', *Mental Retardation* 18, 247–87.

Pearson, L. (2000) 'Money talks? Competing discourses in the implementation of direct payments', *Critical Social Policy* **20** (4), 459–78.

Peters, S. (2000) 'Is there a disability culture? A syncretisation of three possible world views', *Disability and Society* **15** (4), 583–602.

Pfieffer, D. (1996) '"We won't go back": the ADA on the grassroots level', *Disability and Society* **11** (2), 271–83.

Pfieffer, D. (1998) 'The ICIDH and the need for its revision, *Disability and Society* 13 (4), 503–524.

Pfieffer, D. (2000) 'The devils are in the details: the ICIDH2 and the disability movement', *Disability and Society* **15** (7), 1079–82.

Potts, P. (2000) 'Concrete representations of a social category: consolidating and transforming public institutions for people classified as "defective"', in L. Brigham *et al.* (eds) *Crossing Boundaries: Change and Continuity in the History of Learning Disability*. Kidderminster: BILD.

Priestley (1999) *Disability Politics and Community Care*. London: Jessica Kingsley

Qureshi, H. and Nocon, A. (1996) *Report on Expert Seminars on Routine Outcome Measurement in Personal Social Services*. DH 1378, 29 February 1996. York: SPRU.

Rawls, J. (1971) *A Theory of Justice*. Cambridge, MA: Belknap.

Ray, L. (1983) 'Eugenics, mental deficiency and Fabian socialism between the wars', *Oxford Review of Education* **9** (3), 213–25.

Renwick, zR. and Friefeld, S. (1996) 'Quality of life and rehabilitation', in R. Renwick *et al.* (eds) *Quality of Life in Health Promotion and Rehabilitation*. London: Sage.

Riddell, S. and Watson, N. (2000) 'Introduction', *Critical Social Policy* **20** (4), 411–20.

Rioux, M. (1996) 'Overcoming the social construction of inequality as a prerequisite to quality of life', in R. Renwick *et al.* (eds) *Quality of Life in Health Promotion and Rehabilitation*. London: Sage.

Rizvi, F. and Christensen, C. (1996) *Disability and the Dilemmas of Education and Justice*. Milton Keynes: Open University Press.

Rose, H. (1994) *Love, Power and Knowledge*. Cambridge: Polity Press.

Rosenqvist, J. (1993) 'The concept of integration in schools and society in connection with adult quality of life', in S. Moniga, and R. Vianello (eds) *Job Possibilities and Quality of Life for Handicapped People in Europe*. Karlsruhe: European Association for Special Education (EASE).

Roulstone, A. (2000) 'Disability, dependency and the New Deal for disabled people', *Disability and Society* **15** (3), 427–43.

Rummery, K. and Glendinning, C. (1999) 'Negotiating needs, access and gatekeeping: developments in health and community care policies in the UK and the rights of disabled and older people', *Critical Social Policy* 19 (3), 335–351.

Scholl, T. *et al.* (1982) 'Leukaemia and other cancers, anomolies and infections as causes of death in Down's syndrome in the United States during 1976', *Developmental Medicine and Child Neurology* 24, 817–29.

Scraton, P. (2001) *Hillsborough – The Truth*. Edinburgh: Mainstream.

Scope. (1994) *Disabled in Britain*. London: Scope. Published in 3 parts: *A World Apart* (lives of disabled people); *Behind Closed Doors* (parents and carers); *Counting on Community Care* (people's experiences of health and social services).

Shakespeare, T. (1993) 'Disabled people's self organisation: a new social movement?' *Disability, Handicap and Society* **8** (3), 249–64.

Shakespeare, T. (1995) 'Back to the future? New genetics and disabled people', *Critical Social Policy* 15 (Autumn), 22–35.

Shakespeare, T. (1996) 'Rules of engagement: doing disability research', in *Disability and Society* **11** (1), March, 115–19.

Shakespeare, T. (1997) 'Reviewing the past, developing the future', *Skill Journal* 58, 8–11.

Shakespeare, T. (1998) *The Disability Reader: Social Science Perspectives*. London: Cassell.

Shakespeare, T. (2001) Foreword in L. Ward, *Considered Choices? The New Genetics, Prenatal Testing and People with Learning Difficulties*. Kidderminster: BILD.

Shakespeare, T. and Watson, N. (1997) 'Defending the social model', *Disability and Society* **12** (2), 293–300.

Shakespeare, T. *et al.* (1996) *The Sexual Politics of Disability*. London: Cassell.

Shearer, (Initial) (1981) *Disability: Whose handicap?*. Oxford: Blackwell.

Silburn, L. (1993) 'A social model in a medical world: the development of the integrated living team as part of the strategy for younger physically disabled people in North Derbyshire', in J. Swain *et al.* (eds) *Disabling Barriers: Enabling Environments*. London: Sage.

Snowdon (Chair) (1979) *Integrating the Disabled*. Horsham: National Fund for Research into Crippling Diseases.

Soder, M. (1980) 'School integration of the mentally retarded – analysis of concepts, research and research needs', in *Research and Development Concerning the Integration of Handicapped Pupils in the Ordinary School System*. Stockholm: Skoloverstyrelsen.

Stainton, T. (2000) 'Equal citizens? The discourse of liberty and rights in the history of learning disabilities', in L. Brigham *et al.* (eds) *Crossing Boundaries: Change and Continuity in the History of Learning Disability*. Kidderminster: BILD.

Steiner, R. (1994) *How to Know Higher Worlds*. New York: Anthroposophic Press.

Stone, E. (1996) 'A law to protect, a law to prevent: contextualising disability legislation in China', *Disability and Society* **11** (4), 469–83.

Stone, E. (1997) 'From the research notes of a foreign devil: disability research in China', in C. Barnes and G. Mercer (eds) *Doing Disability Research*. Leeds: Disability Press.

Swain, J. and French, S. (2000) 'Towards an affirmation model of disability', *Disability and Society* 15 (4), 569–82.

Szivos, S. (1992) 'The limits of integration', in H. Brown and H. Smith (eds) *Normalisation: A reader for the 90's*. London: Routledge.

Taylor, D. (1989) 'Citizenship and social power', in *Critical Social Policy* 26, 19.

Taylor, S. and Bogdan, R. (1996) 'Quality of life from the individual's perspective', in R. L. Schalock (ed.)

Quality of Life (Vol 1) Conceptualization and Measurement. Washington: American Association of Mental Retardation.

Thomas, D. (1978) *The Social Psychology of Childhood Disability*. London: Methuen.

Thomson, R. G. (1996) *Freakery: Cultural Spectacles of the Extraordinary Body*. New York: New York University Press.

Thomson, R. G. (ed.) (1997) *Extraordinary Bodies: Figuring Physical Disability in American Culture and Literature*. New York: Columbia University Press.

Thomson, R. G. (2001) *The FDR Memorial: Who Speaks from the Wheelchair?* http://chronicle.com/weekly/v47/i20/20b01101.htm

Thorburn, M. and Marfo, K. (eds) (1990) *Practical Approaches to Childhood Disability in Developing Countries: Insights from Experience and Research*. St. John's: University of Newfoundland.

Tomasky, M. (1996) 'Reaffirming our actions', *The Nation* **262** (19), 21–4.

Turk, V. and Brown, H. (1993) 'The sexual abuse of adults with learning disabilities: results of a two year survey', *Mental Handicap Research* 6, 193–216.

Turner, S. (1996) 'Promoting healthy lifestyles for people with learning disabilities: a survey of provider organisations', *British Journal of Learning Disabilities* 24, 138–44.

Turner, S. and Moss, S. (1995) *The Health Needs of Adults with Learning Disabilities and the Health of the Nation Strategy*. Manchester: Hester Adrian Research Centre.

UPIAS (1976) *Fundamental Principles of Disability*. London: Union of the Physically Impaired Against Segregation.

Vernon, A. and Qureshi, H. (2000) 'Community care and independence: self-sufficiency or empowerment?', *Critical Social Policy* **2** (1), 59–80.

VES Newsletter (1988) 'Do we have a duty to die?', *Voluntary Euthanasia Society Newsletter*, January.

Vincent, T. (ed.) (1990) *New Technology, Disability and Special Educational Needs: Some Case Studies in Further Education*. Coventry: Hereward College.

Vincent, T. (1993) 'Foreword', in S. Broadbent and S. Curran (eds) *The Assessment, Disability and Technology Handbook*. Oldham: North West Access Centre.

Walmsley, J. and Rolph, S. (2001) 'The development of community care for people with learning difficulties 1913–1946', *Critical Social Policy* **21** (1), 59–80.

Warnock, M. (Chair) (1978) *Special Educational Needs: Report of the Committee of Enquiry into the Education of Handicapped Children and Young People* (The Warnock Report). London: HMSO.

Warwick, C. *et al.* (eds) (1997) *The Role of Resource Centres in Supporting Integration in Education*. Brussells: HELIOS Group 8.

Werner, D. (1987) *Disabled Village Children*. Palo Alto, CA: Hesperian Foundation.

Whelan, E. and Speake, B. (1977) *Adult Training Centres in England and Wales*. Manchester: University of Manchester Press.

WHO (1976) International Classification Document, A29/1NF.DOC/1.

WHO (1982) *Community Based Rehabilitation. Report of a WHO interregional consultation*, 28 June–3 July 1982, RHB/IR/82.1 Geneva: World Health Organisation.

World Health Organisation (1997) *International Classification of Impairments, Activities and Participation. Manual of Dimensions of Disablement and Functioning, Beta-1 draft for field trials*. Geneva: World Health Organisation.

Wilson, E. (1985) *Adorned in Dreams: Fashion and Modernity*. London: Virago Press.

Wilson, G. (ed.) (1996) *Community Care: Asking the Users*. London: Chapman and Hall.

Wiseman, J. (1978) 'The Research Web', in J Bynner and K. Stribley (eds) *Social Research Principles and Procedures*. London: Longman.

Wood, P. (1980) *International Classification of Impairments, Disabilities and Handicaps*. Geneva: World Health Organisation.

Wolfensberger, W. (1989) 'Human service policies: the rhetoric versus the reality', in L. Barton (ed.) *Disability and Dependency*. Lewes: Falmer.

Wolff, H. (1980) 'Tools for living: a blue print for a major new industry', in A. Brechin *et al.* (eds) *Handicap in a Social World*. London: Hodder & Stoughton.

Wright, T. and Leung, P. (1993) *Meeting the Unique Needs of Minorities with Disabilities*. Washington, DC: National Council on Disability.

Zarb, G. (1993a) 'Ageing with a disability', in J. Johnson and R. Slater (eds) *Ageing and Later Life*. London: Sage.

Zarb, G. (1993b) 'The dual experience of ageing with a disability', in J. Swain *et al.* (eds) *Disabling Barriers: Enabling Environments*. London: Sage.

Index